U.S. Foreign Policy
Toward the
Third World

U.S. Foreign Policy Toward the

Third World

A Post–Cold War Assessment

Edited by

Jürgen Rüland, Theodor Hanf, and Eva Manske

M.E.Sharpe
Armonk, New York
London, England

Library of Congress Cataloging-in-Publication Data

U.S. foreign policy toward the Third World : a post–Cold War assessment / edited by
Jürgen Rüland, Theodor Hanf, and Eva Manske.
   p. cm.
Revised papers originally presented at a conference entitled "Benign Neglect?:
American Third-World Policies After the End of the Cold War" held in Freiburg,
Germany, Oct. 7–8, 2002.
Includes index.
ISBN 0-7656-1620-3 (hardcover : alk. paper)—ISBN 0-7656-1621-1 (pbk. : alk. paper)
  1. Developing countries—Foreign relations—United States—Congresses. 2. United
States—Foreign relations—Developing countries—Congresses. 3. United States—
Foreign relations—1989—Congresses. I. Rüland, Jürgen, 1953– II. Hanf, Theodor.
III. Manske, Eva.

D888.U6U19 2005
327.730172′4′090511—dc22
2005002774

Printed in the United States of America

The paper used in this publication meets the minimum requirements of
American National Standard for Information Sciences
Permanence of Paper for Printed Library Materials,
ANSI Z 39.48-1984.

∞

BM (c)	10	9	8	7	6	5	4	3	2	1
BM (p)	10	9	8	7	6	5	4	3	2	1

Contents

Tables

Preface

This volume was inspired by the devastating terrorist attacks on New York and Washington on September 11, 2001. The fact that the attacks were planned and executed by Islamist extremists of different Arab nationalities gave rise to concerns that they were symptoms of a deepening political, economic, social, and cultural divide between the global North and South. Opinion polls in many parts of the Third World, especially in Islamic countries, suggest that American dominance has contributed to intensifying feelings of powerlessness in the South and that the misery in developing countries is the result of U.S. policies. Such sentiments were even exacerbated in recent years where economic crises wrought havoc in the South. The Asian currency crisis as well as the financial crises in Brazil and Argentina provided a fertile ground for conspiracy theories, with the U.S. figuring as the main culprit.

This volume therefore explores to what extent this seeming decline of U.S. "soft power" in many parts of the global South is the result of a benign or not so benign neglect of these world regions by the United States after the end of the Cold War. Did the United States lose interest in these regions, since with the collapse of the Soviet Union it was seemingly no longer in need of many former Third World allies? Did the United States turn to an inward-looking neo-isolationist foreign policy, only engaging itself where major national interests were at stake? And did the United States abandon Third World development for pushing a neo-liberal project of globalization that not only jeopardized economic perspectives of less developed countries but also eroded cultural identities by Westernization? Did the United States by its seeming neglect—and, by coincidence, other Western nations—unwittingly accept the failing of states, the spread of anarchy and, hence, the emergence of breeding grounds and sanctuaries for international terrorists? What has gone wrong in United States policy toward the global South that such violent and deadly hostile challenges such as September 11 seem to emanate from it?

Answers to these questions are provided by a group of scholars who are either eminent experts of American foreign policy, of major regions of the global South, or both. While the first three chapters outline the global, paradigmatic, and domestic parameters into which U.S. policies toward the global South are embedded in the post–Cold War period, subsequent chapters analyze U.S. policies toward Latin America, the Middle East, South, Southeast and Central Asia, and Africa along four major dimensions: security, economics, democracy, and domestic interests. The volume concludes with an outlook on U.S. policies in the global South as conditioned by the National Security Strategy of September 2002.

The publication of this volume was made possible by the cooperation of many people and institutions. Foremost the editors wish to express their sincere gratitude to the authors. In the process of publication they were repeatedly overrun by events in the turbulent post–September 11 period. They patiently updated their chapters and responded sensibly to the thoughtful comments of two anonymous readers. The editors thank both readers for the time and thoughts they devoted for improving the volume. We also would like to express our gratitude to the institutions that have sponsored an international conference in Freiburg, Germany, where the original versions of these chapters were discussed. The Program Section of the U.S. Embassy in Berlin provided generous travel grants for four of the invited American scholars. The Foreign Office of the Federal Republic of Germany and the BMW Foundation Herbert Quandt (Munich) likewise provided much appreciated financial support. The editors particularly thank Dr. Manfred Stinnes (Program Section of the U.S. Embassy in Berlin) and Dr. Kai Schellhorn (BMW Foundation Herbert Quandt) for their encouragement and active support. Among the people involved in the project at various stages we thank Uta Schöreder (Carl-Schurz-Haus), Ursula Böehme, Christoph Fenner, Astrid Fritz, David Frogier de Ponlevoy, Ingo Geisel, Dr. Anja Jetschke, Desiree Kleiner, Benjamin Köehler, Juergen Müeller, Annette Pöelking, Stefan Rother, Helge Roxin (Department of Political Science, University of Freiburg), Angela Herrmann, and Petra Bauerle (Arnold Bergstraesser

Institute Freiburg). Margeret Rae and John Richardson proofread and edited the German contributions. The final editing and technical preparation of the text was done with great care and competence by Angela Herrmann and Kerstin Priwitzer. The editors express their warmest thanks to all of them.

Abbreviations and Acronyms

ABM	anti-ballistic missile
ACOTA	African Contingency Operations Training and Assistance
ACRF	African Crisis Response Force
ACRI	African Crisis Response Initiative
AFP	Armed Forces of the Philippines
AGOA	Africa Growth and Opportunity Act
AID	Agency for International Development
AIDS	acquired immunodeficiency syndrome
AMF	Asian Monetary Fund
APEC	Asia-Pacific Economic Cooperation
ARF	ASEAN Regional Forum
ASEAN	Association of Southeast Asian Nations
ATA	Afghan Transition Administration
AWACS	airborne warning and surveillance system
BRAC	Bases Realignment and Closure
CANF	Cuban American National Foundation
CARAT	cooperation afloat readiness and training
CENTCOM	Central Command
CEO	chief executive officer
CIA	Central Intelligence Agency
CIS	Commonwealth of Independent States
CJTF-HOA	Combined Joint Task Force–Horn of Africa

CNPC	China National Petroleum Corporation
CSTO	Collective Security Treaty Organization
CTR	cooperative threat reduction
CUSFTA	Canada–U.S. Free Trade Agreement
DAC	Development Assistance Committee
EAI	Enterprise for the Americas Initiative
EAI	Enterprise for the ASEAN Initiative
EIA	Energy Information Administration
EIP	Environment Improvement Project
ETAN	East Timor Action Network
EU	European Union
FBI	Federal Bureau of Investigation
FDI	foreign direct investment
FMF	Foreign Military Financing
FNGO	faith-based NGO
FSA	Freedom Support Act
FTA	free trade agreement
FTAA	Free Trade Area of the Americas
GAM	Gerakan Aceh Merdeka
GATT	General Agreement on Tariffs and Trade
GDP	gross domestic product
GNI	gross national income
GNP	gross national product
HIPC	Heavily Indebted Poor Countries Initiative
HIV	human immunodeficiency virus
IGO	intergovernmental organization
IMET	International Military Education and Training
IMF	International Monetary Fund
IMU	Islamic Movement of Uzbekistan
ISA	Internal Security Act
ISI	import substitution industrialization
ISI	Inter-Services Intelligence
KEDO	Korean Energy Development Organization
LCA	Light Combat Aircraft
LDCs	least developed countries
MCA	Millenium Challenge Account
MCC	Millenium Challenge Corporation
MDS	Missile Defense Shield
MILF	Moro Islamic Liberation Front

MLSA	Mutual Logistics Support Agreement
NAFTA	North American Free Trade Agreement
NATO	North Atlantic Treaty Organization
NEC	National Economic Council
NEPAD	New Partnership for Africa's Development
NGO	nongovernmental organization
NPA	New People's Army
NSC	National Security Council
NSS	National Security Strategy
ODA	Official Development Assistance
OECD	Organization for Economic Cooperation and Development
OPEC	Organization of Petroleum Exporting Countries
PAS	Parti Islam Se Malaysia
PDD	Presidential Decision Directive
PDPA	People's Democratic Party of Afghanistan
PfP	Partnership for Peace Program
PITO	Private Investment and Trade Opportunities
PLO	Palestine Liberation Organization
PRI	Institutional Revolutionary Party
PRTs	provincial reconstruction teams
RMSI	Regional Maritime Security Initiative
SCO	Shanghai Cooperation Organization
SDI	Strategic Defense Initiative
SEAL	Sea Air Land
SEATO	Southeast Asia Treaty Organization
SIPRI	Stockholm International Peace Research Institute
TNI	Tentara Nasional Indonesia
UN	United Nations
UNFPA	United Nations Fund for Population Activities
UNITA	União Nacional para a Independência Total de Angola
USAID	U.S. Agency for International Development
WMD	weapons of mass destruction
WTO	World Trade Organization

U.S. Foreign Policy
Toward the
Third World

1

American Policies Toward the Global South in the Post–Cold War, Post–Bipolar Era

An Introduction

Jürgen Rüland, Theodor Hanf, and Eva Manske

The End of the Cold War: Toward a Peace Dividend?

The end of the Cold War was greeted with much fanfare in the West. For some, the collapse of the socialist bloc even heralded the "end of history," the ultimate triumph of liberal democracy and free-market capitalism over rival ideologies.[1] Although the majority of intellectuals disagreed, many nevertheless looked forward to a peace dividend from the anticipated decline of military spending. There was great hope that the spiraling arms race of the Cold War would give way to arms control, disarmament, and reduced defense budgets. The peace dividend would free resources for alleviating poverty, promoting democracy, and protecting human rights in regions of the global South, where previously the West had given higher priority to anti-communism and containment of the Soviet Union than to development.

A paradigmatic foreign policy shift also became imperative because the North-South divide had considerably widened in the 1980s. Disparities in per capita income between the member countries of the Organization for Economic Cooperation and Development (OECD) and developing countries had increased from 15 to 1 in the mid-1960s to 20 to 1 by the end of the 1980s, and 50 to 1 between OECD members and the least developed countries (LDCs). Income disparities between the highest and lowest quintiles of the global population widened from 45 to 1 in 1980 to 59 to 1 in 1989 (see Table 1.1). Meanwhile, the number of people living in absolute poverty rose from 1.051 billion in 1985 to 1.133 billion in 1990.[2] Indicators for basic needs such as food, shelter, and access to clean water also deteriorated.[3] Particularly worrisome were developmental perspectives for the non–oil-producing LDCs of Sub-Saharan Africa. Their economies had to contend with exploding energy bills caused by the oil crises of the 1970s, deteriorating terms of trade, mounting debts, and the depletion of their natural resources for debt service, resulting in accelerating environmental degradation. Rapid population growth, kleptocratic elites, endemic corruption, the prevalence of primordial loyalties, violent repression of political dissidents, and civil wars aggravated the crisis. Even Latin America, one of the economically more advanced regions of the Third World, was caught in the debt trap. Although the causes of the Latin American debt crisis were partly homemade, the high-interest-rate policy of the Reagan administration and an appreciating U.S. dollar certainly deepened it. Despite re-democratization, Latin Americans still regard the 1980s as the "lost decade." The 1980s were a decade of deep recession and hyperinflation, demanding great sacrifices from the poorer segments of the population. Many inside and outside the region blamed these sufferings on the austerity measures that the International Monetary Fund (IMF) prescribed for the governments of the debt-ridden countries.

The resources freed by the anticipated reduction of defense spending after the Cold War seemed to create a golden opportunity for bringing industrialized countries closer to the objective of spending 0.7 percent of their gross domestic product (GDP) on development aid. By the late 1980s, only the Netherlands, Luxembourg, and the Scandinavian countries had met this goal formulated by the United Nations (UN) in the 1960s. The United States spent less than 0.2 percent; others, such as the Federal Republic of Germany, Italy, Australia, and Canada, barely 0.5 percent.[4] Moreover, freed from the need to support corrupt and dictatorial, but anti-communist regimes, prospects increased that development aid could henceforth be spent more effectively. Instead of focusing on opaque state bureaucracies and the class of rent-seekers controlling them, development aid could be increasingly channeled to nongovernmental organizations (NGOs) and other civil society representatives working for poverty alleviation and grassroots empowerment.

Table 1.1

Income Disparities Between Highest and Lowest Quintile of World Population, 1960–89 (in percent of global income)

Year	Lowest quintile	Highest quintile	Ratio highest to lowest quintile	GNI coefficient
1960	2.3	70.2	30 : 1	0.69
1970	2.3	73.9	32 : 1	0.71
1980	1.7	76.3	45 : 1	0.79
1989	1.4	82.7	59 : 1	0.87

Source: United Nations Development Report, *Human Development Report 1992* (New York/Oxford: 1992), p. 36.

Another anticipated positive development was the enhanced role of the UN in conflict resolution through peacekeeping missions. Festering ethnic and anti-regime conflicts, which had become the dominant type of violent conflict in the post–World War II era, would no longer become the "southern dimension" of the East-West conflict.[5] The civil wars in Southern Africa (Angola, Mozambique, and Namibia), Central America (Nicaragua, El Salvador, and Guatemala), and Southeast Asia (Cambodia, East Timor, and the Philippines) were examples of internal conflicts that became intertwined with the superpowers' struggle to extend their own position or contain their adversary in the so-called Third World. The blood toll of these conflicts and the human suffering they caused were immense; between 1945 and 1983 more than 20 million died and more than 30 million became refugees or displaced persons.[6]

With the "new concert of powers" and the UN Security Council less divided and less frequently paralyzed by the veto of one of its permanent members,[7] peace missions would henceforth be confronted with fewer obstacles than during the Cold War. In the years immediately preceding the collapse of the Soviet Union, a time of marked superpower rapprochement, UN peace missions had already increased in number and adopted more extensive functions, such as organizing and monitoring elections (see Table 1.2 and Table 1.3). The UN also played a key role in monitoring the fragile peace in Central America, in the decolonization of Namibia, and the Soviet withdrawal from Afghanistan. This raised hopes that in the post–Cold War period the resolution of intrastate conflicts would not have to wait until one of the external powers withdrew or hostilities died down due to exhaustion of the warring local parties.[8]

Table 1.2

Vetos in the UN Security Council, 1945–90

Country	Number of vetos
Soviet Union	114
United States	69
United Kingdom	30
France	18
China	3
Total	234
Number of vetos 1991–2001	32

Source: Peter J. Opitz, *Die Vereinten Nationen. Geschichte, Struktur, Perspektiven* (München: Fink, 2002), p. 32.

Table 1.3

UN Peacekeeping Missions, 1945–2002

Period	Number of peacekeeping missions
1945–88	13
1989–2002	41

Source: Peter J. Opitz, *Die Vereinten Nationen. Geschichte, Struktur, Perspektiven* (München: Fink, 2002), pp. 32 and 54–55.

Thus, the end of the Cold War seemingly strengthened the UN in one of the core functions accorded to it by the UN Charter, that is, securing peace in the world. For the first time since its foundation, conditions existed in which the principle of collective security was more than an empty conceptual shell. The annexation of Kuwait by Iraqi dictator Saddam Hussein in August 1990 became the first test case. The UN-mandated military coalition led by the United States unequivocally conveyed the message to aggressors that they would be held accountable if they breached international law. Less than a year later, the UN extended the mandate for peacekeeping missions to cases in which failing or failed states are unable to avert human disasters or in which genocide or other crimes against humanity are being committed or are imminent. The UN resolution authorizing the establishment of protection zones for the Kurds after the Gulf War in 1991 and the U.S.-led mission to Somalia in 1992 were the first humanitarian interventions. The latter marked a departure from the UN Charter's principle of national sovereignty or noninterference in the domestic affairs of other states. By responding to gross human rights violations, the concept of humanitarian intervention also contributed to the creeping individualization of the hitherto primarily state-based nature of international law.

The end of the Cold War also seemed to coincide with a long-term trend in international relations, in which economics and "soft power" increasingly replaced military power as the main means of influencing the outcome of interactions between states. Under the impact of economic globalization, there was growing interdependence between states and societies, making military power increasingly less effective as a power resource. While globalization seemed to erode the policy-making capacities of the nation-state in many policy fields, most notably economics, many governments in the Third World responded to these pressures by forming or joining regional organizations. This "new regionalism" differed from the old regionalism of the 1950s and 1960s through its informality, "soft" law, "shallow" institutionalization, and an aversion to supranational integration.[9] Although many of these newly formed regional groupings were organizationally weak, governments joined them in an effort to strengthen their bargaining power in multilateral forums such as the World Trade Organization (WTO) and the UN, to name the most important. The result was an increasing vertical and horizontal differentiation of international institutions, which became part of a fledgling system of global governance.[10] The latter found its expression in the emergence of new layers of international cooperation such as inter- and transregional dialogues, the rise of subregional transborder cooperation schemes, and a proliferation of international regimes.[11] Thus, even outside the OECD, international politics became increasingly complex, with international institutions and transnational actors challenging the nation-state as the dominant actor in international relations.

In a world increasingly governed by institutions and norms, "soft power" became another important power resource.[12] Soft power refers to the agenda-setting capabilities of states in and outside institutional arenas and the ability of states to influence the behavior of other actors through values they find worth imitating. It is—as explained by Joseph S. Nye—"more than persuasion or the ability to move people by argument. It is the ability to entice and attract."[13]

In the wake of these changes, there was great optimism that, more than ever before, institutions and universally accepted norms would matter in the shaping and unfolding of the new international order.[14] These beliefs were also mirrored in the paradigmatic changes of international relations research. More than once, realism was pronounced dead.[15] Approaches to the study of international relations accordingly shifted toward neo-institutionalism and social constructivism. Liberal institutionalism and other approaches highlighting the paradigm of co-operation took the lead even in regions like Asia, which had hitherto played only a negligible role in the theorizing on international relations or where the majority of studies were guided by realist orthodoxy.[16]

For many who pinned their hopes on a cooperative new world order, much depended on the foreign policies of the United States.[17] The United States entered the post–Cold War era as the only remaining superpower in what Charles Krauthammer called a "unipolar moment."[18] Would the United States—following its idealist and internationalist traditions of foreign policy making—make its unrivaled power and resources available to a transformation of international relations so as to facilitate sustainable development, social justice, democracy, human rights, preventive diplomacy, and conflict prevention in the global South? And would Washington—in line with the assumptions of hegemonic stability theory—throw its political weight behind a multilateral order and contribute to sustained international institution building with the objective of strengthening the fledgling structures of global governance? Or would America turn to a more inward-looking, neo-isolationist foreign policy equivalent to a disengagement from the Third World? Such disengagement would at best be benign neglect; in many cases, however, such neglect would be less than benign.

Toward a New World Disorder?

For a moment in the early 1990s, the prospects for a multilateral American foreign policy and increased global engagement by the United States appeared more real than it did in retrospect. To a much greater extent than the Reagan administration, President George H.W. Bush, despite his predilections for a pragmatic foreign policy, seemed intent on relying on multilateralism and international institutions. The war against Iraq was based on a UN mandate and when the Iraqi invading forces were expelled from Kuwait, Bush complied with the limited UN mandate.

He refrained from marching on Baghdad and toppling the regime of Saddam Hussein as influential commentators in the United States had called for.[19] The older Bush's multilateral credentials include moves to replace the Canada-U.S. Free Trade Agreement (CUSFTA) with the North American Free Trade Agreement (NAFTA)—thereby including Mexico—and to launch the Enterprise of the Americas Initiative (EAI). The latter envisioned a free trade zone in the Western hemisphere ranging from Alaska to Tierra del Fuego by 2005.[20]

Before long, however, it became clear that these high hopes and expectations would not be met due to U.S. domestic politics as well as to international factors.

On the domestic front, many analysts saw the United States in a state of progressive decline in the late 1980s and 1990s. Paul Kennedy, for instance, attributed the seeming decline of U.S. power to an "imperial overstretch." According to this view, the overextension of commitments abroad had been a persistent drain on American resources and thus severely weakened the U.S. economy. Because military power was regarded as a variable dependent on economic prowess, America's decline was measured mainly in terms of economic malperformance. Key indicators were the declining American share of world GDP and global trade, the slump in industrial productivity, and the deterioration of the education and transportation systems. The view of the nation as being in a "growth crisis" assumed alarming proportions when America's economic performance was compared with the "miracle economies" of Japan, China, and the East Asian "tigers."[21] The mounting U.S. trade deficit with these trading partners was seen as a reflection of a disturbing decline in American competitiveness. Some conservative observers even went so far as to relate American weakness to the increasing decadence of values prevailing in the West, such as the disintegration of the family, hedonism, rampant crime, and drug addiction. To put the West in general—and the United States in particular—back on the road to economic growth, it was held that Western societies needed an infusion of Confucian values, which were identified as the root causes of East Asia's unprecedented economic success.[22] More sober voices like that of Joseph S. Nye, who rejected the "Western decline" hypothesis, went more or less unheard at the time. Nye argued that such assessments were based on false yardsticks. It was misleading to compare America's contemporary position in the world with the immediate post–World War II era when U.S. military and economic power was indeed unprecedented. It meant comparing a normal distribution of power with that in an exceptional period.[23]

While Nye maintained that there was no alternative to a continued internationalist U.S. foreign policy, the "Western decline" debate nevertheless facilitated a shift toward "soft" or "tempered isolationism."[24] Although the incoming Clinton administration did not explicitly rule out internationalist orientations, it made clear it would concentrate primarily on rebuilding the domestic fundamentals of American power. While committing himself to policies promoting democracy and human rights in the first two years of his presidency, Clinton later increasingly pursued a foreign policy agenda clearly subordinated to America's economic interests.[25] The formation of an Economic Security Council, presided over by President Clinton himself, underscored his administration's priorities.[26]

At least at a rhetorical level, free-market fundamentalism became the platform on which the United States built its relations with the developing world. This policy echoed the so-called Washington Consensus, which rests on the three pillars of open markets, free trade, and democracy.[27] It is guided by the belief that open markets, a liberal investment regime, privatization, and financial deregulation are the best recipes for sustained economic growth.[28] Democracy and good governance are viewed as prerequisites for a free-market economy. The reverse relationship, that is, that a liberal economic order facilitates democratization, has also become one of the articles of faith of the adherents of a neoliberal economic order. With this revival of modernization theory in its most simplistic form, the United States sought to regain superiority in its three-way competition with the European Union (EU) and Japan by implanting the American model of capitalism in as many parts of the world as possible.

Although the United States sought to give its neoliberal development strategy global reach by supporting the structural adjustment policies of the IMF and the World Bank, in practice economic relations with the global South became quite opportunistic. Broadly speaking, this policy concentrated on the big emerging markets in East and Southeast Asia, Latin America, and Southern Africa and a few big emerging sectors such as telecommunication, environmental technologies, and services in which the United States had a competitive edge.[29] China, South Korea, Indonesia, Singapore, Brazil, Argentina, Mexico, South Africa, Turkey, and, after the inauguration of economic liberalization policies in 1991, India, became the main addressees of U.S. economic policies. Moreover, pressuring developing countries to adhere to neoliberal orthodoxy did not prevent Washington from resorting to protectionist policies when it fitted American interests. What in U.S. parlance is called "fair trade" is often enforced by unilateral imposition of antidumping measures and countervailing duties on its trading partners under Article 301 of the Omnibus Trade and Competitiveness Act of 1988. While rhetorically still adhering to the free trade paradigm, the act marked a shift in American trade policies toward "reciprocal trade" and "managed trade." With the end of the Cold War, increasing competition, and increasing trade dependency—as illustrated by the rise of trade as a percentage of GDP from 12 percent in 1970 to 25 percent in 1997—there were no more compelling reasons to tolerate "free riders."[30]

"Unprincipled multilateralism" also marked the American response to the Asian financial crisis of 1997–98.[31] While spells of anti-Americanism were a recurring phenomenon in much of Southeast Asia, the United States nevertheless enjoyed considerable "soft power" in the region. This capital was, however, jeopardized by the American refusal to assist Thailand, from where the Asian currency crisis originated. Whereas during the 1994–95 Mexican peso crisis Washington committed more than $20 billion to bail out its southern neighbor, during the Asian crisis it delegated responsibility for crisis management to the IMF.[32] Not surprisingly, the seeming lack of U.S. concern, America's dominant position in the IMF, and the IMF's mishandling of the crisis fueled conspiracy theories in the region. The seeming triggering of the crisis by (Western) currency speculators and the heavy-handed conditionalities attached to rescue packages of the IMF were interpreted in Southeast Asia as a ploy to sabotage high-performing economies that had mutated into formidable competitors for the West.[33] American opposition also derailed attempts of Asian and, in particular, the Association of Southeast Nations (ASEAN) countries to set up an Asian Monetary Fund (AMF) as a regional institution entrusted with the management of future financial crises.[34]

The Clinton administration embraced multilateralism only when it had to act out of a position of relative weakness.[35] A case in point is the free trade agenda vigorously pushed by Clinton in the Asia-Pacific Economic Cooperation (APEC). Many Asian members of APEC suspected, not without reason, that the free trade policy was a thinly veiled strategy to pry open Asian markets in economic sectors such as telecommunications, information technology, and services in which the United States had a competitive edge.[36] By contrast, Ecotech, the aid component of APEC—launched under the pressure of Southeast Asian developing countries—hardly ever went beyond lip service and received little commitment on the part of the United States.[37] Other multilateral initiatives of the United States such as NAFTA and the envisioned Free Trade Agreement of the Americas (FTAA) were, like APEC, first and foremost institutional balancing strategies. They intended to balance European moves toward monetary union and they served as regional alternatives in the event of a failure of the Uruguay trade liberalization round of the General Agreement on Tariffs and Trade (GATT). More concretely, they were also used to extract concessions from the EU in the liberalization of agriculture, which had become the greatest impediment to the conclusion of the Uruguay Round.

To a considerable extent, these policies of pursuing national economic interests also reflected the prevailing mood in the United States, where both houses of Congress were controlled by the Republican Party from 1994 onward. The Republican majorities were particularly critical of American development aid, which they viewed as ineffective and a waste of scarce resources. Development aid is certainly no panacea for alleviating poverty and initiating an economic "take-off" in the countries of the South. Indeed, critics have a point when they claim that aid disbursements frequently do not reach their target groups. Yet, the neoliberal recipes prescribed by the Washington Consensus can hardly be considered a better medicine. "Trade for aid" sounds persuasive in principle, but in practice it amounts to a perpetuation of the typical colonial trade structure whereby poor countries export unprocessed raw materials to the United States and other industrialized economies. It is no coincidence that U.S. investments in Africa are heavily geared toward the oil sector and that 71 percent of U.S. imports from Sub-Saharan Africa in 1996 were energy related.[38] Nor did the Heavily Indebted Poor Countries Initiative (HIPC) of the World Bank contribute much to alleviating the debt burden of African LDCs.[39] If it was a key objective of the Clinton administration to help Africa to integrate into the world economy, it failed. At the same time foreign aid declined from $12 billion in 1989 to $6.5 billion in 1996.[40] U.S. aid to Latin America fell from $1.6 billion in 1991 to $681 million in 1996; the decline in aid was somewhat less dramatic in the case of Sub-Saharan Africa but it still fell from $1.5 billion in 1993 to $1.1 billion in 1996. By the late 1990s, U.S. aid to LDCs had declined to less than 0.03 percent of its GDP.[41] Overall, at the beginning of the new millennium, development aid had dropped to barely 0.1 percent of U.S. GDP (see Table 1.4). This is only about one-third of European aid levels and the lowest percentage among the world's major donor nations.[42] Taking into account that the lion's share of this aid went to a few strategically important countries such as Egypt, Israel, and Jordan, the amount available for all other developing countries was negligible.[43]

While democracy promotion is one of the pillars of the Washington Consensus, in practice economic objectives and democratization may conflict. Structural adjustment—if not slowed down or cushioned by social policies (thereby diluting austerity measures)—easily undermines the legitimacy of governments and provides a fertile ground for more or less extreme forms of populism.[44] The weakening of democracy in Latin America and the rise of populist leaders such as Thaksin Shinawatra in Thailand and Joseph E. Estrada in the Philippines are cases in point.[45]

In other cases, democracy promotion was clearly subordinated to economic objectives or considerations of political stability, as, for example, with the Clinton administration's Africa policy, which courted a group of "new African leaders," consisting of Yoweri Museveni of Uganda, Isaias Afwerki of Eritrea, Meles Zenawi of Ethiopia, and Paul Kagame of Rwanda. This "new generation of leaders" had in common a certain commitment to structural adjustment and the ability to provide some political stability in countries that had experienced protracted civil wars and autocratic rule. Particularly embarrassing for Clinton was the fact that three months after his much publicized visit to Africa in March 1998, Ethiopia and Eritrea became embroiled in a war that cost the lives of tens of thousands, while Museveni and Kagame became key players in the civil wars in Eastern Congo. Criticism by NGO activists and Africanists of the more than dubious democratic credentials of these leaders and their questionable human rights record was brushed aside or ignored by the administration. Even if the Clinton presidency in its second term must be credited with a more activist Africa policy, it was largely a matter of symbolic politics. With no prospect of any rival power capable of challenging U.S. interests in Africa, insignificant trade relations and investment levels, and no vital domestic interests involved, it was difficult to persuade Congress of the need to channel resources into Africa.[46] Much of the responsibility for Africa's quagmire was still attributed to Europe's colonial legacy.

Table 1.4

Official Development Aid of Selected Industrial Countries, 1990–2002 (in percent of GNI)

Country	1990[a]	1991[b]	1992	1993[b]	1994	1995	1996	1997[c]	1998	1999	2000	2001	2002
Australia	0.34	0.38	0.36	0.35	0.34	0.36	0.30	0.28	0.27	0.26	0.27	0.25	0.26
Canada	0.44	0.45	0.46	0.45	0.43	0.38	0.32	0.37	0.30	0.28	0.25	0.22	0.28
Denmark	0.94	0.96	1.02	1.04	1.03	0.96	1.04	1.05	0.99	1.01	1.06	1.03	0.96
Germany	0.42	0.40	0.36	0.37	0.33	0.31	0.33	0.31	0.26	0.26	0.27	0.27	0.27
France	0.60	0.62	0.59	0.63	0.64	0.55	0.48	0.49	0.40	0.39	0.32	0.32	0.38
Italy	0.31	0.30	0.34	0.31	0.27	0.15	0.20	0.13	0.20	0.15	0.13	0.15	0.20
Japan	0.31	0.32	0.30	0.26	0.29	0.28	0.20	0.22	0.27	0.27	0.28	0.23	0.23
Netherlands	0.92	0.88	0.86	0.82	0.76	0.81	0.81	0.81	0.80	0.79	0.84	0.82	0.81
Norway	1.17	1.13	1.12	1.01	1.05	0.87	0.85	0.90	0.89	0.88	0.76	0.80	0.89
Sweden	0.91	0.90	1.03	0.98	0.96	0.77	0.84	0.86	0.72	0.70	0.80	0.77	0.83
United Kingdom	0.27	0.32	0.30	0.31	0.31	0.29	0.27	0.29	0.27	0.24	0.32	0.32	0.31
United States	0.21	0.20	0.18	0.15	0.14	0.10	0.12	0.12	0.10	0.10	0.10	0.11	0.13

Sources: Development Assistance Committee (DAC) of the Organization for Economic Cooperation and Development (OECD), available at www.oecd.org/dataoecd/43/26/1894401.xls, accessed July 11, 2004.

[a]United Nations Development Programme, *Flows of Aid From DAC Member Countries*, available at www.undp.org/hdr2003/indicator/pdf/hdr03_table_15.pdf, accessed July 24, 2004.

[b]Bundesministerium für wirtschaftliche Zusammenarbeit und Entwicklung, ed., *Medienhandbuch Entwicklungspolitik 1995* (Bonn: BMZ, 1995). p. 50.

[c]Bundesministerium für wirtschaftliche Zusammenarbeit und Entwicklung, ed., *Medienhandbuch Entwicklungspolitik 2002* (Bonn: BMZ, 2002). p. 358.

In fairness to the Clinton administration, in other cases its strategy of "enlargement," that is, widening the circle of democracies in the world, was pursued more vigorously, albeit not necessarily more consistently.[47] Military aid for Indonesia, for instance, was successively reduced in the 1990s in response to the involvement of the Indonesian military in gross human rights violations during the Suharto era. It was terminated altogether due to the complicity, if not active participation, of Indonesian troops in the massacres committed by pro-Indonesian militias after the East Timor independence referendum in September 1999. Military cooperation with Thailand was temporarily interrupted between May and September 1992 after troops had violently suppressed the country's democracy movement in May 1992.[48] Sanctions were also imposed on the military junta in Myanmar in response to its repressive policies, the use of forced labor, and its alleged involvement in drug trafficking.[49] In Malaysia, during the 1998 APEC summit in Kuala Lumpur, Vice President Al Gore endorsed *reformasi* and took Prime Minister Mahathir Mohamad to task for the harsh treatment of his former deputy, Anwar Ibrahim.[50] The United States also played a leading role in the restoration of democracy in Haiti.[51] The fact, however, that the administration was much less strident in its criticism of nondemocratic practices and human rights violations in Russia and China subjected Washington to persistent criticism of double standards and a lack of a consistent democracy promotion policy.

At a global level, the incoming Clinton administration was confronted with the troubling experience that by the early 1990s the number of armed conflicts in the world had risen from forty-eight in 1990 to an unprecedented high of fifty-two in 1992, before declining again in the second half of the 1990s. From 2001 to 2003, it hovered between thirty-four and thirty-nine (see Table 1.5).[52] As in previous decades, most of these were internal conflicts and, as before, 90 percent of them raged in the global South. Yet, with the civil wars in the former Yugoslavia and the wars in the Caucasus, these conflicts reached the European periphery. Moreover, it was clear that their roots went far deeper than the East-West conflict. For many, the new world order seemed to have degenerated into a "world disorder." Cooperation and the institutionalist paradigm of international relations seemed to be in constant retreat, replaced by the more pessimistic outlook of the revitalized realist strand of international relations theory. Foremost among the prophets of doom was Samuel P. Huntington, who predicted that

Table 1.5

Number of Wars After the Cold War

Year	Number of wars
1990	48
1991	52
1992	52
1993	45
1994	41
1995	37
1996	29
1997	29
1998	33
1999	35
2000	34
2001[a]	37
2002	39
2003	35

Sources: Peter J. Opitz, *Die Vereinten Nationen. Geschichte, Struktur, Perspektiven* (München: Fink, 2002), p. 59; Konfliktbarometer.

[a]Project Ploughshares, *Armed Conflicts Report 2002,* available at www.ploughshares. ca/content/ACR/ACR00/ACR02-PrefaceIntroduction.html, accessed July 27, 2004.

international relations in the twenty-first century would be marked by a clash of civilizations.[53] Alain Minc predicted an atrophy of the Westphalian order in the form of a "New Middle Age," while Robert D. Kaplan deplored a "Coming Anarchy."[54]

Initially the United States responded favorably to the heightened need for peace missions, taking the lead in the Operation Restoration Hope in Somalia. However, as the operation moved from humanitarian intervention to robust peacemaking, U.S. soldiers became involved in a conflict with Mohammed Farah Aidid, a notorious Somali warlord. After American soldiers were killed in action and their corpses dragged through the streets of Mogadishu, Clinton, under mounting pressure at home, pulled U.S. troops out of Somalia in March 1994. The Somalia debacle marked a turning point in American participation in peace missions and humanitarian interventions. Shortly after the Somalia pullout, Clinton released Presidential Decision Directive 25 (PDD 25), which stipulated a number of conditions to be fulfilled for U.S. involvement. Perhaps even more damaging for multilateral collective security policies under the aegis of the UN was the fact that the Clinton administration backpedaled from its earlier commitment to the creation of a UN army and ruled out placing American troops under UN command.[55]

Relying more on its own strength than on multilateral institutions, the United States did not cut its defense budget. On the contrary, defense spending rose constantly in the second half of the 1990s and ballooned after September 11, 2001. By 2002, it had reached a staggering $347 billion, an increase of more than $100 billion since 1996, and an amount seven times that of global spending on development aid. According to the Stockholm International Peace Research Institute (SIPRI), the United States accounted for 43 percent of military spending worldwide. The increases in defense spending went hand in hand with a revolution in military technology, which facilitated a streamlining of the military apparatus. At the same time, the newly developed precision weapons immensely increased the effectiveness and the firepower of the U.S. army, securing U.S. military dominance for the next decades. In the second half of the 1990s, the United States also became the largest exporter of military equipment: between 1998 and 2002 the United States was the supplier in 41 percent of all registered arms deals.[56] Most of the arms sales went to the Middle East and, until the Asian financial crisis, to Southeast Asia.

The retreat from the administration's initial "assertive multilateralism" was evident in the refusal of the United States to participate in a peace mission to Rwanda in 1994.[57] Most observers agree that a UN mission could have averted the ensuing genocide, which claimed nearly half a million lives. That the United States was clearly reverting to a pragmatic, realist policy of intervention was shown in the case of Haiti in the same year. Whereas in the case of Rwanda the U.S. government argued that there were no immediate American interests at stake, this was different in the case of Haiti, where the United States led a mission to restore democracy and return ousted President Jean-Bertrand Aristide to power.

Substantial American efforts to resolve the Arab-Israeli conflict were of a mainly bilateral nature. These efforts—after temporary progress—are now once more in limbo after the collapse of the Camp David II negotiations in July 2000, the second Intifada, Israeli reprisals, and lack of progress with the post–Iraq War Road Map.[58]

American displeasure with the UN and some of its subsidiary organizations motivated a downgrading of the UN in American foreign policy, reflected in the nonpayment of its dues to the world organization.[59] In fact, the second Clinton administration moved sharply toward unilateralism. A striking example was American policies toward Third World rogue states. While in the first North Korean nuclear crisis in 1993–94 the Clinton administration still pursued a multilateral path with the formation of the Korean Energy Development Organization (KEDO), in the case of Iraq and Iran it shifted from the Bush administration's policy of a balance of power to a strategy of "dual containment."[60] The Helms-Burton Act (targeting Cuba) of 1996 and the D'Amato Act (targeting Iran) explicitly called for extraterritorial application, threatening even close allies with sanctions should they trade with the targeted countries. However, neither the Clinton administration nor the succeeding Bush administration did in fact implement these laws with respect to America's allies.[61]

The United States in the Global South:
A Case of Benign Neglect?

The terrorist attacks orchestrated by Muslim extremists on New York and Washington on September 11, 2001, seem to have vindicated the more pessimistic analysts of world politics and, in particular, Huntington's prognosis of an international disorder marked by cultural conflict.[62] Others, who were averse to constructing a direct link between the September 11 attacks and deepening cultural conflict, referred to the growing inequity between rich and poor countries caused by neoliberal globalization as factors facilitating terrorism and religious extremism. For them, the challenges for Western and American security would come mainly from the impoverished, economically stagnant global South. Though more research is needed on the roots and dynamics of international terrorism, it is not farfetched to conclude that cultural and distributional conflicts in the international arena converged in the September 11 attacks.

This volume does not seek to explore and explain the linkages between the September 11 attacks and American policies toward the global South. It does, however, take September 11 as a symptom of deep-rooted problems in America's relations with the global South and calls for a reappraisal of U.S. policies toward the developing world in the post–Cold War period.[63] It raises the question of whether these problems arise from sheer neglect—benign or otherwise. Or are they the result of high-handed unilateralism, interpreted in the South as an

American grand design to establish U.S. global hegemony based on superior military power and aggressive Westernization that erodes the cultural identity of non-Western societies? If this is the case, it would indeed—as Joseph S. Nye warned—dangerously undermine American "soft power" in the Third World.[64]

Organization of the Volume

The contributors to this volume, all renowned specialists on American foreign policy and acclaimed regional experts, explore U.S. policies in key regions of the Third World. The first two chapters following the Introduction discuss American post–Cold War foreign policies from a more general perspective. Chapter 2 discusses the broad parameters of American post–Cold War foreign policies and Chapter 3 examines how domestic actors such as the branches of government, bureaucratic interests in the foreign policy and security apparatus, NGOs, economic lobbies, pro–South lobbies, the media, and think tanks influence policy toward countries of the global South. Chapters 4 to 9 provide historically informed, policy-oriented analyses addressing American foreign policy toward Latin America, the Middle East, Southeast Asia, South Asia, Central Asia, and Africa. East Asia has been excluded, although China with its vast social and spatial disparities is still an ambiguous case. Although the Chinese government considers the People's Republic a developing country, the United States categorized it as an industrialized country during the negotiations on China's membership of the WTO. At the core of this dispute lay trade concessions China may claim as a developing country, which would exacerbate America's trade deficit with the People's Republic. However, our decision not to include East Asia in the volume was influenced less by these considerations than by the fact that the region's socioeconomic indicators differ markedly from the rest of Asia and even more so from all other regions of the global South. Chapter 10 concludes with an assessment of U.S. policies toward developing countries after September 11, 2001, and the war against Iraq that takes Washington's new National Security Strategy (NSS) as its point of departure.

Regional chapters focus on four major parameters of U.S. foreign policy raised in the introduction: security, economics, democracy, and domestic politics.

Security was the overwhelming concern in American foreign policy and, by extension, in its relations with the global South during the Cold

War. The end of the Cold War and the demise of the Soviet Union have alleviated these concerns without, however, removing them from the agenda. One may agree with James M. Scott and A. Lane Crothers when they state that the post–Cold War period may be "more benign," but it is also characterized by "more threat ambiguity."[65]

Post–Cold War security concerns in the American foreign policy community concentrated on potential challengers and strategic competitors such as China, Japan, and even the EU (according to a Pentagon study authored by Paul Wolfowitz in the early 1990s). As far as the global South is concerned, Washington saw to it that no powers inside or outside these regions could threaten American security. In the second half of the 1990s, it also increasingly devoted attention to so-called nontraditional security issues such as organized crime, drug trafficking, piracy, terrorism, money laundering, international migration, and environmental hazards. Yet, much more than in the decade before, because of September 11, 2001, security issues have dramatically and unequivocally returned to the top of U.S. foreign policy agenda, leading some observers to speak of a "second Cold War."[66] These paradigmatic changes in America's foreign policy are reflected in the priority that the authors of the regional chapters give to security.

In the Clinton administration, economics became a foreign policy issue on a par with security. Underlying this new policy thrust were the impact of intensifying economic competition driven by globalization and the perceived economic decline of the United States in the late 1980s and early 1990s. As this volume concentrates on America's ties with the global South, the question arises of the extent to which America's economic relations with these countries have spurred or impeded development in the regions of the South.

The Third Wave of democratization has reversed the erstwhile dominance of authoritarian regimes in much of the Third World. Although in the early 1970s two-thirds of all countries had authoritarian governments, at the beginning of the new millennium the same proportion were democracies of one kind or another. At least at a rhetorical level, promotion of democracy, good governance, and human rights policies are now elements in the foreign policies of Western governments. Beyond the normative dimension, the democratic peace hypothesis has become for them a key rationale for promoting democracy. It assumes that a democratic environment will reduce security threats in the world. As has been pointed out above, American administrations, though with varying emphasis, have also raised "building democracy" to a foreign policy objective during the post–Cold War period.

Globalization and regionalization have increasingly eroded the traditional congruence of political and social space as defined by state borders. In view of the cross-border nature of many environmental, economic, and security-related issues, transnational actors have become important players in foreign policy making. They have not only contributed to a pluralization of foreign policy making, but also blurred the boundaries between domestic and foreign policy making. In these "intermestic issues," foreign policy making increasingly resembles domestic policy making; it has, as Helen M. Ingram and Suzanne L. Fiederlein argue, become a public policy arena.[67] The ensuing "foreign policy decentralization" once more underscores the fact that a given objective national interest, as suggested by classical and structural realists, does not exist for foreign policy makers.[68] Foreign policy analysis must therefore encompass more than the realist billiard model and, as far as possible, take into account the domestic forces molding foreign policy. This also has repercussions for the scope of action of foreign policy makers, which is determined by the win-sets of the two-level games linking the international and the domestic chess boards.[69]

Following this introductory chapter, Chapter 2, by Hanns W. Maull, discusses the long waves of American foreign policy traditions, providing a map for assessing and evaluating U.S. post–Cold War policies toward the global South. Maull develops the provocative argument that the present foreign policy thrust, which has been denounced by critics as unilateralist, preemptive, interventionist, and marked by disdain for international institutions, is the rule rather than an aberration in U.S. history. Whenever the United States did pursue a multilateral approach, it was never "principled multilateralism." Imbued with a sense of exceptionalism, it served mainly as a justification for American interventions, including the use of force, where and when it fit American interests. But the current "robust multilateralism" in which "America defines the tasks, determines the strategy, and leads the implementation—always reserving the right to go it alone and, if necessary, strike pre-emptively," will hardly suffice to deal effectively with the post–September 11 terrorist threat. Instead of merely relying on superior military power, effective responses to international terrorism must tackle its political and economic roots. But even then the United States faces a dilemma: if, for instance, democracy is one of the recipes for overcoming terrorism, as proposed by the Bush administration, counter-terrorism could well undermine it as did counter-insurgency during the Cold War. While current policies may oscillate on the multilateralism-unilateralism axis, Maull nonetheless concludes that there will be no return to isolationism and that U.S. foreign policy will be guided by the tenets of realpolitik, even if the United States pursues a multilateral approach.

James M. McCormick (Chapter 3) examines the extent to which the lack of coherence of American foreign policies in the post–Cold War era toward regions in the global South might be attributed to the absence of forceful advocates within American society championing the cause of development and seeking to influence American policies toward poor countries. McCormick shows that far from a decline of so-called Third World groups, American foreign policy making has been characterized by an increasing pluralism of actors and topics since the end of the Vietnam War. As long as security issues dominated U.S. foreign policy, NGOs and civil society groups were largely excluded from decision making. However, the new economic, environmental, sociocultural, and other nonconventional security issues dominating the security agenda since the end of the Cold War have opened more avenues for societal actors to become involved. Not only has congressional involvement become more assertive, NGOs and many single-issue interest groups such as ethnic and religious lobbies, human rights organizations, and anti-globalization movements have also become active players in foreign policy making. Most of these groups target Congress more than the administration, and occasionally succeed in mobilizing congressional majorities for their cause. All in all, however, their impact has been limited. Most of the issues they stand for find little support in the wider public. Members of Congress primarily interested in reelection are more inclined to work for the bread-and-butter issues of their constituents than to engage in issues their voters perceive as remote from their daily lives. After September 11, 2001, foreign policy again became a predominantly executive domain, a development in which Congress readily concurred by rallying behind the president.

Howard J. Wiarda (Chapter 4) argues that it would be misleading to characterize American foreign policy toward Latin America as "benign neglect." Although U.S. policy toward Latin America is frequently criticized as low priority, incompetent, and culturally insensitive, U.S.–Latin American relations are more complex. Major changes in both the United States and Latin America in the 1990s have promoted a closer relationship that is neither unilateral nor one of "benign neglect." The "Hispanization" of the United States, increasing economic interdependencies, and, in the seeming absence of alternatives, the acceptance of the premises of the Washington Consensus by Latin American elites, are at the core of these changes. Moreover, at lower policy levels, often ignored by the media, U.S. policy in Latin America is vigorous and activist. The foreign policy-making bureaucracies, the external relations of local governments, NGOs, and private sector engagement can be named in this respect. Another important facet is the post–Cold War shift from strategic, political, and diplomatic issues in U.S. relations with Latin America toward economic ones. This shift has been accompanied by a decline in public foreign aid and the promotion of private foreign direct investment (FDI). Intensifying trade relations, spurred by free trade agreements such as NAFTA and the envisioned FTAA, further underline the new quality of relations. Close bilateral relations, in particular with Mexico, though less so with Brazil and Argentina, also contradict the allegation of "benign neglect." All in all, post–Cold War U.S. policies in Latin America are characterized by continuity. Even the administration of President George W. Bush has largely followed the policies of its predecessors as there is currently little terrorist threat from Latin America.

After a brief overview of American interests in the Middle East during the Cold War period, William B. Quandt (Chapter 5) explores U.S. policies in that region for the post–Cold War era. The prevention of Soviet domination of the region, access to its oil resources, and the security and well-being of Israel were major U.S. interests before 1990; with the end of the Cold War this traditional list changed significantly. No longer did Washington have to contend with Moscow or any other external major power. The new challenges came from within—radical regimes such as Iraq and Iran, Islamic extremism, and, after September 11, the phenomenon of terrorism. The key to containing or even solving these problems was held to be an Arab-Israeli settlement, toward which the Clinton administration devoted much of its energy, but which ultimately failed due to the intransigence of both sides.

Quandt registers a major change in U.S. policy toward the Middle East after September 11, 2001. Since then the region has become a test case for the new strategic doctrine of "dominance" which—as the Iraq policy illustrates—even includes preemptive military strikes. Under the current Bush administration, the United States abandoned Clinton's more even-handed position in the Arab-Israeli conflict and increasingly tilted toward Israel, seemingly giving Prime Minister Ariel Sharon a free hand to retaliate against Palestinian suicide bombings. Hawks in the Bush administration see U.S. policy toward Islamic extremism and Middle Eastern rogue states as part of a civilizational conflict in Huntington's terms, with regime change, democratization, development, and modernization as possible, albeit vague and uncertain, remedies. In sum, it would be wrong to speak of a policy of U.S. "benign neglect" toward the Middle East. Development and military aid have remained at persistently high levels, and America was actively involved in the Arab-Israeli peace process throughout the Clinton presidency.

Amitav Acharya (Chapter 6) examines U.S. policies in Southeast Asia. While it would go too far to categorize U.S. policies toward this region as outright "neglect," Acharya nevertheless shows that U.S. attention has continued to decline since the end of the Vietnam War. Greater priority has been attached to Northeast Asia with its focal points of the Taiwan Strait and the Korean peninsula. With no major security threats originating from Southeast Asia, trade with ASEAN member states and foreign direct investment in the region soared in the 1980s and 1990s. However, the lack of support for Southeast Asian states hit by the Asian currency crisis, the perceived association of Washington with the heavy-handed IMF austerity regime, and what was seen as a pro-Israeli policy of the United States fueled anti-American sentiment in the region.

September 11 has led to a major shift in U.S. policies toward Southeast Asia, bringing about a "reengagement" of the United States in Southeast Asian security. Southeast Asia, which includes Indonesia, with the world's largest Muslim population, Malaysia, a Muslim majority state, and the Philippines, with its Islamic Moro minority in the south, was labeled a "second front" by U.S. strategists. The responses of Southeast Asian states to the U.S.-led war against terror varied. While the Philippines and Singapore cooperated closely with Washington, reactions from Malaysia and Indonesia were more circumspect and critical of the wars against the Taliban and Iraq. At the multilateral level, the United States used the ASEAN-U.S. dialogue, the ASEAN Regional Forum (ARF), and APEC as platforms for forging its anti-terrorism coalition. Muslim societies were particularly angered by what they perceived as double standards. Whereas the United States attacked Afghanistan and Iraq, it did little to resolve the Arab-Israeli conflict. The U.S.-ASEAN Joint Declaration for Cooperation to Combat International Terrorism has been celebrated by some observers as a landmark agreement, although its nonbinding nature raises many questions about its effectiveness. Amid growing fears in the region of U.S. unilateralism, Acharya cannot discount the possibility that "the increased security push by the United States undertaken in the name of the war on terror will have a polarizing impact on the region, because of a disjunction between U.S. strategic objectives and the domestic political imperatives and national (read regime) security objectives of Southeast Asian governments."[70]

Sumit Ganguly and Brian Shoup (Chapter 7) argue that South Asia has been relatively neglected by U.S. foreign policy. Like Howard J. Wiarda's diagnosis of the Latin American case, Ganguly and Shoup maintain that the region received greater attention only during major crises, for example, after the Soviet invasion of Afghanistan in 1979. The policy of propping up Zia-ul-Haq's dictatorship in Pakistan as a bulwark against further Soviet inroads into the region was, however, short lived; moreover, to complicate matters, it strained relations with India. As a consequence of the latter's close relations with the Soviet Union, which appeared to conflict with New Delhi's credentials as a nonaligned country, U.S.-Indian relations have never been warm. However, support for Pakistan was scaled back considerably in the 1990s, reflecting American objections to Pakistan's nuclear policies. In a parallel development, the Clinton administration engineered a rapprochement with India when—after the collapse of the Soviet Union—the latter began to reorient its foreign policy and open up its economy. Yet, criticism of India's nuclear policies defined the limits of U.S.-Indian relations. After September 11, 2001, the United States downplayed its nonproliferation policies, emphasizing Pakistan's role as a major ally in the war against the Taliban in Afghanistan and international terrorism. This time, India's concerns were treated more sensitively, building on the policies of the Clinton administration. Nevertheless, levels of cooperation with South Asia are comparatively modest—a fact also corroborated by low levels of development aid, trade, and investment.

Conrad Schetter and Bernd Kuzmits (Chapter 8) show that America's difficult position in Afghanistan in the post–September 11 period is less the result of previous benign neglect than inconsistent policies based on expectations of short-term gains and changing domestic political constellations. During the Cold War, U.S. engagement in Afghanistan was primarily a response to the changing fortunes in the superpower rivalry with the Soviet Union. After the withdrawal of the Soviet occupation troops from Afghanistan in 1988, the U.S. missed the opportunity to devise a road map to peace and Afghanistan subsequently disintegrated into a battlefield of warring mujahidin armies. After the rise of the fundamentalist Taliban to power by the mid-1990s, U.S. policies wildly fluctuated between complicity with the new rulers for the sake of American oil firm interests and increasing demonization after Madeleine Albright took over as secretary of state in 1997. After September 11, 2001, and the ensuing war on terror, security concerns took precedence over all other interests. This is evidenced by Operation Enduring Freedom designed to remove the Taliban regime from power and continued U.S. military presence to flush out remnants of Al-Qaeda and the Taliban. After the hostilities, the U.S. has become the main donor in the reconstruction of Afghanistan.

As far as the former Soviet republics in Central Asia are concerned, Schetter and Kuzmits reject the widespread notion that the U.S. presence in these countries is merely a pretext for securing long-term economic and geopolitical interests. While the United States has undeniably exhibited interest in the region's energy resources, oil and gas deposits are less than anticipated and do not justify the expectation of another "great game" emerging. Moreover, U.S. presence in the region was much less a watershed than in Afghanistan, because after initial neglect of the region it practically commenced with the extension of the NATO Partnership for Peace to Central Asian republics in the mid-1990s. Yet, the U.S. military presence, which expanded after September 11, complements operations in the war against terror in Afghanistan and elsewhere in South Asia. While flows of U.S. development assistance to these countries increased markedly in the post–September 11 period, it is less than expected by the region's governments and is primarily security related. This puts the U.S. in a similar dilemma as during the Cold War in much of the global South. For security and strategic reasons Washington is forced to support authoritarian regimes, the repressive policies of which may increasingly alienate the population from the U.S. At the same time, by gradually shifting to a multidirectional foreign policy, Central Asian governments are balancing U.S. influence by nurturing closer ties with Russia and China. Although the U.S. shares with Russia and China important security interests in the region, the simultaneous great power rivalry exposes the U.S. to pressures by Central Asian rulers. Schetter and Kuzmits conclude by predicting that the U.S. presence in Afghanistan and Central Asia will continue for an extended period of time.

Peter J. Schraeder (Chapter 9) provides a comprehensive review of U.S. African policies. Although there were fluctuations over time, since the Cold War era U.S. African policies are characterized by low priority and continuity. This continuity is the result of presidential disinterest, congressional neglect, bureaucratic conservatism, and intra-bureaucratic rivalries. Schraeder shows that, as far as Africa is concerned, the end of the Cold War has not freed the United States of the conceptual and ideological shackles of its Cold War competition with the Soviet Union. Under the impact of September 11, the more proactive Africa policies of Clinton's second term have been replaced by a de facto return to the geopolitical and security concerns of the Cold War era. But even Clinton's more proactive policies were far from consistent: development aid and poverty alleviation measures declined markedly and were more often than not sacrificed on the altar of narrow economic interests. The same can be said of democracy promotion after September 11, which, beyond the rhetoric, is overshadowed by national security interests and priorities determined by the war against international terrorism. The preoccupation with stability and anti-terrorism has led to the cultivation of strong links with Africa's leading regional powers, South Africa and Nigeria, and the isolation and containment of regional pariah states, most notably Libya and Sudan. Conspicuous by its absence is an American contribution to the resolution of internal civil conflicts and peacekeeping missions, which were suspended after the disastrous experience of the Somalia intervention. The Bush administration has displayed an even stronger aversion to U.S. involvement in peacekeeping operations, favoring African military solutions under the guise of "African solutions for African problems." The participation of a small contingent of U.S. troops in the Nigerian-led peacemaking mission in Liberia is a cautious readjustment of that policy. The chapter ends on a skeptical note, raising the specter of an Africa policy guided primarily by U.S. geopolitical interests in the ongoing war against terrorism. It may be subsumed under the motto: "Forget democracy and development and boost anti-terrorism."

The concluding chapter (Chapter 10) summarizes the main findings of the volume before making conjectures about the future of U.S. policies toward the global South. Its point of departure is the new National Security Strategy (NSS) of the United States as promulgated on September 20, 2002. Jürgen Rüland argues that the unfolding post–September 11 and, in particular, post–Iraq War United States is informed by a generally realist vision, thereby retarding the development of global governance. Although the NSS is more than a merely unilateralist policy blueprint, what has been mistaken by observers for multilateralist elements is little more than coalition building in the quest for U.S. dominance. Furthermore, the seemingly idealist components of the NSS, development aid, and democratization, are subordinated to a realist policy bias in which the highest priority is given to America's national interest. While it is laudable that the Bush administration intends to markedly step up development aid, poverty alleviation, and funds for fighting AIDS, aid policies are closely linked to the necessity of fighting international terrorism and a neoliberal economic growth strategy. Promotion of democracy as a strategy to enhance U.S. security creates a dilemma, because the United States's need to align itself with autocratic regimes in its fight against terrorism undermines the credibility of this strategy. Moreover, the domino democratization envisioned in the Middle East has been flawed from the very beginning and the longer the U.S.-led occupation forces remain in Iraq, the more disastrous its consequences become.

Notes

1. Francis Fukuyama, *The End of History and the Last Man* (New York: Free Press, 1992).

2. World Bank, *Implementing the World Bank's Strategy to Reduce Poverty: Progress and Challenges* (Washington, DC: World Bank, 1993), p. 5.

3. Franz Nuscheler, "Entwicklungspolitische Bilanz der 80er Jahre—Perspektiven für die 90er Jahre," in Dieter Nohlen and Franz Nuscheler, eds., *Handbuch der Dritten Welt: Grundprobleme, Theorien, Strategien* (Bonn: Verlag J.H.W. Dietz Nachf., 1993), pp. 157–59.

4. In 1998, eighteen members of the Development Assistance Committee (DAC) of the Organization for Economic Cooperation and Development (OECD) spent 0.36 percent of their GDP on development aid. Bundesministerium für wirtschaftliche Zusammenarbeit und Entwicklung, *Journalistenhandbuch Entwicklungspolitik 1991/92* (Bonn: 1990), p. 66.

5. Rudolf Hamann, *Die "Süddimension" des Ost-West-Konfliktes: Das Engagement der Supermächte in Krisen und Kriegen der Dritten Welt* (Baden-Baden: Nomos, 1986).

6. Volker Matthies, *Kriegsschauplatz Dritte Welt* (Munich: Beck'sche Reihe, 1988), p. 129; Peter J. Opitz, "Jenseits der Solidarität—Kriege und Konflikte in der Dritten Welt," in Peter J. Opitz, *Grundprobleme der Entwicklungsländer* (Munich: Beck'sche Reihe, 1991), p. 293; and Franz Nuscheler, *Internationale Migration: Flucht und Asyl* (Opladen: Leske & Budrich, 1995), p. 55.

7. Richard Rosecrance, "A New Concert of Powers," *Foreign Affairs* 71, no. 2 (Spring 1992): 64–82.

8. Edward Luttwak, "Give War a Chance," *Foreign Affairs* 78, no. 4 (1999): 36–44.

9. Norman Palmer, *The New Regionalism in Asia and the Pacific* (Lexington, KY: Lexington Books, 1991); Kenneth W. Abbott and Duncan Snidal, "Hard and Soft Law in International Governance," *International Organization* 54, no. 3 (2000): 421–56; Jürgen Rüland, "'Dichte' oder 'schlanke' Institutionalisierung? Der neue Regionalismus im Zeichen von Globalisierung und Asienkrise," *Zeitschrift für Internationale Beziehungen* 9, no. 2 (Dec. 2002): 175–208.

10. On global governance, see James N. Rosenau, "Governance, Order, and Change in World Politics," in James N. Rosenau and Ernst-Otto Czempiel, eds., *Governance Without Government: Order and Change in World Politics* (Cambridge, UK: Cambridge University Press, 1992), pp. 1–30; Dirk Messner and Franz Nuscheler, "Global Governance: Organisationselemente und Säulen einer Weltordnungspolitik," in Dirk Messner and Franz Nuscheler, eds., *Weltkonferenzen und Weltberichte: Ein Wegweiser durch die internationale Diskussion* (Bonn: Stiftung Entwicklung und Frieden, 1996), pp. 12–36.

11. Wolfgang H. Reinecke, *Global Public Policy: Governing Without Government?* (Washington, DC: Brookings Institution Press, 1998); Rüland "'Dichte' oder 'schlanke' Institutionalisierung?"

12. On the concept of "soft power," see Joseph S. Nye, "Soft Power," *Foreign Policy*, no. 80 (Fall 1990): 153–71; and Joseph S. Nye, Jr., *The Paradox of American Power: Why the World's Only Superpower Can't Go It Alone* (Oxford: Oxford University Press, 2002), pp. 8–9.

13. Nye, *The Paradox of American Power*, p. 9.

14. On the role of norms in international relations, see Judith Goldstein and Robert O. Keohane, eds., *Ideas and Foreign Policy: Beliefs, Institutions, and Political Change* (Ithaca, NY: Cornell University Press, 1993).

15. A good example is the literature on international politics in the Asia-Pacific region, which was hitherto almost exclusively dominated by realist approaches. See Richard Higgott, "Ideas, Identity and Policy Coordination in the Asia-Pacific," *Pacific Review* 7, no. 4 (1994): 367–79; Amitav Acharya, "Ideas, Identity, and Institution-Building: From the 'ASEAN Way' to the 'Asia-Pacific Way,'" *Pacific Review* 10, no. 3 (1997): 319–46; and Jörn Dosch, *Die ASEAN: Bilanz eines Erfolges. Akteure, Interessenlagen, Kooperationsbeziehungen* (Hamburg: Abera, 1997).

16. For these theoretical debates, see Higgott, "Ideas, Identity and Policy Coordination in the Asia-Pacific"; Tim Huxley, "Southeast Asia in the Study of International Relations: The Rise and Decline of a Region," *Pacific Review* 9, no. 2 (1996): 199–228; Acharya, "Ideas, Identity, and Institution-Building"; Amitav Acharya, "Realism, Institutionalism and the Asian Economic Crisis," *Contemporary Southeast Asia* 21, no. 1 (1999): 1–19; and Jürgen Rüland, "ASEAN and the Asian Crisis—Theoretical Implications and Practical Consequences for Southeast Asian Regionalism," *Pacific Review* 13, no. 3 (2000): 421–51.

17. On the balance of power, see classical realists such as Hans J. Morgenthau, *Politics Among Nations: The Struggle for Power and Peace,* 5th ed., rev. (New York: Alfred A. Knopf, 1978) and structural realists in the tradition of Kenneth Waltz; for the balance of threat argument, see Stephen M. Malt, *The Origins of Alliances* (Ithaca, NY: Cornell University Press, 1987).

18. Charles Krauthammer, "The Unipolar Moment," *Foreign Affairs* 70, no. 1 (1991): 23–33.

19. Christian Hacke, *Zur Weltmacht verdammt: Die amerikanische Außenpolitik von J.F. Kennedy bis G.W. Bush* (Munich: Econ Ullstein List Verlag, 2001), p. 484.

20. On the Enterprise of the Americas Initiative, see Martina Zellmer, *Die "Enterprise for the Americas Initiative": Eine neue Entwicklungspolitik der USA gegenüber Lateinamerika?* Freiburger Beiträge zu Entwicklung und Politik no. 15 (Freiburg: Arnold-Bergstraesser-Institut, 1994).

21. Nye, *The Paradox of American Power,* p. 125. On the "Asian miracle," see World Bank, *The East Asian Miracle: Economic Growth and Public Policy* (Oxford: Oxford University Press, 1993).

22. See, for instance, Ezra Vogel, *Japan as Number One: Lessons for America* (Cambridge, MA: Cambridge University Press, 1979).

23. Joseph S. Nye, *Bound to Lead: The Changing Nature of American Power* (New York: Basic Books, 1991).

24. Nye, *The Paradox of American Power,* pp. 134, 154; Rick Travis, "The Promotion of Democracy at the End of the Twentieth Century: A New Polestar for American Foreign Policy?" in James M. Scott, ed., *After the End: Making U.S. Foreign Policy in the Post–Cold War World* (Durham, NC: Duke University Press, 1998), p. 253.

25. James M. McCormick, *American Foreign Policy and Process,* 2nd ed. (Itasca, IL: F.E. Peacock, 1998), p. 217.

26. Hacke, *Zur Weltmacht verdammt,* p. 544.

27. On the Washington Consensus, see also the contribution of Howard Wiarda in this volume.

28. William Minter, "America and Africa: Beyond the Double Standard," *Current History* 99, no. 637 (May 2000): 202–3.

29. Hacke, *Zur Weltmacht verdammt,* p. 545.

30. Stefan A. Schirm, *Neue Strategien U.S.-amerikanischer Außenhandelspolitik?* (Universität Stuttgart: Arbeitspapiere zur Internationalen Politik, 2000), p. 1.

31. On unprincipled multilateralism, see the contribution of Hanns W. Maull in this volume.

32. Steven W. Hook, "Inconsistent U.S. Efforts to Promote Democracy Abroad," in Peter J. Schraeder, ed., *Exporting Democracy: Rhetoric vs. Reality* (Boulder, CO: Lynne Rienner, 2002), p. 109–28; Jörg Faust, "Die mexikanische Krise und ihre regionalen Auswirkungen," *Aussenpolitik* 46, no. 4 (1995): 394–404.

33. For a critique of the IMF's role in the Asian financial crisis, see Heribert Dieter, *Die Asienkrise: Ursachen, Konsequenzen und die Rolle des Internationalen Währungsfonds* (Marburg: Metropolis Verlag, 1998); and Joseph E. Stiglitz, *Globalization and Its Discontents* (New York: Norton, 2002).

34. Heribert Dieter, "Asia's Monetary Regionalism," *Far Eastern Economic Review* (July 6, 2000): 30.

35. For a study of American multilateralism in the Asia-Pacific region, see Jörn Dosch, *Die Herausforderung des Multilateralismus: Amerikanische Asien-Pazifik Politik nach dem Kalten Krieg* (Baden-Baden: Nomos, 2002).

36. Helen E.S. Nesadurai, "APEC: A Tool of U.S. Regional Domination?" *Pacific Review* 9, no. 1 (1996): 31–57.

37. On the development aid component of APEC, see Mohamed Ariff, *APEC and Development Cooperation* (Singapore: Institute of Southeast Asian Studies, 1998).

38. Minter, "America and Africa," p. 203.

39. Ibid., p. 204; Salih Booker, "Bush's Global Agenda: Bad News for Africa," *Current History* 100, no. 646 (May 2001): 199.

40. Hacke, *Zur Weltmacht verdammt,* p. 586.

41. Hook, "Inconsistent U.S. Efforts to Promote Democracy Abroad," p. 119.

42. Nye, *The Paradox of American Power,* p. 146; OECD press release, Paris, May 13, 2002.

43. On levels of aid to Middle Eastern countries, see also the contribution of William B. Quandt in this volume.

44. Thomas Carothers, "Promoting Democracy and Fighting Terror," *Foreign Affairs* 82, no. 1 (Jan./Feb. 2003): 84–97.

45. On Latin America, see Nikolaus Werz, "Alte und neue Populisten in Latein-amerika," in Nikolaus Werz, ed., *Populismus: Populisten in Übersee und Europa* (Opladen: Leske & Budrich, 2003), pp. 45–64; on Thailand, see Michael L. Nelson, "Thailand's House Elections of January 6, 2001: Thaksin's Landslide Victory and Subsequent Narrow Escape," in Michael L. Nelson, ed., *Thailand's New Politics, KPI Yearbook 2001* (Bangkok: King Prajadhipok's Institute & White Lotus, 2002), pp. 283–342.

46. For the difficulties of Africa lobbies in mobilizing congressional support, see Peter J. Schraeder, *United States Foreign Policy Toward Africa: Incrementalism, Crisis and Change* (Cambridge, UK: Cambridge University Press, 1995); Henry Kissinger, *Does America Need a Foreign Policy? Toward a Diplomacy for the Twenty-first Century* (New York: Simon & Schuster, 2001), p. 201.

47. McCormick, *American Foreign Policy and Process,* p. 220.

48. Kay Möller, "ASEAN and the United States: For Want of Alternatives," in Jörn Dosch and Manfred Mols, eds., *International Relations in the Asia-Pacific: New Patterns of Power, Interest, and Cooperation* (Hamburg: Lit, 2000), p. 162.

49. For a more critical assessment, see Amitav Acharya's chapter on Southeast Asia in this volume.

50. Sheldon W. Simon, "Is There a U.S. Strategy for East Asia?" *Contemporary Southeast Asia* 21, no. 3 (Dec. 1999): 338.

51. McCormick, *American Foreign Policy and Process,* pp. 242ff.

52. See Peter J. Opitz, *Die Vereinten Nationen: Geschichte, Struktur, Perspektiven* (Munich: Fink, 2002), p. 59 and Project Ploughshares, *Armed Conflicts Report 2002,* available at www.ploughshares.ca/content/ACR/ACR00/ACR02-PrefaceIntroduction .html, accessed July 27, 2004.

53. Samuel P. Huntington, "The Clash of Civilizations?" *Foreign Affairs* 72, no. 3 (Summer 1993): 22–43; Samuel P. Huntington, *Kampf der Kulturen: Die Neugestaltung der Weltpolitik im 21. Jahrhundert* (Munich: Europa Verlag, 1996).

54. Alain Minc, *Das neue Mittelalter* (Hamburg: Hoffmann und Campe, 1994); Robert D. Kaplan, "The Coming Anarchy: How Scarcity, Crime, Overpopulation, Tribalism, and Disease are Rapidly Destroying the Social Fabric of Our Planet," *Atlantic Monthly* 273, no. 2 (1994): 44–76.

55. McCormick, *American Foreign Policy and Process,* p. 221. See also Peter Rudolf, "Friedenserhaltung und Friedenserzwingung: Militärinterventionen in der amerikanischen Außenpolitik," in Peter Rudolf and Jürgen Wilzewski, eds., *Weltmacht ohne Gegner: Amerikanische Außenpolitik zu Beginn des 21. Jahrhunderts* (Baden-Baden: Nomos Verlagsgesellschaft, 2000), pp. 304–6.

56. *Süddeutsche Zeitung* (June 18, 2003): 9. See also Hacke, *Zur Weltmacht verdammt,* p. 545.

57. The term "assertive multilaterialism" was coined by then U.S. ambassador to the UN and later secretary of state, Madeleine Albright.

58. The Road Map is a new peace proposal of the U.S. government presented by former secretary of state Colin Powell in April 2003, in *Die Zeit* (April 30, 2003): 3.

59. Part of the dues was paid shortly after the September 11 terrorist attacks.

60. McCormick, *American Foreign Policy and Process,* p. 250.

61. Hacke, *Zur Weltmacht verdammt,* p. 594; and Wolf Grabendorff, "Die Lateinamerika-Politik der USA unter der Lupe: Das Konzept einer Westlichen Hemisphäre," *Internationale Politik,* no. 9 (2001): 35.

62. See also the contribution of William B. Quandt in this volume.

63. For a more recent study of the Cold War era, see Peter L. Hahn and Mary Ann Heiss (eds.), *Empire and Revolution: The United States and the Third World Since 1945* (Columbus: Ohio State University Press, 2001).

64. Nye, *The Paradox of American Power,* p. 73.

65. James M. Scott and A. Lane Crothers, "Out of the Cold: The Post–Cold War Context of U.S. Foreign Policy," in James M. Scott, ed., *After the End: Making U.S. Foreign Policy in the Post–Cold War World* (Durham, NC: Duke University Press, 1998), p. 20.

66. See Peter J. Schraeder in this volume.

67. For the term "intermestic issues," see James M. Scott and A. Lane Crothers, "Out of the Cold," p. 19; Helen M. Ingram and Suzanne L. Fiederlein, "Traversing Boundaries: A Public Policy Approach to the Analysis of Foreign Policy," *Western Political Quarterly* 41, no. 4 (Dec., 1988): 725–45.

68. James M. Scott, "Interbranch Policy Making After the End," in James M. Scott, ed., *After the End: Making U.S. Foreign Policy in the Post–Cold War World* (Durham, NC: Duke University Press, 1998), p. 401.

69. Robert D. Putnam, "Diplomacy and Domestic Politics: The Logic of Two-Level Games," *International Organization* 42, no. 3 (1988): 426–60.

70. See the contribution of Amitav Acharya in this volume.

2

American Foreign Policy

Between Isolationism and Internationalism, Unilateralism and Multilateralism

Hanns W. Maull

> I dread our own power and our own ambition; I dread our
> being too much dreaded. . . . We may say that we will not
> abuse this astonishing and hitherto unheard of power. But
> every other nation will think we will abuse it. . . . Sooner or
> later, this state of things must produce a combination
> against us which may end in our ruin.
>
> —*Edmund Burke, quoted in Harris Owen,* "The
> Anglosphere Illusion," *in* The National Interest

The foreign policy of the Bush administration has recently come under heavy fire, mostly from Europe. Put in a nutshell, the accusation is that this policy does not much care about international commitments, international institutions, international law, or about what America's allies and the rest of the world think about U.S. policies. As Jürgen Habermas wrote:

> The United States, which for half a century could rightly be considered as the pacemaker [on the way toward the rule of cosmopolitan law] through the war in Iraq has not only destroyed that reputation and her role as the guarantor of international law. But with the illegal attack on Iraq, she has set a devastating example for future superpowers. Let's not delude ourselves: America's moral authority is shattered.[1]

In short, the Bush administration stands accused of unilateralism. On top of this, it is suspected of a penchant for preemptive military strikes and of following a doctrine of military preemption, clearly in breach of international law. The case at hand is war in Iraq and the forced removal of Saddam Hussein and his regime through the U.S. policy of regime change.

More broadly, many observers are concerned about the heavy emphasis this administration is putting on military power and worldwide power projection, as expressed in its decision to raise military spending. The insistence on military supremacy when there is no serious military competitor in sight anywhere strikes many as out of sync with the realities of today's interconnected world. Consider this quote: "In pursuing advanced military capabilities that can threaten other powers, America is following an outdated path that, in the end, will hamper its own pursuit of national greatness."[2] The phrase may be thought to describe well the concern of many friends and allies of America about American foreign policy responses to September 11, 2001. Yet it is taken, with only slight modifications, from the September 2002 National Security Strategy of the United States of America, addressed to China.[3] Of course, the Bush administration would reply, America is different; you cannot compare America to China, even if both seem to be behaving in a similar fashion. This is but one of many examples in this document that reflects America's exceptionalism as a great power, both in terms of its self-perception and in its foreign policy identity and behavior. That is, America does not only think of itself as exceptional, but its policies in many ways are exceptional by historical comparison with other great powers.

The quote on China thus clearly illustrates that what is regarded as legitimate and appropriate for America by America itself will not necessarily be considered legitimate or appropriate for everyone else. More generally, America's foreign policy reserves the right for America to do what it feels necessary to achieve security, including the threat and use of overwhelming force, without undue concern about international support and legitimacy.

This exceptionalism is, of course, not new but has been part of American foreign policy since its beginnings, eventually turning the United States into the "Imperial Republic" (Raymond Aron).[4] For, as Pierre Hassner has noted, "Americans are absolutely against any encroachment on their own sovereignty but absolutely in favor of intervention against others. And that by definition betrays an imperial mentality."[5]

The Bush administration's foreign policy therefore seems less an aberration than a reincarnation of the powerful foreign policy traditions of America's exceptionalism. This is the first key contention in this chapter: In the coming years, U.S. foreign policy will be guided by motivations and strategic preferences with a long and venerable tradition, and therefore represent a continuation of past policies adapted to new circumstances, rather than a fundamental departure. From a longer historical perspective, it may well be that U.S. foreign policy in the Cold War will turn out to have been exceptional in its willingness to engage in efforts of nation-building, democratization, and international institutional architecture, while since the end of the 1980s America will have been returning to its traditional foreign policy inclinations.

U.S. foreign policy toward the Third World, in particular, may come to resemble its policies toward the Western hemisphere in the last years of the nineteenth and the early years of the twentieth century. Then, America pursued an agenda of commercial penetration and political "democratization" (i.e., self-government, though often under heavy U.S. tutelage) with diplomatic vigor and frequent military interventions. Depending on one's point of view, that arrangement could be called an "Empire of Liberty," "U.S. hegemony," or "imperialism on the cheap." The reality was, and is likely to be, a mixture of all three elements. What we can rule out, probably for good, is American "isolationism": in fact, America has never been isolationist in its whole history, although it initially was too weak to act as an internationalist great power. America's policies toward the Third World as a whole are therefore unlikely to follow "benign neglect" (though some parts of that world may indeed be neglected). Rather, they seem likely, for the foreseeable future, to be driven by a few key themes: war against terrorism and the struggle against the axis of evil; the search for military supremacy (notably vis-à-vis China); the pursuit of America's commercial interests, and its missionary democratic zeal, probably in that order.

My second key assertion is that—assuming U.S. foreign policy will indeed remain engaged in this sense—its policy stance will not only be inherently contradictory (as any grand strategy will inevitably be), but that the dilemmas of American foreign policy are already acute and will become even more so, as a result of the shift toward more traditional inclinations, for two reasons: First, America's strategy in its war against terrorism seems inherently ambiguous and contradictory, and, second, an increasingly complex and difficult foreign policy environment will vastly complicate the pursuit of any grand strategy, let alone this strategy.

In the following, this argument will be fleshed out in greater detail. In doing so, I will first assess the underlying motives of U.S. foreign policy and its traditional strategic inclinations. This will be contrasted with an assessment of the new international environment and the reasons why it will be so difficult for America to shape it. Finally, I will highlight a few dilemmas arising for American foreign policy out of this clash between its traditional foreign policy inclinations and its new environment.

America as the "Exceptional Power"

What motivates American foreign policy? In his study on America's role in the world from 1945 to 1973, Raymond Aron has not only brilliantly analyzed but also aptly summarized America's role in world politics in the title of his book: America is indeed "The Imperial Republic," a power of extraordinary influence over others and over world affairs, but also a country reluctant to assume the mantle (and to carry the burden) of empire. Those contradictory foreign policy inclinations—which aim to mold the world in America's image yet refuse to do so in truly imperial fashion—will, I argue, also shape American foreign policy in this new age.

But what specifically are these traditional foreign policy inclinations?

• First, a strong missionary impulse: America sees itself as the "city upon the hill" (Governor Winthrop), as a shining example to others, but also as an active promoter of freedom, democracy, and human rights elsewhere (including by military means: for example, President Woodrow Wilson repeatedly tried, but failed, to achieve regime change in Mexico through military intervention).[6] This missionary impulse has been ambivalent—it implies, for other states, the right to self-rule but may in practice involve the United States defining what constitutes an appropriate government, historically often with very low or dubious standards and considerable behind-the-scenes interference by America.[7] For international relations, America's missionary impulse has at times (most notably, under Presidents Woodrow Wilson and Franklin D. Roosevelt) seen Washington promote concepts and institutions of international order modeled loosely on America's domestic political system, based on the right to self-determination for all peoples, the rule of international law and institutions, and quasi-democratic decision making by consensus or through a quorum, such as in the UN Security Council. In all of its manifestations, the missionary impulse has tended to produce Manichean views of the world, dividing it into "them" and "us," into friends and foes. President Bush expressed that Manichean world view perfectly when he asked other governments to chose between supporting America's war against terrorism, or being against America.[8] Al-Qaeda, of course, is trying to project and impose on the Muslim world a similarly Manichean view of the world, and there is a certain danger that Al-Qaeda's attempt to engineer the "clash of civilizations" between the West and the Islamic world predicted by Samuel P. Huntington could turn into a self-fulfilling prophecy through America's tendency to lump together all Islamic radical forces under the label of enemy. The religious foundations of America's missionary impulse in its foreign policy tradition appear indirectly, in its secularized forms, in the Wilsonian tradition of liberal internationalism, but also more directly in what the American historian Walter Russell Mead has described as the Jacksonian tradition, which is religious, populist, and interventionist.[9] Today, this tradition has resurfaced and acquired considerable influence, for example, through a new foreign policy alliance between the Jewish lobby and the Christian Right, which—partly for religious reasons—supports a pro-Israeli U.S. policy in the Middle East. On the other hand, the Bush administration's support for a Palestinian state, for democratic change in the Arab-Islamic world in particular, and for a considerable expansion of U.S. development assistance, reflects the continuing relevance of the Wilsonian tradition even to this administration's foreign policy.[10]

• The second key element in America's foreign policy tradition is economic expansionism. America's rugged individualism, its insistence on the individual's right to pursue happiness, has from the beginning included a keen pursuit of material and commercial opportunity, as settlers in the West, as farmers, traders, and entrepreneurs—where necessary, with the support of the government. The aggregate effect of this tendency has been to create a highly dynamic, powerfully expansive economy, which rapidly turned toward commercial penetration of the rest of the world in its search for industrial markets and investment opportunities. This penetration of world markets was achieved by and large on American, rather than on principled liberal terms—that is, with governmental, and specifically with U.S. foreign policy, intervention where considered necessary or useful. In practice, the policy implications of the principles of liberalism (namely, the opening of national economies to free trade) often coincided with the interests of American companies, given the competitive strengths of U.S. firms. The diplomatic expression of this foreign policy tradition has, of course, been the demand for "open doors" for U.S. commerce and investors abroad, which served as a diplomatic lodestar for U.S. foreign policy even before those demands were enshrined in the two "open door" notes issued in 1899–1900.[11] Initially, commercial expansion abroad focused on the Western hemisphere, but also on the Pacific and East Asia—witness the successful opening of Japan by Commander Perry in 1853, the less successful parallel efforts to pry open the Hermit Kingdom of Korea, and above all the efforts to obtain access to China, where American traders were soon followed by large numbers of missionaries.[12] Today, the lowering of barriers for American commercial activities abroad continues as a key foreign policy concern, as witnessed by the considerable emphasis that free trade is given in the National Security Strategy document of September 2002. Chapter 6 ("Ignite a New Era of Global Economic Growth Through Free Markets and Free Trade") spells out the present-day policy conclusions drawn from this key element in America's foreign policy tradition: The goal is worldwide economic expansion, led by America through further liberalization. This is to benefit, in particular, the poor worldwide (but, and this remains unmentioned, American companies could of course also be expected to be the main beneficiaries of such expansion).[13] The principle of "open doors" today is also reflected in U.S. interest in the hydrocarbon resources of Central Asia and the Arabian/Persian Gulf, and in its attitudes to capital market liberalization.

• The third key element of the American foreign policy tradition pulls in a somewhat different direction. It also springs from the important place individualism and individual freedom from government interference enjoy in America's political culture. America's missionary impulses and its politico-commercial expansionism were often held in check by the insistence of America's electorate on lean government and by a system of political checks and balances. As a result, foreign policy has not been a natural focus of the American people. America also never became a colonial power in a very serious way, and where it did—as in the Philippines from 1899 to 1946—this created considerable opposition at home. The only substantial acquisitions made during America's quasi-colonial expansion in the nineteenth century that remain today as part of U.S. territory are Hawaii and Puerto Rico. American troops also occupied parts of Panama, Nicaragua (1910–33), and Haiti (1915–33) for longer periods of time. Still, this traditional American reluctance to get entangled abroad in a big way could be overcome if there was a serious threat and—or—if the missionary inclinations of America's exceptionalism aroused support for expansive foreign or national security strategies. This happened after the Japanese attack on Pearl Harbor in December 1941, it happened during the Cold War, and it may now happen again. Clearly, the Bush administration tries to use the war on terrorism to mobilize and even militarize American society. This has already led to infringements of civil liberties that could pose a threat to America's democracy—as they did, in a similar situation, in the late 1940s McCarthy era with its witch hunts against real or alleged communists. But there are also signs of resistance to this drive for greater government power: for example, public opinion initially reacted rather skeptically toward the notion of "regime change by war" in Iraq, and Congress was unwilling to give the administration the completely free hand that it wanted. Resistance to efforts to reconstruct the national security state under anti-terrorist auspices may well grow in the future. Still, the clarion call invoking national security clearly still resonates powerfully in American society.

In short, American foreign policy has, from its very beginnings, been motivated by a sense of exceptionalism and of a mission of America in the world and by America's dynamic capitalist economic expansionism. Both were tempered, however, by a shrewd sense for power realities and America's leverage, and by the basically skeptical attitude of Americans toward their government. Still, European-style foreign policy realism, as advocated, for example, by the European immigrants Hans J. Morgenthau or Henry Kissinger, never had a chance to thrive in America.[14] The alleged paradigm shift in American foreign policy, which supposedly was initiated by President Woodrow Wilson, who firmly set America on its course to become the world's first democratic superpower, in reality seems not so much a shift in paradigm as recognition of America's power and influence in the world. As Kissinger reluctantly recognizes, it was Wilson's foreign policy that resonated with the unique "American experience," rather than Teddy Roosevelt's or Nixon's realpolitik approach.[15]

The American Way of War and Diplomacy: Strategies and Foreign Policy Instruments

To pursue its foreign policy objectives, America has used the whole gamut of foreign policy instruments, from public and intergovernmental diplomacy in bilateral and multilateral settings through the unilateral imposition of demands under the threat of force, up to full-scale war and intervention. In this rich choice of instruments, multilateral diplomacy, permanent alliances, and the establishment of international institutions have been rather recent phenomena. The dominant theme throughout, however, has been insistence on freedom of action. Since the war of independence and the farewell address of George Washington through the Monroe doctrine to the George W. Bush doctrine, America—in line with its exceptionalism—has tried to keep its options open and to avoid entanglements as much as possible even when it entered into formal commitments.[16]

It was only after World War II, and in its confrontation with the Soviet Union, that the United States engaged in serious, sustained, and comprehensive efforts at international institution building. Out of those efforts grew the present international order, which in many ways still bears the handwriting of its American founding fathers. A key element of this order has been the facilitation of transnational economic interactions—first and foremost in trade, but later on also in capital movements. The political corollary was the expansion of this form of government throughout the world, beginning with occupied Germany and Japan, and close and institutionalized cooperation between liberal democracies.

Those core ideas of the Pax Americana—peace, democracy, and prosperity through free trade—have turned out to be extraordinarily powerful: not only did they engulf the rest of the world and eventually destroy the Soviet empire and its very system, they also enmeshed the United States itself in an ever denser web of interdependence and vulnerability.[17] For a while, it also seemed as if this experience would thoroughly change the direction of American foreign policy. But the Cold War, which saw the heyday of American multilateralism, may still turn out to have been an exceptional period. After 1989, U.S. principled multilateralists were soon put on the defensive, and when President Clinton's flirt with multilateralism came to a bad end in Somalia in 1993, the shift toward a new form of multilateralism in which America pursued its own, national agenda using multilateral channels if and when it deemed this the most effective way to do so, was all but complete.

This new style of multilateralism has been characterized by American observers, famously, as "multilateralism à la carte" (Richard Haass) or, more critically, as "predatory multilateralism."[18] It is disliked by many Europeans, who accuse America of being "unprincipled."[19] Nor are they impressed by arguments that this approach to multilateralism has been the result of a struggle between congressional unilateralism and executive multilateralism.[20] President Clinton, they would retort, allowed himself to be dragged along by Congress without much resistance, while President George W. Bush, in any case, led the charge himself. Today, principled multilateralists have all but disappeared from the policy-making establishment. The Bush administration's foreign policy team seems dominated by the right wing of the Republican Party, made up of populist, religiously inspired ideologues, and the technocrats of American military supremacy. A second group, which appears to be weaker but better grounded in the complex realities of today's international relations, is moderate conservatives, who want to use multilateralism to advance American interests in a pragmatic fashion. What unites them is their reluctance to accept constraints on America's freedom of maneuver.[21]

A second recurring theme in the history of American foreign policy has been America's willingness to rely on force. America secured its independence through war against Britain, and even leaving aside the Indian wars and those against Spain on the North American continent itself, America's political and commercial expansion overseas from the mid-nineteenth century onward owed much to force. From 1800 to 1934, experts have counted no less than 180 interventions, starting in 1804–11 with the Barbary Coast expedition. America's frequent involvement in small wars (statistically, more than one per year on average), already suggests that those wars were often fought for far less than vital national interests. They were also often waged with little public support, and sometimes led to prolonged deployment of U.S. military, including also what we would today call "peacekeeping" duties.[22] Again, this ready reliance on force reflects the American historical experience and its specific political culture, in which the right to carry guns is considered fundamental. As *The Economist* recently pointed out, while European societies no longer support war as a meaningful and promising political choice, the American sociology of warfare is different: after the trauma of the Vietnam War, pro-war lobbies have made a comeback in America, supported by the lure of high-tech warfare and its promise of "zero casualties," at least for American soldiers.[23]

Yet, the highly successful high-tech wars in Afghanistan and Iraq and their relatively small American casualties notwithstanding, America probably still shares with European societies a deep reluctance to accept the loss of lives, and in particular American lives, in the conduct of warfare.

America, as do the other industrialized countries, lives in the "post-heroic age of warfare."[24] As in its attitude toward multilateralism, America's attitude toward the use of force thus remains ambivalent. Moreover, military intervention and war are rarely solutions to problems in themselves; their consequences may in fact be worse than the original threat. As the United States first recognized in 1945, and now very recently again in Iraq, military victory needs to be secured through political, economic, and cultural efforts to rebuild the foundations of political stability, peace, and prosperity, within states and between them. This can be a time-consuming, difficult, and expensive task.

Will America be wise enough to recognize the limits to military force? And will it again find the farsightedness, the determination, and the patience to take on the burdens of state- and international institution-building to sustain its achievements? On balance, it seems more likely that the United States will continue to be a skeptical, sometimes even a cynical, multilateralist and rely more on military force and interventions than may be palatable to its allies and good for its own purposes. America has probably never been multilateralist in the principled European sense. The United States has always wished to remain in control of the agenda, and to reserve the right to act unilaterally whenever it deemed this necessary. The real difference between America and Europe thus is not that between unilateralist and multilateralist foreign policies. Rather, America generally leans toward instrumental multilateralism and tends to overestimate the utility of force and to underestimate the important— if indirect—structural benefits provided by vibrant international institutions, while Europe professes principled multilateralism but refuses seriously to address unresolved issues of force and violence permeating today's international "order."[25]

Transformation of Context: September 11, 2001, as a Defining Moment for a New Age in International Relations

The problem with the European approach is that it takes for real what by and large still is an aspiration: the rule of law and order in international relations. The world is still a very violent place, and order—in the sense of peaceful management of conflicts and change—is still far from embedded. In that sense, American foreign policy is more "realistic" than European approaches tend to be. The problem with America's policy is that it may overestimate American power and underestimate the difficulties of securing the future, for international relations have entered an era of unprecedented complexity and danger. To quote again the Bush administration, the world stands "at the crossroads of radicalism and technology."[26] It is shaped by globalization—that is, the interplay of extraordinarily powerful forces of social change driven by technological advances—and by its implications, which include all-pervasive vulnerability to hostile acts by even small groups of radical adversaries.

The growing complexity and turbulence of international relations is well described in the CIA report "Global Trends 2015."[27] James Rosenau was perhaps the first to systematically explore that condition from the perspective of "turbulence," in the sense of chaos theory.[28] I myself have argued that international relations may be experiencing "entropy," that is, a decline in order.[29] At the core of this change lie advances in science and technology (by "technology" I mean applied, that is commercialized, science) that have empowered individuals and social organizations exponentially. Among the implications are important new opportunities for bettering the lot of mankind but equally dramatic risks. Thus, the evolutionary path of modern technology points toward a situation in which a very small number of individuals may be able in one stroke to destroy mankind. Even today, as September 11, 2001, has shown, small groups with sufficient skill, determination, and a ruthless willingness to sacrifice themselves and others are able to wreak enormous destruction. At the same time, the growing complexity of international relations owing to the proliferation of actors, both state and non-state, the exponential growth of transactions of all kinds, and the erosion of all forms of authority make it that much harder to control and contain threats and risks.

What are the implications of this new context of international relations? Here are some of my own conclusions:

• First, the boundaries between international and domestic affairs are weakening. Foreign policy thus needs to begin at home, and the effects of foreign policy actions in distant places will be felt domestically ever more strongly. This has been hammered home to Americans by the terrorist attacks of September 11, 2001. It means that politics in many ways now has to be conceived as a seamless web, in which national and international patterns of order and anarchy are indissolubly intertwined. Policies will therefore also become increasingly Janus-faced, looking both inward and outward, and employing both peaceful persuasion and enforcement. This has now also been fully recognized in the U.S. government's National Security Strategy Document 2002.[30]

• Second, the growing difficulties of managing change politically are felt throughout the world in escalating problems of governance at all levels and in all corners of the world. The most visible consequences of this problem are failing or failed states and the proliferation of low-level violence in the so-called new wars.[31] In other parts of the world, the difficulties are less dramatic and less visible; industrial democracies, in particular, by and large have been flexible enough to weather the new turbulences, at least so far. They should be under no illusion, however: the political readjustment has just begun, and even in those more resilient and flexible political systems the capacity to govern the forces of globalization and change has probably declined, rather than increased, over the last decade.

• Third, threats to national security and international peace no longer emanate only or even primarily from states. Rather, the world of states is now confronting non-state actors, using sanctuaries and support provided by failed or rogue states, and diffuse, non-intentional security threats such as organized crime, the spread of pandemics, and possible catastrophic environmental changes.[32] Although this does not imply that traditional, state-based threats to national security will no longer be relevant, the broadening of security policy challenges requires drastic conceptual and operational adjustments.

In this new, turbulent, and entropic world of international relations— the "age of terrorism," as it already has been called—the political challenge will be to secure the capacity to control and manage the risks and threats of globalization, while exploiting its opportunities.[33] This capacity is provided by power and authority, that is, by the whole range of policy instruments and institutions of effective governance, from the local to the global level. The state will remain at the center of global governance, but it will have to adjust in a double sense: first, it will have to change internally in line with a changing socioeconomic environment, becoming what Richard Rosecrance has called a "virtual state," that is, a lean, efficient state capable of discharging successfully a broad variety of governing functions.[34] In reality, such states are of course still rather rare, and many Third World states are a very long way off.

Second, states will have to upgrade and enhance structures of governance above the national level, that is, regional and global institutions of governance and international regimes, as national security, peace, and international stability will become increasingly dependent on a functioning, sustainable international order. National foreign and security policy will thus have to rely more and more on effects secured through international order, and therefore will come to depend—more than hitherto—on the capacity of other countries to govern their own realm and their external relations well. Where this international order is deficient, and where specific states fall short of what is expected of them, there will have to.be cooperative international efforts to strengthen international arrangements, rebuild failed states, and reeducate and reintegrate rogue states. This will require patient policy efforts and often also extensive resources over prolonged periods of time. National power, even the unique power of the United States, will in such instances be vastly insufficient. Only effective and efficient international cooperation will be able to gather the critical mass needed.

American Responses: Dilemmas of U.S. Foreign Policy in the "Age of Terrorism"

To achieve security under such circumstances will demand the sustenance and development of political order across the whole spectrum of politics, from the local to the global, in principle on a worldwide basis, for there are no longer any "remote" areas. Structures of national, regional, and international order will have to be intertwined for maximum synergies in ways that will have to go far beyond the present scope of global governance.[35]

This is a tall order for American foreign policy, whose traditional inclinations are not well geared to it, and the United States may not only have to learn a great deal of new tricks, but also to unlearn some of the key tenets of its exceptionalist foreign policy tradition. Yet America will be the only state capable of pulling off such a broad-based system of international governance. For the simple truth is this: What international order there is, is basically made in America, and continues to be relevant only by courtesy of the U.S. government. As the "war against terror" gathered momentum, U.S. policy seemed to lose sight of the need for broad-based international cooperation and of the importance to strengthen the underpinnings of international order, both in terms of vibrant international institutions and functioning statehood. While the National Security Strategy 2002 explicitly recognized the importance of both, proposing, for example, new initiatives to strengthen the liberal international trading system and expand official development assistance, the Bush administration policies in practice often impatiently shunted aside international institutions and already existing cooperative efforts. Tellingly, the Bush administration "forgot" to propose a budget line for the reconstruction in Afghanistan; Congress had to correct that oversight. And while America's expressed commitment to promote freedom and democracy worldwide, and particularly in the Islamic world, holds promise for the broader tasks of strengthening international order, its professed commitment unfortunately smacks of opportunism, given the long-standing ties of America with autocratic Islamic governments and Washington's rather recent conversion to regime change in Iraq.[36]

At present, America thus seems likely to rely on a very robust form of multilateralism, in which America defines the tasks, determines the strategy, and leads the implementation—always reserving the right to go it alone and, if necessary, strike preemptively when deemed necessary. Others are invited to join on America's terms, and to contribute what they can and will.[37] In recruiting such ad hoc coalitions of the willing, America will not be squeamish: witness American support for President Musharraf in Pakistan and its close cooperation with the Central Asian successor states of the Soviet Union.

Some of this new American foreign policy may turn out to be ephemeral, and many of its rough edges will no doubt eventually be smoothened by domestic and international constraints on American executive power. Still, the bias in American foreign policy against policies that would effectively strengthen international order is likely to prevail into the future. If this is so, this policy will, however, sooner or later run into some rather serious dilemmas:

• Perhaps the greatest and most fundamental dilemma is that America simultaneously both upholds and challenges the international status quo. Today, America has every reason to defend an international order in which it occupies a uniquely powerful military, political, economic, and cultural position. And many of America's foreign policy activities are indeed directed at sustaining that order—its policies toward China, for example, or those toward many parts of the so-called Third World, including importantly the Israeli-Arab conflict. Yet, America also actively challenges the status quo, and thus contributes to international disorder.[38] For example, America's insistence on a new arms race against the limits of what is technologically feasible will inevitably not discourage adversaries. Rather, they will follow America's lead, or if they cannot follow, they will seek to exploit the opportunities of asymmetric warfare. America also acts as an anti–status quo power through its support for democracy and human rights, invoked, with somewhat menacing undertones, by pro-Israeli, war-on-Iraq advocates in the Bush administration against the rulers of some of America's oldest allies in the Middle East (e.g., the Saudi Arabian monarchy), through alliances with regional powers that then turn their U.S.-supplied guns against America and its interests in those regions (e.g., Iran, Iraq), but most fundamentally through its embrace of capitalist expansionism.[39] Modern capitalism is profoundly disruptive of existing social and therefore ultimately also political arrangements, and its inherent expansionist tendencies demand constant upgrades in national and international arrangements of governance. By pushing for a better, more democratic, and more prosperous world, America also challenges, and often undermines, the prevailing political status quo, both nationally (in the case of autocratic political systems) and internationally (with regard to international order and international institutions). If America fails to compensate for its drawdowns on international order through efforts to enhance it, the implications are likely to threaten its own security.

• The second dilemma concerns the tension between America's missionary foreign policy ideology and realistically achievable objectives. Thus, what exactly are the objectives in America's war against terror, and in its confrontation with the axis-of-evil states? Michael Howard has rightly pointed to the profound difficulties raised by defining the struggle against Al-Qaeda as a "war."[40] Who exactly is the enemy? How is victory to be defined? The same goes for the "axis of evil," or rogue states: Why those states? Why not others? What is the objective in confronting them? Disarming them? Replacing their regimes? If so, how? With what perspective? Can America realistically expect to define the answers to those questions alone? If not, how will inevitable compromises square with the defined "mission?"

• The third dilemma lies in a potential mismatch between power and purpose. Even American power, impressive as it is, will—as the NSS 2002 document readily admits—be insufficient for many of the tasks at hand. How can America mobilize the power resources needed? Can it really expect to do so on its own terms, without compromising its independence and freedom of maneuver? And how useful will American military supremacy, and its capacity to project overwhelming force over huge distances really be in achieving America's aims? Will America be willing to support not only the burden of war, but the much more cumbersome and time-consuming tasks of peace-building and nation-building?

• This leads to dilemma number four: How can America reconcile its global ambitions with its reluctance to commit public resources to underwrite such ambitions? And if it tries to do so, what will be the price? Will America once more go down the road of a national security state, again become an "imperial presidency" with its inherent temptations of abuse of power? If so, under what ideological auspices, given that such mobilization is conceivable only through ideology? What would this mean for U.S. democracy?

Confronting, and eventually hopefully resolving, those dilemmas will no doubt be a messy process. Yet the world needs America to get it right, which would mean four things:

• First, America will have to find, review, and constantly redefine a judicious balance between persuasion and enforcement, between leadership and integration, between its desire to act alone and the advisability to take others on board.

• Second, America will have to rely on its traditional allies, and notably on Europe, as well as on the empowerment of international institutions in explicitly formulated, mutually agreed strategies involving a division of labor.

• Third, America will have to accept that it is itself part of the international order, not only its creator and upholder. Only an America willing to follow the rules it wants to see respected by others can expect to mobilize the support it will need, for this support would then no longer only be support for America, but built on perceptions of shared interests and a common good.

• Fourth and last, America will need to build the domestic foundations for such a foreign policy around politically credible visions of world order and an enlightened internationalism.

Clearly, that is a tall order. Yet, as Winston Churchill once famously suggested, you can always rely on America getting it right in the end—after having tried out everything else.

Notes

1. Jürgen Habermas, "Was bedeutet der Denkmalsturz?" *Frankfurter Allgemeine Zeitung* (Apr. 17, 2003): 33.

2. White House, *The National Security Strategy of the United States of America* (Washington, DC: Sept. 2002; printer version), p. 19.

3. I have substituted "other powers" for the words "its neighbors in the Asia-Pacific region" and "America" for "China" in the original text.

4. Charles W. Kegley, Jr., and Eugene Wittkopf, eds., *American Foreign Policy: Pattern and Process,* 5th ed. (New York: St. Martin's Press, 1996), pp. 31ff; Walter LaFeber, *The American Age: United States Foreign Policy at Home and Abroad Since 1750* (New York: W.W. Norton, 1989), passim; Raymond Aron, *The Imperial Republic: The United States and the World, 1945–1973* (London: Weidenfeld & Nicolson, 1975).

5. Pierre Hassner, *The United States: The Empire of Force or the Force of Empire?* Chaillot Papers no. 54 (Paris: ISS, 2002), p. 47.

6. LaFeber, *The American Age,* pp. 261ff.

7. A recent example for this ambiguity was the demand by President Bush for a more representative and democratic Palestinian National Authority: this was clearly meant as a suggestion to the Palestinian people to get rid of their Chairman Arafat and choose another leadership. The new leadership, however, equally clearly had to be palatable to Washington and Jerusalem, regardless as to who the Palestinians would prefer to represent them.

8. Michael Hirsh, "Bush and the World," *Foreign Affairs* 81, no. 5 (Sept./Oct. 2002):18–43.

9. Walter Russell Mead, *Special Providence: American Foreign Policy and How It Changed the World* (New York: Knopf, 2001).

10. See. G. John Ikenberry, "America's Imperial Ambition," *Foreign Affairs* 81, no. 5 (Sept./Oct. 2002): 44–60.

11. LaFeber, *The American Age,* pp. 204ff.

12. Arthur Power Dudden, *The American Pacific: From the Old China Trade to the Present* (Oxford: Oxford University Press, 1992).

13. See The White House, *The National Security Strategy of the United States,* pp. 13ff.

14. Henry A. Kissinger, *Diplomacy* (New York: Simon & Schuster, 2000).

15. Ibid., pp. 21–55 (esp. pp. 54–55).

16. Arguably, multilateralism began to make a serious appearance in U.S. foreign policy in 1895, when Theodore Roosevelt brokered an international settlement of the war between Japan and China. After World War I, Woodrow Wilson's efforts to construct a new international order largely failed, but his successor Harding succeeded, at least to some extent, in Asia-Pacific. The Washington Treaties of 1922–23 for a while successfully stabilized political and economic relations across the Pacific, not least through arms control agreements. See Akira Iriye, *The Origins of the Second World War in Asia and the Pacific* (London: Longman, 1987).

17. Michael Mandelbaum, *The Ideas That Conquered the World: Peace, Democracy and Free Markets in the Twenty-first Century* (New York: Public Affairs, 2002).

18. Vinod K. Aggarwal, "Strategy Without Vision: The U.S. and Asia-Pacific Economic Cooperation," in Jürgen Rüland, Eva Manske, and Werner Draguhn, eds., *The Asia-Pacific Economic Co-operation (APEC): The First Decade* (London: Routledge/Curzon, 2002), pp. 87–118 .

19. Matthias Dembinski, *Unilateralismus vs. Multilateralismus: Die USA und das spannungsreiche Verhältnis zwischen Demokratie und Internationaler*

Organisation, HSFK Report, 4/2002 (Frankfurt am Main: Hessische Stiftung für Friedens und Konfliktforschung); Robert Kagan, *Macht und Ohnmacht: Amerika und Europa in der neuen Weltordnung* (Berlin: Siedler, 2003).

20. Jürgen Wilzewski, "Demokratie und Außenpolitik: Friktion zwischen Präsident und Kongreß," in Peter Rudolf and Jürgen Wilzewski, eds., *Weltmacht ohne Gegner: Amerikanische Außenpolitik zu Beginn des 21. Jahrhunderts* (Baden-Baden: Nomos, 2000), pp. 35–61.

21. Peter Rudolf, *Wie der 11 September die amerikanische Außenpolitik verändert hat. Bilanz nach einem Jahr* (Berlin: Stiftung Wissenschaft und Politik, SWP Aktuell 33, Sept. 2002).

22. Max Boot, *The Savage Wars of Peace: Small Wars and the Rise of American Power* (New York: Basic Books, 2002); idem., *Everything You Think You Know About the American Way of War is Wrong,* E-Notes, Sept. 12, 2002, available at www.fpri.org/enotes/americawar.20020912.boot.americanwayofwar.html, accessed July 8, 2004.

23. "Unlike any other democracy, with the possible exception of Britain, America has a strong war lobby." "A Year On, Night Fell on a Different World," *The Economist,* internet edition, published Sept. 5, 2002, available at www.economist.com/PrinterFriendly.cfm?Story_ID=1313880, accessed Apr. 22, 2003.

24. Edward N. Luttwak, "Towards Post-Heroic Warfare," *Foreign Affairs* 74, no. 3 (May/June 1995): 109–22.

25. Hanns W. Maull, "Die 'Zivilmacht Europa' bleibt Projekt: Zur Debatte um Kagan, Asmus/Pollack und das Strategiedokument NSS 2002," *Blätter für deutsche und internationale Politik* (Dec. 2002): 1467–78.

26. The White House, *The National Security Strategy of the United States,* pp. 5ff.

27. CIA, *Global Trends 2015: A Dialogue About the Future with Nongovernment Experts,* NIC 2000–2002 (Washington, DC: National Intelligence Council, Dec. 2000).

28. James N. Rosenau, *Turbulence in World Politics: A Theory of Change and Continuity* (New York: Harvester, 1990).

29. Hanns W. Maull, "Containing Entropy, Rebuilding the State: Challenges to International Order in the Age of Globalisation," *Internationale Politik und Gesellschaft* 2 (2002): 9–28.

30. White House, *The National Security Strategy of the United States,* pp. 15ff.

31. Robert I. Rotberg, "The New Nature of Nation-State Failure," *Washington Quarterly* 25, no. 3 (Summer 2002): 85–96; Herfried Münkler, *Die neuen Kriege* (Reinbek: Rowohlt, 2002).

32. Christopher Coker, *Globalisation and Insecurity in the Twenty-first Century: NATO and the Management of Risk,* Adelphi Paper no. 345 (London: Oxford University Press for the International Institute for Strategic Studies, 2002).

33. Audrey Kurth Cronin, "Rethinking Sovereignty: American Strategy in the Age of Terror," *Survival* 44, no. 2 (Summer 2002): 119–40.

34. Richard Rosecrance, *The Rise of the Virtual State: Wealth and Power in the Coming Century* (New York: Basic Books, 1999).

35. Significantly, the need to do so was initially clearly recognized by this administration in its response to the terrorist attacks of Al-Qaeda: Bush tried to put together a very broad coalition, comprising not only America's traditional allies but also Russia and China, among others.

36. As President Reagan's special envoy, Donald Rumsfeld had courted Saddam Hussein during a visit to Baghdad. This was part of a broader drive of U.S. foreign policy at the time to balance Iraq against revolutionary Iran. Cf. Michael Dobbs, "Not So Long Ago, Washington Made Iraq a Valued Ally," *International Herald Tribune* (Dec. 31, 2002–Jan. 1, 2003): 2.

37. Donald H. Rumsfeld, "Transforming the Military," *Foreign Affairs* 81, no. 3 (May/June 2002): 20–32.

38. Hanns W. Maull, "Amerikanische Außenpolitik an der Schwelle zum 21. Jahrhundert," in Winand Gellner and Gerd Strohmeier, eds., *Identität und Fremdheit: Eine amerikanische Leitkultur für Europa?* PIN-Politik im Netz Jahrbuch 2001 (Baden-Baden: Nomos, 2001), pp. 25–38; Francois Heisbourg, "American Hegemony? Perceptions of the U.S. Abroad," *Survival* 41, no. 4 (Winter 1999/2000): 5–19.

39. The case of Iraq is instructive: During the 1980s, Iraq not only received critical satellite imagery to help it prevail in the war it had launched against Iran in 1980, but also extensive support for its biological weapons program and tacit encouragement in its deployment of chemical arms. All this was done to contain revolutionary Iran (whose Islamist regime was simultaneously courted, surreptitiously, by presidential emissaries) and thus stabilize U.S. influence in the Middle East. America's continued reliance on repressive and unstable regimes (such as, in earlier times, the Iran of the shah, or today, the Pakistan of President Musharraf or the Uzbekistan of President Karimov) may well come to haunt it again in the future, just as in the case of Saddam Hussein.

40. Michael Howard, "What's in a Name?" *Foreign Affairs* 81, no. 1 (Jan./Feb. 2002): 8–13.

3

Decision-Making Processes and Actors in American Foreign Policy Formulation

Is There a Third World Lobby?

James M. McCormick

In a recent analysis, Stephen Zunes and Ben Terrall argued that Third World lobby groups, primarily human rights activists, were crucial in changing American policy toward the situation in East Timor. A primary locus of this lobbying was the U.S. Congress, where the East Timor Action Network (ETAN) was able to affect American policy toward Indonesia and thus alter how the United States responded to East Timor. While Zunes and Terrall acknowledge that other factors were at work in the change in American policy, they also contend that "one cannot ignore the effectiveness of the pressure applied by human rights activists."[1]

As this case suggests, interest groups can and do make a difference in addressing Third World issues within the United States. Yet an important question is whether this instance is typical for Third World issues and whether the American foreign policy-making process affords such groups ready access to the political arena. Put differently, how generalizable are the findings from this case? Are there identifiable sets of interest groups, much like business, labor, and ethnic groups, who regularly work to advance the interests of the Third World? In light of the current global environment and America's war on terrorism, do these groups have a role to play in the foreign policy-making process today? Most importantly, how effective are these groups in shaping American foreign policy?

In this chapter, we undertake several tasks to begin to answer these questions. First, we identify the changing foreign policy-making process within the United States, and suggest how it has impeded or facilitated interest group activity in affecting foreign policy over the years. Second, we discuss how that environment has changed since the end of the Cold War and since the events of September 11, 2001. For the current era, we identify some Third World interest groups—and groups promoting Third World interests—and discuss how they operate within the foreign policy-making arena today. Finally, and importantly, we provide a preliminary assessment of the relative effectiveness of Third World lobbies on the operation of American foreign policy.

Models of American Foreign Policy Making

In his recent book, *The Paradox of American Democracy,* political analyst John Judis identified three models of how the American political system works "and how it should work."[2] In his view, the electoralist, the pluralist, and the populist/Marxist models are three apt ways to describe and analyze the functioning of American politics over the history of the republic. The electoralist model assumes that what the American government pursues was largely a function of the candidates and parties selected by the voters; the pluralist model assumes that the government does more of what is in tune with the views of organized groups or interests than what the voters or the parties want; and the populist/Marxist model assumes that "important government decisions [are] shaped and made by a small, interlocking group of business, political, and military leaders who prevailed regardless of who won the election."[3] Although Judis's analysis is focused more on American domestic politics than on foreign policy, his three models offer an excellent point of departure for discussing foreign policy decision making since the end of World War II. In essence, these three models capture the two most prominent ways foreign policy making has been described and raise the possibility of a third approach as foreign policy issues become more salient to American voters.

These three models, however, leave out a fourth possible model of policy making, the "autonomous state" or the "strong state" model. This "ideal-type" model of policy making assumes that the administrative power and capacity of the state are sufficiently strong that the state can "resist societal pressure" and "persuade private groups to follow policies that are perceived as furthering the national interest."[4] In one sense, this model is akin to Judis's third model, albeit with more robust dominance by government officials and with no effect from interest groups. Indeed, Stephen Krasner notes that this model may apply to some limited strategic foreign policy questions where the executive is given broad latitude (e.g., protecting the homeland), but that it is not applicable to all foreign policy issues (e.g., foreign economic policy).[5]

More generally, though, the United States bears little resemblance to this model because its governmental system is structurally and functionally a "weak state." That is, the constitutional structure of the United States, with its separation of powers and its system of "checks and balances" among different institutions, operates against governmental dominance. Instead, the structural arrangements invite the participation of societal groups in the policy-making process. In addition, several other factors also contribute to this weak state status for the United States— the lack of a serious threat of foreign invasion, an "unusually cohesive" American society with "dominant social values" without government efforts, and the strength of the American economy—that has largely militated against governmental intervention to promote prosperity.[6] As a result, the conditions within the American polity have largely operated against the "strong state" or "autonomous state" status for the United States and instead facilitate interest group involvement. In short, then, while the "strong state" label might be applicable in a very narrow time period (at the beginning of the Cold War or immediately after September 11, 2001), this strong state quality is likely to be short-lived, since the American polity is ultimately accessible to outside groups. In this sense, the three models advanced by Judis seem to capture the nature of the American experience more fully, especially since World War II.

The Cold War Years

The best-known policy-making model in discussions of U.S. foreign policy is probably Judis's third model, essentially the elitist view of foreign policy making. This model assumes that only a small group of decision makers affects the foreign policy-making process and that this elite group has been very successful in shaping the direction of America's role in the world. In this connection, the public has little interest in, or knowledge of, foreign policy, and their representatives in Congress have only a limited impact on foreign policy. Instead, the foreign policy-making process is "executive-dominated," with the major responsibility for foreign affairs resting with the president and his principal advisors.[7]

The elitist model appears to have considerable face validity, especially when applied to the early years of the Cold War as the United States emerged as a major global participant. After President Franklin Delano Roosevelt had firmly established important presidential prerogatives in the foreign policy arena at the beginning of World War II, succeeding presidents strengthened executive dominance with their actions. President Harry Truman's unilateral actions regarding Korea in 1950, Eisenhower's overwhelming bipartisan support for his foreign policy initiatives, and Kennedy's handling of the Cuban Missile Crisis, all enhanced presidential preeminence.[8] In all, these immediate post–World War II administrations pursued their own foreign policy agenda with limited opposition from Congress or the public. During this time, too, the Cold War consensus, a common set of foreign policy values and beliefs about the American role in the world, succeeded in largely knitting together the public and the elites to support the principal direction of American foreign policy.[9]

Other conditions reinforced this executive dominance during the Cold War years. First, the emphasis on the principles of realism in the conduct of foreign policy aided presidential control. In the realist paradigm, foreign policy making largely follows the rational actor perspective in which the unitary state pursues its national interest. The principal representative of the unitary state, as Justice Sutherland so aptly wrote in *U.S. v. Curtiss-Wright*, is the executive: "The President alone has the power to speak or listen as a representative of the nation."[10] As such, the role of multiple domestic actors in the foreign policy-making process—parties, interest groups, and the public at large—was often difficult to accommodate or incorporate for students of realism. Second, the perceived threat posed by international communism during the Cold War greatly assisted elite dominance as well. Because American foreign policy focused so singularly on the threat posed by the Soviet Union, the concentration of power in the executive branch was understandable and necessary to respond to that threat. After all, the presidency provided a unity and decisiveness not found elsewhere in government. As a result, other potential foreign policy participants were either largely excluded from the process or lent their support to presidential actions.

The Cold War environment limited the role or impact of interest groups for several reasons. First, since foreign policy was executive led, interest groups had considerable difficulty in gaining access to the process. As Bernard Cohen has pointed out in his analysis of the process in the early 1970s, interest groups sought to influence executive bureaucracies, but they rarely succeeded.[11] While Congress was also a potential target for interest groups during these years, its foreign policy role tended to be limited, further eroding the ability of interest groups to affect policy. Second, most foreign policy issues were seemingly remote from the lives of most American citizens. As such, it was difficult to rally public support for interest groups' activity on foreign affairs. Third, many of the foreign policy issues during this period were security driven and were likely to be manifested as crisis issues. Crisis issues, as contrasted with strategic or structural issues, were not very susceptible to interest group activities or at least not subject to effective interest group action.[12] Crisis decision making, by its very nature, is usually concentrated in a small group, and such decisions usually required a quick response. Interest groups thus were not well positioned to challenge largely executive decision making on these issues. Finally, and specific to our concerns here, Third World interest groups were largely excluded from the process, since East-West security issues dominated the foreign policy agenda. To the extent that foreign aid issues or intervention issues appeared on the agenda, interest groups could have some impact, but given the pervasiveness of the Cold War consensus, the impact of Third World interest groups was usually negligible.

From an academic perspective, too, analysts have documented the executive dominance in foreign policy making during these years, albeit in different ways. In 1956, for example, sociologist C. Wright Mills wrote *The Power Elite* in which he identified interlocking elites as the source of American foreign (and domestic) policy.[13] These dominant elites—across parties and interest groups—favored a strong defense, the promotion of capitalism, and a dominant role for the United States in global affairs. A decade later, Aaron Wildavsky identified the American policy-making environment in a more differentiated way but with the same effect for foreign policy. In his classic "Two Presidencies" article, Wildavsky argued that two presidencies exist in the United States, one for foreign policy and another for domestic policy.[14] In the former, the president was remarkably successful in working his will on other potential foreign policy participants—Congress, bureaucracies, interest groups, and the public at large—even as domestic policy making was much more of a contest among these multiple participants. Indeed, Wildavsky shows that from the late-1940s through the mid-1960s presidents obtained about 70 percent of their foreign and defense policy initiatives from Congress but only about 40 percent of their domestic initiatives.[15] In 1973, historian Arthur Schlesinger summarized the policy-making environment in yet a third way by labeling it the "imperial presidency."[16] This description was particularly applicable to the foreign policy realm in that the executive had come to dominate the policy-making process with his unilateral actions. In essence, Schlesinger contended that the president had been allowed to become too dominant and that Congress and other foreign policy participants needed to respond to this overwhelming power concentrated in the executive branch.

From Vietnam to the Cold War's End

By the late 1960s and early 1970s, the American foreign policy-making process began to change in the direction of a more pluralist one. The impetus for this change was the opposition to the Vietnam War—by the public, coalitions of interest groups, and Congress. Public demonstrations by coalitions of groups opposed to the war, and congressional hearings by the Senate Foreign Relations Committee, led by Senator J. William Fulbright, were early manifestations of the changing political landscape for foreign policy decision making. In turn, these public and congressional pressures over Vietnam had the effect of demanding a more open political process and more public debate on foreign policy.

The immediate consequences were calls for greater congressional involvement in the foreign policy-making process and for Congress to assert more fully its constitutional powers in the foreign policy area. As a result, Congress passed a series of procedural measures requiring the executive branch to involve the legislative branch more fully in the conduct of foreign policy. These congressional initiatives ranged from legislation requiring reports on commitments abroad made by the executive branch, imposing procedural requirements on American arms sales overseas, seeking to limit presidential use of American armed forces through the War Powers Resolution, and employing various kinds of conditionalities on American aid and trade policy. Although the aggregate impact of these pieces of legislation has been modest in constraining executive actions over the years, they did require the executive branch to calculate the possible response of Congress to foreign policy actions in a way not done previously.

Several internal reforms within Congress were simultaneous with these procedural actions and thus allowed wider legislative participation on both foreign and domestic issues. Starting with the Legislative Reorganization Act of 1970, several committee reforms (e.g., opening up committee hearings, electing committee chairs, expanding the jurisdictions of committees, enlarging staff) produced a legislative body more open and accessible to outside influences. More points of access were now available to potential participants both inside and outside Congress to try to affect policy. As a result, interest groups and the public generally could have greater effect on Congress and the political process.

These internal reforms were also fueled by the changing membership in Congress, and especially by the changing membership on the principal foreign policy committees of the Congress (e.g., House Foreign Affairs [now International Relations] Committee, Senate Foreign Relations Committee).[17] The new members were increasingly drawn from the wings of their political parties and thus were more ideological in their policy positions (i.e., Republicans as a group were more conservative and Democrats more liberal than past members). In turn, foreign policy issues were now increasingly a source of interest (and debate) for these new members, and conflict with the executive branch over foreign policy direction was now more routine. The result was the rapid erosion of the kind of congressional bipartisanship from an earlier era, and the increasing bifurcation of foreign policy positions between Republicans and Democrats within Congress. Indeed, the major foreign policy issues from the late 1970s through the 1990s (e.g., debates over the Panama Canal treaties, the nuclear freeze issue, contra aid, trade and aid policy, national missile defense) were sharply drawn along partisan and ideological lines, as several studies reveal.[18] In an environment where foreign policy conflict was now more pronounced, the opportunity for interest groups to impact the foreign policy-making process became increasingly possible—and likely—since such groups could exploit these divisions to promote their own views.

As the Congress was moving toward greater involvement and debate on foreign policy and as the political parties were increasingly divided on these issues, the public followed suit. The systematic analyses of the Chicago Council on Foreign Relations quadrennial surveys from 1974 through 1998 demonstrate that the American public was divided on major

American foreign policy questions into identifiable and stable groups. Research by Eugene Wittkopf has demonstrated that the public was not only divided over whether the United States should be involved in foreign affairs (along the isolationism-to-internationalism continuum), but it was also divided over how (along the militant-to-cooperative action continuum).[19] These two dimensions, moreover, divided the American public into four groups, roughly in equal proportions: hardliners, internationalists, accommodationists, and isolationists. Two other key research findings by those working in this area further demonstrate the increasingly divisive nature of foreign policy: (1) these four groups were primarily divided by the domestic political ideology they held—along the liberal to conservative continuum; and (2) the proportion of the public in these four groups differed from the proportion of the political elites in these same four groups—the elites are more internationalist and accommodationist than the public. The implications of such findings are again important for understanding interest groups and their potential effect on foreign policy. With the public's views of foreign policy divided into stable and identifiable groups and with the composition of these groups different from the political elite groupings, the opportunity for interest groups to seek to close these fissures or build coalitions across them increases substantially.

In sum, the foreign policy-making process by the 1970s and 1980s had moved in the direction of a pluralist one, fueled by a changing Congress, a divided public, and partisan/ideological divisions on foreign policy among elites and the public. In such an environment, foreign policy interest groups were no longer under the restraints that operated at the height of the Cold War.

After the Cold War

Indeed, as the Cold War ended, the changes in the foreign policy-making process, already in progress, were accelerated, with the implosion of the Soviet Union, the dramatic changes in Eastern Europe, and the rise of new issues and new participants in this changed environment. With the threat of communism no longer serving as the "North Star" of American foreign policy making, new economic, environmental, social-cultural, and security issues emerged on the foreign policy agenda. More often than not, these new issues divided the American public, members of Congress, and the executive branch. Congressional approval of the

North American Free Trade Agreement (NAFTA) and the World Trade Organization (WTO), for instance, divided President Clinton from members of his own Democratic Party and alienated important members of his political base, namely working class union members. The efforts to grant most-favored nation trading status (or permanent normal trading relations) to China, for instance, produced unusual coalitions of supporters and opponents. They ranged from liberal and conservative free traders and foreign policy realists from both political parties in support of such action to liberal human rights activists and religious conservatives in opposition.

Environmental and sociocultural issues produced the same effect. To be sure, seeking to manage the effects of global warming or working to promote human rights abroad may garner widespread public support when asked in the abstract. Yet the policy implications of employing conservation efforts to obtain the former or promoting trade openness to achieve the latter have differential effects on various regions, constituencies, and individuals within American society. In this respect, and in contrast to the Cold War years when the Soviet Union was the dominant focus and could galvanize support across the political spectrum, it was now more difficult to identify a policy position that was not divisive to a portion of the American public and its leadership. With new regional, ethnic, and religious conflicts (e.g., Somalia, Bosnia, Haiti, Iraq), the public and its leaders are often sharply divided over specific actions, as Wittkopf's four groupings among the public and elites would surely suggest.

As a result, a "new tug-of-war," as Jeremy Rosner aptly called it, emerged between Congress and the executive branch on foreign policy.[20] The president had an increasingly difficult time getting his way on foreign policy and had to be directly involved if he was to succeed. The other important implication of this new environment was that interest groups were afforded even greater access and potential involvement than before. Interest groups were, in effect, invited to mobilize, seek support from the public, and attempt to influence policy in the executive and legislative arenas. Indeed, we have witnessed an explosion of new participants on foreign policy issues, led most notably by the large increase in nongovernmental organizations (NGOs), but also including a sharp increase in traditional interest groups (now with a new foreign policy focus), the rise of single-issue foreign policy interest groups, and the emergence of foreign nations lobbying within the United States. Although we will discuss some of these interest groups shortly, the upshot of these changes is a more disjointed and untidy foreign policy-making process with a broad array of actors seeking to direct American foreign policy.

An important corollary to the changes in issues and actors at the end of the Cold War was the changes in the kinds of issues that they represent and the locus of where those issues were decided. Although the Cold War years often generated foreign policy crisis issues (and thus restricted interest group activity), the post–Cold War years have increasingly generated structural and strategic foreign policy issues. Strategic policy issues involve those that deal with specifying "the goals and tactics of defense and foreign policy." The appropriate policy toward a particular region (e.g., the Middle East), a country (e.g., Iraq), or issue (e.g., weapons of mass destruction) would constitute strategic policy questions. Structural issues are those that focus on "procuring, deploying, and organizing military personnel and material . . . [and deciding] which countries will receive aid, what rules will govern immigration," and so on.[21] The appropriate number of military bases at home or abroad, the size and shape of defense expenditures, and the amount and allocation of foreign aid would constitute structural issues. More concretely, the debate over what to do about Saddam Hussein and Iraq epitomizes the nature of a strategic issue, while the implementation of a national missile defense illustrates a structural one.

Although strategic and structural issues involve both executive and legislative actions (including the appropriating of funds for structural questions), these issues are usually decided over some discernible time span in both branches of government. Interest groups thus have more points of access and more time to affect the policy-making process. In sum, if these two kinds of issues are indeed more prevalent today and Congress and the president are more involved in deciding them, as we contend, interest groups are indeed advantaged today.

After September 11, 2001

One important complicating factor to this assertion about the increase in strategic and structural issues is the impact of the events of September 11, 2001, on the issue agenda and the foreign policy-making process. After all, those events replaced the emphasis on the range of issues that had gained a place on the foreign policy agenda and seemed to provide a new "North Star" (i.e., the war on terrorism) for American foreign policy as well. In that kind of environment, the policy-making process initially reverted to a more executive-dominated one since security issues, not strategic and structural issues, once again dominated the policy agenda. Indeed, in the immediate days and months after September 11, 2001, Congress reverted to a more familiar role of supporting the president and granting him broad discretion in fighting terrorism. By a vote of 98 to 0 in the Senate and 420 to 1 in the House, Congress passed Senate Joint Resolution 23, which authorized the president to employ force "against those nations, organizations, or persons, *he determines* planned, authorized, committed, or aided the terrorist attacks" against the United States (emphasis added). In addition, Congress passed the USA Patriot Act, which granted even more authority to the executive branch to pursue terrorist suspects. About a year later, Congress was almost equally supportive of President Bush's request over Iraq. By a vote of 296 to 133 in the House and 77 to 23 in the Senate, Congress authorized the president to use force "as he determines to be necessary and appropriate in order to defend the national security of the United States against the continuing threat posed by Iraq and enforce all relevant United Nations Security Council Resolutions regarding Iraq."

Beyond these legislative actions, the focus of Congress seemingly had been sharply altered by September 11, 2001. As former representative Lee Hamilton, who served in the House from 1965 to 1999, noted: "Congress is very focused on terrorism. This is the most dramatic shift in the foreign policy agenda of Congress in a very short time that I have ever seen." Another former member of Congress, Mickey Edwards, put it this way: "Members of Congress understand that politically they have to be supportive of the president and that the public is not going to put up with people playing politics."[22] Finally, and more directly germane to our discussion, the events of September 11, 2001, diminished the influence of ethnic groups on the foreign policy-making process. American supporters of India, for example, lost foreign policy influence as the George W. Bush administration embraced Pakistan to fight terrorism.[23] In this sense, the policy-making process seemingly had changed and the more pluralist process of the 1970s through the 1990s had been transformed.

With the events of September 11, 2001, receding into the background, the pluralist policy-making process has begun to return, albeit slowly, much as political scientist Robert Jervis suggested.[24] As he noted with regard to terrorism specifically: "It is yet possible that the shock we have all felt will be translated into greater agreement and effective measures to deal with the world's ills, but I suspect that differences in diagnosis, values, and interests will continue to characterize how we understand terrorism and conduct world politics."[25] Indeed, we have already witnessed that. Note the fissures in the policy-making process between Congress and the White House and within the executive branch itself over the anti-terrorism campaign and the debate and demonstrations over going to war against Iraq. While virtually all representatives and senators continue to provide general support for the president's war on terrorism and only a few voices are regularly heard in dissent over Iraq, differences between members of Congress and the White House do emerge on particular policies and actions.

By summer 2002, some differences were evident by the debate and disagreements over attacking Iraq and Saddam Hussein, but they have begun to occur on other issues as well (e.g., the trade-off between protecting domestic civil liberties and fighting terrorism). Within the administration, too, there were key officials with differing views on attacking Iraq: Secretary of State Colin Powell raised concerns about the "risks and complexities" over an attack, while the civilian leadership in the Pentagon (Secretary of Defense Rumsfeld and Deputy Secretary of Defense Paul Wolfowitz) were much more anxious to carry out such a mission.[26] While the intra-branch divisions over Iraq were muted by fall 2002 and early 2003, the inter-branch disputes between Senate majority leader Tom Daschle and President Bush perhaps reached a crescendo in late September 2002. What is most germane for our purposes is that various kinds of interest groups have been activated on the Iraq issue—ranging from public demonstrations over the proposed attack to the comments by former governmental officials over the wisdom of this course of action. Although these voices may ultimately be muted, foreign policy has remained an issue that produces debate in the post–September 11, 2001, world, and presidential prerogatives and presidential direction on foreign policy gained renewed potency after September 11, 2001.

In sum, then, some interests were again entering the discussions over foreign policy direction and foreign policy actions. Although September 11, 2001, may have muted the foreign policy debate and altered the decision-making process, the opportunities for interest groups to affect policy continued, albeit in a much more muted way than before those tragic events.

Interest Groups and Foreign Policy

Although the changed foreign policy-making process over the years may afford interest groups the opportunity to impact policy, it has been the tremendous growth in the number and activities of such groups that have allowed them to try to do so. The sheer growth in interest groups, including groups representing the Third World and Third World interests, is the first important phenomenon to note. Three aggregate indicators highlight the magnitude of interest groups involved in the American foreign policy-making process and indicate their potential to influence policy.

The first is the number (and growth) of non-governmental organizations (NGOs) worldwide. By one recent estimate, there are now 5,600 NGOs; another suggests 25,000, and yet a third estimate puts the total at 100,000 in the global arena today.[27] Whatever the exact number, the growth in NGOs has been meteoric, with only about 400 of these organizations a century ago. These organizations, with their ties to states and intergovernmental organizations (IGOs), can and do have a considerable impact on policy through the information they provide about global conditions, through the services they deliver, and through the information they share with policy makers. In this way, NGOs can serve as important sources of lobbying within a state and the global community. NGOs, for example, have been instrumental in promoting global environmental efforts, advocating women's rights, and promoting arms control agreements across the international community and within individual states. Perhaps more important for this analysis, NGOs have been active in issues related to the Third World. They have promoted the rights of children, helped the poor and disabled, supported indigenous peoples, and campaigned for human rights generally, among many other issues.[28]

The second aggregate indicator is the sheer number of groups with active lobbying efforts in Washington, DC. As compiled by *Washington Representatives 1999,* there are about 17,000 lobbyists in the nation's capital, representing 11,000 organizations and firms.[29] These Washington representatives cover a wide array of interests, ranging from traditional corporate lobbyists, government agencies with their own in-house representatives, foreign countries that rely on their embassies, law firms, or public relations firms to represent their interests, to religious and coalition groups lobbying on a broad number of concerns. While these lobbyists and organizations do not focus all of their attention on foreign policy issues, an increasing number of them do, especially as globalization and the domestication of foreign policy continue.

A third indicator of the increasing role of interest groups is the rise of more and more think tanks in Washington and elsewhere in the United States that also affect the policy-making process. Although well-known think tanks, such as the Brookings Institution, the Heritage Foundation, the Hoover Institution, the American Enterprise Institute, and the Center for Strategic and International Studies, have been around for many decades and their policy relevance is recognized, the rise of many new think tanks (and consulting agencies) with a narrow issue agenda is an important new phenomenon that has provided added clout to interest groups and their activities. Officials in these think tanks are often well-connected individuals in the Washington community who lead their organization for a time and then move into a government agency as an administration changes or the personnel within an administration move on. In this way, think tanks (or interest groups) not only seek to influence policy, but they capture control of policy direction through placing former personnel in policy-making roles. No longer does an interest group (or think tank) seek to influence policy; its former personnel can now make policy directly. Andrew Natsios, current head of the U.S. Agency for International Development (USAID), fits this pattern, with his previous role as vice president of World Vision U.S. and other international relief agencies, but he is far from the only one. Moreover, the pattern is often one of a revolving door, where an official leaves an administration, joins or sets up a think tank, and returns to another administration later on.

As an initial way to assess the role of Third World interest groups, let us discuss several different types of groups from these areas and indicate how they can and do lobby on Third World issues, much as ETAN did so successfully over the question of East Timor recently in the U.S. Congress. By Third World issues, we are referring to issues that particularly affect nations and peoples primarily outside of North America, Europe, and East Asia. In an age of globalization issues, of course, hard-and-fast demarcation of them is often difficult to draw and nearly impossible to sustain over time. Still, issues dealing with authoritarian governments, civil and ethnic conflicts, development, human rights, and global poverty are among some of the concerns that Third World countries and peoples are most interested in. Among the many interest groups that focus upon Third World issues in the United States, we have selected five different groups to provide some sense of the nature of the "Third World lobby" currently operating in American society. The five are (1) new ethnic lobbies, (2) foreign lobbies, (3) religious organizations, (4) human rights groups, and (5) anti-globalization groups. The aim in discussing these groups is to identify their breadth, their mechanisms for seeking influence, and their relative success in affecting American foreign policy. It is also to show that some groups are Third World lobbies directly (e.g., foreign or ethnic lobbies), while others lobby on behalf of Third World interests (e.g., religious groups, human rights groups, and anti-globalization groups).

Ethnic Lobbies

Ethnic groups are perhaps the oldest foreign policy lobby within the United States. These are groups of Americans who lobby on behalf of the interest of their country of origin. The aim of such groups is to shape American policy in a favorable way toward that country, or at least to dissuade American policy from assisting an adversary of that country. The best-known ethnic lobbies are the Jewish, Greek, and Irish lobbies, but other, newer ethnic groups are emerging to try to affect the American foreign policy-making process, too. An increasing number of these groups now promote issues and interests of the global South, albeit often narrow and country-specific ones. A few illustrations of these newer ethnic lobbying groups will suggest their magnitude and their effect.

Shortly after the collapse of the Soviet empire and the Soviet Union itself in the early 1990s, eighteen ethnic associations from that part of the world (e.g., Armenian Americans, Belarusian Americans, Hungarian Americans, Czech Americans, Estonian Americans, Georgian Americans, Latvian Americans, Ukrainian Americans, and others) formed the Central and East European Coalition. The aims of this coalition were to promote the expansion of NATO to include the countries of Eastern and Central Europe and to seek greater foreign assistance for them as well. Indeed, the coalition was credited by the Clinton administration with helping gain congressional approval for NATO expansion.[30] Such a group as this would not only lobby in Washington, but, like all ethnic lobbies, would seek to rally its adherents to send letters to members of Congress and to the White House over this issue.

The Armenian Assembly, a separate lobbying group among this large ethnic coalition, has been particularly effective in influencing foreign aid policy, although it has suffered a setback after September 11, 2001. The assembly, for instance succeeded in obtaining earmarked economic and military aid for Armenia and for prohibiting aid to Azerbaijan, its adversary in the Caspian Sea region in the 1990s— for fiscal year 2003, for instance, Armenia received $90 million in economic aid and $4 million in military aid.[31] After the events of September 11, 2001, however, Congress, at the urging of Secretary of State Colin Powell, passed legislation allowing the president to waive aid restrictions to Azerbaijan in an effort to fight terrorism, much as with previous restrictions on Pakistan. In part, then, the events of September 11, 2001, weakened the policy impact of some ethnic lobbies, especially within Congress.[32]

Two other important ethnic lobbies illustrate the range of Third World issues on the agenda of some ethnic lobbies. The Cuban American lobby has a relatively narrow agenda, while the African American lobby has a broader one. The Cuban American National Foundation (CANF), largely composed of Cubans who fled the island nation and their descendants, is the principal Cuban American lobbying group. Its primary goal has been to continue the embargo against Cuba, and it has been very successful maintaining the embargo. As a member of Congress noted several years ago, this ethnic lobby "uses difficult, difficult tactics whenever you disagree with them."[33] That is, this lobby has extensive contacts and ties with Congress, and it plays a considerable role in presidential elections since several key states (most notably, Florida) have important Cuban American constituencies.

There is some evidence that CANF's success may be fading a bit lately, especially after the death of its founder, Jorge Mas Canosa, in 1997. By one assessment, for instance, CANF is increasingly divided between older and younger Cuban Americans.[34] In addition, several other lobbying groups (e.g., Americans for Humanitarian Trade with Cuba, a bipartisan group of former American governmental officials, and USA*Engage) have emerged that are more favorable to trade with Cuba or at least want to explore alternate policy options. Nonetheless, CANF remains a formidable lobbying group on an important single issue (although, by one account, it has extended its interests to include general Central American and African policy issues) and illustrates how an ethnic lobby can be influential on American foreign policy.[35]

Trans-Africa is the most prominent African American lobby and has had several recent foreign policy successes over the past two decades.

This group was very instrumental in gaining passage of the Anti-Apartheid Act of 1986 over President Ronald Reagan's veto. In 1993 and 1994, Trans-Africa was also pivotal in pressuring the Clinton administration to take stronger measures against the military rulers in Haiti. Eventually, this pressure, along with the work of the Congressional Black Caucus, led to intervention by the United States to restore democracy to that country. In 1999 and 2000, however, Trans-Africa opposed the African Growth and Opportunity Act that was before Congress, but failed to halt its passage. That legislation, with its promotion of U.S.-Africa trade and the duty-free access for particular products from Africa, stimulated the involvement of other ethnic groups and interests on African issues (e.g., Africare, the African American Institute, and prominent members of the Congressional Black Caucus).[36]

Finally, a sizeable ethnic group, the Mexican American community, does not yet have the impact on foreign policy as some of these others, but it may potentially in the near future. The growing presence of Hispanics of Mexican descent throughout the United States (but particularly in states such as California, Arizona, and Colorado) provides a ready political base of support for promoting favorable policy positions toward Mexico, Central America, or elsewhere. The Mexican American community, however, has not been as well organized or as cohesive as, for example, the Cuban American community. As a result, its role in promoting Third World issues remains considerably less than the others mentioned so far, although it supported NAFTA and closer ties with Mexico. Yet, as an analysis discovered several years ago, the attitudes of Mexican Americans on several issues were not markedly different than the American public as a whole.[37]

While we often think of ethnic groups as lobbying the executive and legislative branches from outside those institutions, the emergence of ethnic caucuses within Congress is yet another way for these interests to try to affect foreign policy. Congressional caucuses are informal organizations of House or Senate members (or members from both chambers) with an interest in a particular country or issue. In the 107th Congress in 2002, these caucuses totaled 176.[38] Several of these congressional caucuses, moreover, are explicitly focused on ethnic groups and interests. In 1988, for example, there were six such congressional caucuses with an ethnic focus; in 1997, there were fifteen.[39] By the 107th Congress (2001–2), there were now nineteen congressional ethnic caucuses. These caucuses included the Albanian Issues Caucus, Congressional Caucus on Armenian Issues, Congressional Caucus on Hellenic Issues, Congressional Caucus on India and Indian Americans, Congressional Ukrainian Caucus, Congressional Asian Pacific Caucus, and Congressional Hispanic Caucus, among others. While such caucuses often come and go, they illustrate a more direct way for ethnic groups—and especially small and Third World groups—to have more direct access to the political process and to attempt to influence foreign policy.[40] Although it would be an exaggeration to suggest these caucuses significantly influence policy, their proximity to the political process surely assists them.

Foreign Lobbies

Foreign lobbies, or more accurately, lobbies representing foreign countries, are the newest and perhaps the most pervasive foreign policy interest groups today. Table 3.1 gives some sense of the number of countries in various regions of the world and the number of individuals representing these countries in Washington from 1977 to 1999.[41] Over these years, there has been an increase in the number of countries represented in Washington and in the total number of groups representing those countries. While the foreign lobbies from Western Europe, Asia, and North America (as might be expected) are most active, countries from Africa, Eastern Europe, the Middle East, and South America (and individuals or firms representing them) have increased their lobbying as well. Representatives from Japan, Canada, and Britain (and the rest of Western Europe) still account for most of the total foreign lobbying, but China, Russia, and countries of the former Soviet Union have increasingly sent or hired representatives to make their positions known in Washington.

Foreign lobbies use various mechanisms to get their message out. Embassies, of course, are the first component of this representation in Washington, but most countries hire law and public relations firms to present their views to both Congress and the executive branch. These firms are wholly familiar with American politics and, more often than not, are well connected in official Washington. Some of these countries also contract with ex-officials in the American government to represent their interests on Capitol Hill or the executive branch. These officials would be especially effective in promoting a country's interests. Finally, these foreign lobbies often form coalitions with American business interests and U.S. firms as a way to strengthen their lobbying.[42]

Table 3.1

Foreign Interest Groups in Washington by Region, 1977, 1986, 1996, and 1999

Region	Year 1977	1986	1996	1999
Africa				
Total countries	13	26	33	36
Total representatives	30	46	72	74
Asia				
Total countries	16	18	21	24
Total representatives	80	256	257	222
Pacific				
Total countries	5	3	7	7
Total representatives	23	20	26	16
Western Europe				
Total countries	19	18	21	21
Total representatives	155	207	254	230
Eastern Europe				
Total countries	10	6	24	25
Total representatives	44	17	92	71
Middle East				
Total countries	14	10	18	12
Total representatives	38	57	108	64
North America				
Total countries	23	20	23	26
Total representatives	95	176	210	242
South America				
Total countries	10	7	13	12
Total representatives	43	58	83	73

Sources: The data for 1977, 1986, and 1996 are taken from Table 7.1 in James M. McCormick, "Interest Groups and the Media in Post–Cold War U.S. Foreign Policy," in James M. Scott, ed., *After the End* (Durham, NC: Duke University Press, 1998), p. 183. See also the *Directory of Washington Representatives of American Associations and Industries* and earlier *Washington Representatives* volumes. The 1999 data were compiled from *Washington Representatives*, 1999, 23rd ed. (Washington, DC: Columbia Books, 1999).

Particularly germane to this discussion is the large number of Third World countries having hired representatives in Washington. Nigeria, Rwanda, Swaziland, Mauritania, and Congo from Africa, Indonesia and India from Asia, and Haiti, Mexico, and Guatemala from the Caribbean and Latin America are but some of the countries with hired lobbyists in Washington. Various political factions in foreign countries (e.g., Sinn Fein and the Ulster Unionist Party from Ireland and

Northern Ireland; factions from Iran and Kashmir) have also hired representatives to promote their views in Washington—both to the executive and legislative branches.[43]

Sometimes, too, the actions of these foreign lobbies brush right up against—and even cross—American legal limits in their efforts to influence the American political process. During the 1996 election campaign, for example, the Clinton administration received contributions from groups and individuals from several Third World countries (e.g., Indonesia, Taiwan, Thailand, South Korea, and China). Over the years, members of Congress have received gifts or assistance from individuals from foreign countries (e.g., Koreagate scandal, Torricelli case) in which the apparent intent is to influence American foreign and domestic policy action, even if indirectly.[44] And at other times, foreign governments employ economic or social retaliation against American firms or individuals that do not support or promote their interests in Washington.[45] In all, both aggregate and individual case data show that representatives of other countries are increasingly common and prominent actors in the American foreign policy-making process.

Religious Lobbies

Religious organizations have always been an important component of the American social and political fabric, but only in recent decades have they been viewed as playing a prominent public role in seeking to affect American foreign policy. During the Vietnam War in the 1960s and 1970s, the conflict in Central America in the 1980s, and the nuclear freeze issue of the 1980s, several religious organizations actively sought to promote their views on these issues. In the 1990s and to the present, religious groups have been involved in discussing the need and possibilities of humanitarian interventions due to the massive human rights violations during several ethnic and civil conflicts (e.g., Bosnia, Haiti, Rwanda, and Kosovo).[46] Furthermore, religious groups have long been interested in (and actually participants in) helping poor countries and development efforts around the world. In all, their principal goal, motivated by the social gospel that they believe, preach, and practice, has been to add a moral dimension to foreign policy.

Although the number of religious organizations with foreign policy lobbying activities is difficult to measure precisely, there are probably as many as one hundred different religious lobbies in Washington.[47] These religious lobbies include most of the mainline Protestant denominations (e.g., Methodists, Presbyterians, Baptists), the Roman Catholic Church, and Jewish organizations. In addition, these lobbies include conferences, councils, or committees of these religions, such as the National Council of Churches, the National Conference of Catholic Bishops, the American Friends Service Committee (Quakers), and the Mennonite Central Committee. They also include several faith-based NGOs (or FNGOs), such as World Vision (representing evangelical Protestants), World Council of Churches (representing mainline Protestants), and Catholic Relief Services (representing Roman Catholics).

These FNGOs actively seek to influence the foreign policy of the United States. Andrew Natsios, current head of USAID and previously vice president of World Vision U.S. and executive director of World Vision Relief and Development, succinctly outlined the techniques these religious organizations use to impact policy and especially foreign assistance policy worldwide.[48] First, these organizations use newsletters and magazines to keep their donors informed on current or emergency crisis situations around the world. Second, they may ask their donors to contact or write governmental officials to seek some kind of intervention. Third, many of the larger FNGOs have Washington officials who directly lobby members of Congress and the executive branch. At the time of the genocide in Rwanda in 1994, Natsios notes, "representatives of Catholic Relief Services, World Vision, and Africares visited Dick Clark, the National Security Council's director of peace-keeping operations, to urge military intervention to stop the slaughter." Fourth, sometimes these groups "go public" with appeals through the media, mailings to Congress, and radio and television interviews. In 1998 several FNGOs, in collaboration with other groups, engaged in a wide array of public activities to stop an amendment that would have ended American aid to North Korea. Fifth, FNGOs also affect the making of American foreign policy through the information that they provide to policy makers. FNGOs' information about a problem or crisis abroad is often better for one fundamental reason: their information "derives from a relatively permanent presence on the ground with a large number of staff who speak to a great many local people." As a result, these NGOs "are sometimes asked to White House, State Department, and USAID meetings during major crises" because of the unique perspective they can provide.

In these various ways, then, FNGOs can and do seek to influence policy, although the overall effect may still be somewhat limited (as we discuss below). Nonetheless, FNGOs are more numerous than many might suspect, and they increasingly participate in the agenda setting and the policy-making process, especially in light of the humanitarian crises brought on by civil and ethnic wars and by large-scale famines in recent years. By doing so, they offer another dimension to Third World lobbying that is often overlooked.

Human Rights Lobbies

Human rights lobbies are the fourth important type of interest groups that often promote Third World interests. These human rights groups include those that focus on improving human rights worldwide and those that focus on human rights in particular countries or regions. In the former category, Amnesty International and Human Rights Watch are two such major groups. These kinds of groups invariably represent Third World interests and lobby the public and official Washington to promote global human rights. They employ a full array of techniques, ranging from utilizing informative web sites, developing extensive human rights reports (on all countries or on specific situations in particular countries), engaging in testimony and lobbying on Capitol Hall, and using regular contacts with offices in the executive branch. Their reports and their testimony can be highly influential in Congress, both for the impact they have in stimulating congressional hearings and by the detailed and nonpartisan information they provide about the conditions of global human rights.

Human rights groups or interests focused on a particular issue or a particular region are also important lobbying groups for Third World interests in Washington. In the 1980s, for example, such interests were especially active over American policy toward Central America. An analysis of the interest groups active over aid to the Nicaraguan contras identified about one hundred interest groups involved on both sides of the issue.[49] While not all of these groups were human rights groups, an important theme of many of them was the magnitude of human rights violations. In the 1990s, other groups emerged to lobby for actions in Bosnia and Rwanda as the human rights conditions in those countries were increasingly recognized as abysmal. Most recently, too, the significant and sustained action of the ETAN illustrates how these specialized human rights groups can get their message out—and alter American policy.

Anti-Globalization Lobbies

With the emergence of globalization at all levels—whether economic, political, and social—there has been a reaction to that phenomenon, and a large number of interest groups have arisen within the United States and elsewhere throughout the world to protest against it. Most of these interest groups are supporting and working on behalf of Third World states and interests, and they are challenging what they see as social and economic dislocations for Third World countries and peoples as economic liberalization moves across the globe.

As part of globalization, for instance, transnational corporations, largely based in developed countries, have moved their operations to developing countries to take advantage of cheaper labor and have engaged in "boom and bust" investments within these countries as well. The result too often has been that these countries are left in dire economic straits when these investments fail or the investors leave. The host countries in turn have few options but to accept the conditionalities imposed by outside institutions, notably the International Monetary Fund (IMF), to try to right their economies. The Asian currency crisis of 1997–98, for example, epitomizes the downside of this globalization process and the serious economic and political dislocations that it produced in that region of the world and beyond.[50]

A recent analysis by Manfred Steger identifies several of these interest groups and outlines the array of activities they engage in as part of their effort to affect this process.[51] Third World Network, the International Forum on Globalization, Global Exchange, and Focus on the Global South are four such groups. These groups, largely headquartered abroad (although Global Exchange is headquartered in California), provide numerous publications, reports, seminars, and teach-ins to educate the public about the dangers they see from globalization. These organizations, Steger reports, also undertake local initiatives to activate other groups and interests over globalization issues (e.g., sweatshops and other labor violations). While the target of these groups is often more the public than the political elites, their activities undoubtedly also have an impact on politics.

Other groups and interests have undertaken more direct action to publicize their opposition to globalization and to target political elites. Indeed, violent protests have resulted at a number of international economic meetings in recent years. At the Third Ministerial Meeting of the WTO in Seattle during November and December 1999, the first of these protests took place, and the so-called Battle for Seattle got enormous attention in the United States and the rest of the world. Other such protests followed in Davos, Switzerland, in February 2000, Washington, DC, in April 2000, Quebec City, Quebec, Canada, in April 2001, and Washington, DC, in September 2002. Indeed, the G-8 countries met in an isolated spot in Kananaskis, Alberta, Canada, in summer 2002 in part to forestall massive demonstrations.

Foreign Policy Influence of Third World Lobbies

Do these various lobbies discussed so far (and others not discussed) form an effective and successful Third World lobby in the shaping of American foreign policy? The answer is difficult to determine in any definitive way for at least two reasons. First, empirical measures of interest group impact on policy outcomes have been difficult to obtain and are often missing from such assessments. Instead, assessments rely upon qualitative appraisals that may well invite challenges by others, even as they provide some evaluation of an interest group's impact. Second, the standards of evaluation of group success are also elusive. How much interest group success is sufficient to claim that such lobbying made a difference? Let us comment on both of these dimensions.

To be sure, systematic measures of lobbying activities would clearly provide a fuller assessment of an interest group's influence on policy, but Lawrence Rothenberg has provided several reasons why such measures are difficult to obtain. First, gaining access to policy makers and comparing lobbying with the impact of other factors are very demanding tasks. Even if this access were possible, "teasing out exactly the degree to which behavior is a function of group effects" is extraordinarily challenging and labor intensive. Second, assessing interest group effects is also problematic, because "it has often been unclear what exactly [an] organization [has] to furnish . . . to have an impact." For example, how much information or political pressure by a group makes a difference? Third, sometimes interest groups overreach for what they want to obtain and thus hinder their prospects of making a difference. Or, as Rothenberg puts it, "under some conditions organizational processes result in group goals that are ripe for activities and in other instances they produce objectives that are difficult to attain."[52] In light of the limitation of access to these Third World lobbies, our measures of their policy impact must be more qualitative and somewhat impressionistic, albeit informed by several specific examples.

The standard of evaluation also complicates any qualitative (or quantitative) assessment of interest group impact. That is, does the impact need to be regular and sustained, or can it be episodic? Can it be even more infrequent and still be successful? Once again, Rothenberg, and his careful assessment of the impact of the non-profit organization Common Cause on the MX missile development program in the mid-1980s, provides us with some insights in thinking about evaluative standards. As he reports, lobbying by Common Cause made a difference—albeit "around the margins" and more in modifying the missile development than in canceling it altogether—as measured both by his quantitative and qualitative (or interview) assessments. Still, this limited success was noteworthy, especially when some tend to dismiss (or fail to confirm) interest group effects.[53] Put differently, limited impact can have policy consequences.

In the case of Third World lobbies in this analysis, then, we consider three levels of evaluation in our assessment. First, if we set the standard of evaluation for success as regular, sustained impact on the direction of policy, then we must conclude that these groups have little effect, since they are often more interested in addressing a narrow singular issue or narrow sets of issues. Moreover, these groups are still sufficiently disparate in their approach and goals to impact foreign policy more routinely. Second, if the standard is more episodic achievement of success, the record is better, since many of these groups have achieved significant successes from time to time. Third, if the standard is weaker still, the extent to which these groups affect the foreign policy agenda, the record gets better yet. By that standard, these Third World lobbying groups play a more continuous role in American foreign policy by keeping some items on the agenda, bringing up others, and stopping or slowing down particularly harmful policy actions. In all, the second and third standards seem the more apt and overarching ones for describing the impact of the Third World lobbies.

Successes and Failures

In the aggregate, groups lobbying for the global South have surely had some successes and have produced tangible policy effects—albeit often limited ones. Several ethnic groups, for example, have had substantial and continuous effects on specific aspects of American foreign policy. The impact of the Jewish or Cuban American lobby on America's Middle East or Cuba policy is hardly debatable, nor, more recently, is the effect of the Armenian Assembly or the Greek lobby on policy toward countries and regions of interests to those ethnic groups. Yet, it is hard to argue that other ethnic lobbies, and especially some of the newer ones, have had a sustained effect. Witness the setback of the Indian lobby and even the Armenian lobby in the post–September 11 period.

Foreign lobbies also illustrate the same limited effect. While the Chinese lobby has been markedly successful in obtaining permanent normal trading relations and the Japanese lobby has been successful in protecting its market, other foreign lobbies have hardly been as successful. The one identifiable Third World foreign lobby that proved remarkably successful was Saudi Arabia over the AWACS' sale in the early 1980s.[54] The religious lobbies certainly have had their successes in promoting humanitarian aid to the neediest part of the world and have been important distributors of American government aid programs. In 1998, for instance, major FGNOs utilized about $325 million in governmental funds in their aid endeavors.[55] Yet, foreign aid budgets within the American political system have always been a great struggle to fund and have declined in recent decades. In this sense, and as Mark Amstutz argues, FNGOs "play only a modest, indirect role in the development and implementation of [American] foreign policy."[56]

Similarly, human rights and anti-globalization groups can claim several specific successes. Amnesty International and Human Rights Watch, among many others, have been instrumental in adding human rights conditions to the distribution of American assistance around the world and lobbying for cutting off aid to governments that are chronic violators of human rights. Notably, too, groups opposed to globalization succeeded after the "Battle for Seattle" in getting President Clinton to pledge to incorporate labor and environmental standards in future discussions of liberalizing the international trading order. Still, these groups have not been successful in transforming their concerns into the focal point of foreign policy. In short, then, while the record of Third World lobbying is hardly bare, the impact of such lobbying is hardly robust in shaping the general direction of American foreign policy.

While these limited successes of Third World lobbies should not be eschewed, their overall impact is probably less measurable and more intangible. That is, Third World lobbies are more likely to affect the agenda of American foreign policy in a continuous way, even as they do not regularly shape policy. Moreover, the five groups that we have discussed illustrate the differing ways Third World lobbies can affect the policy agenda. The religious organizations, for example, do so by providing a moral dimension to American foreign policy decision making. As Amstutz puts it, "Religious communities can help to structure debate and illuminate relevant moral norms."[57] And as Andrew Natsios adds, "FNGOs do bring the moral dimension to the foreign-policy debate, which is usually dominated by political calculations that may ignore a policy's cost in human life."[58] The ethnic and foreign lobbies are important for maintaining some issues on the agenda for their particular nation of origin, although these agenda issues are usually very specific rather than broader foreign policy goals. Finally, the human rights groups and the anti-globalization groups are especially important for bringing new issues to the agenda and reminding American policy makers of issues that they are not addressing sufficiently. Importantly, then, the sheer fact that these groups can affect the agenda in Washington is not unimportant. From time to time, then, these agenda items enter the policy-making process, and Third World lobbies can and do then impact American foreign policy.

Constraining Factors on Third World Lobbies

Several reasons appear to account for why Third World groups have not done better at affecting foreign policy. Each of these reasons deserves further study. First, the growth and strength of other lobbying groups in American society often overshadow groups representing interests of the global South. As we have noted, Third World lobbies have expanded dramatically in recent decades, but, importantly, interest groups across the political spectrum have as well. Powerful American economic interest groups (fundamentally major transnational organizations—whether business or labor) are arguably more consequential in the bureaucratic and policy-making area than are the new civil society Third World groups that we have discussed in this analysis. In this sense, the new groups promoting Third World interests continue to face major challenges.

Second, and related to this first reason, American media coverage of Third World interests continues to be limited and public support for Third World issues remains low. Although the events of September 11, 2001, have expanded the American public's interest in international events and information about other countries, that attention is largely confined to the dominant news of the day (i.e., the situation with Iraq and with North Korea).[59] There is little sustained or systematic coverage of the global South. Indeed, some evidence suggests that international coverage by the American media has actually declined in recent decades, despite the movement toward a more globalized world.[60] In short, then, public support for Third World issues is weak, due to the limited media coverage and limited knowledge or concern about such issues.

Third, although coalition building across some Third World groups does occur (e.g., anti-hunger groups and religious lobbies and the various anti-globalization groups), these joint efforts need to be enlarged and enhanced if these lobbies are to gain more impact upon American foreign policy. Since Third World interest groups are often underfunded and understaffed, coalition building between and among them is often yet another challenge.

Finally, bureaucratic procedures (despite more recent access for interest groups) and the continued priority of some issues over others within the American political system militate against the effectiveness of Third World lobbies. That is, some interest groups enjoy easier access to the policy-making process than others do because of the perceived interest and importance of those issues to the American public. In this sense, Third World lobbies are still disadvantaged. Furthermore, with the sustained focus of the Bush administration on the war on terrorism, the ability of Third World groups to gain a prominent place on the foreign policy agenda remains a continuing difficulty.

Conclusion

America's foreign policy decision-making process has evolved from a relatively closed one during the Cold War years toward a more pluralist one since the end of the Vietnam War. The formal end of the Cold War accelerated that pluralist decision-making process, but the events of September 11, 2001, muted that process somewhat. Still, interest groups have a much greater prospect of influencing and shaping the direction of American foreign policy over the years for several important reasons. As American foreign policy making became more open, the number of actors, the types of foreign policy issues, and the divisiveness of foreign policy issues changed. Increasingly, foreign policy issues were no longer the exclusive purview of the executive branch, and crisis (or security) issues no longer dominated the foreign policy agenda. As a result, Congress, interest groups, and the public at large were now part of the political process to address this broader agenda. These actors were aided by the emergence of more strategic and structural issues—issues that often require the involvement of the executive and legislative branches and often demand more deliberation and debate than crisis issues did. In turn, the foreign policy issues often sparked debate and controversy among the array of actors involved in the process. In such an environment, interest groups can and do attempt to exploit the divisions among the White House, Congress, and the American public to try to shape foreign policy for their own ends.

The events of September 11, 2001, halted for a time the accelerated pluralist model of foreign policy making in the years immediately after the Cold War. In this sense, there was a movement back in the direction of an elitist or executive-dominated model of decision making so prevalent during the Cold War years. To be sure, the George W. Bush administration sought to embrace such a model and succeeded in gaining support for it for a time. In this context, the potency of interest groups, including the Third World lobbies, was diminished. As criticism of the war on terrorism emerged and the Iraq War and its ensuing complications developed, the fundamental pluralism of the American political structure reemerged. Challenges once again began to occur over foreign policy direction, and the avenues of access for interest groups remained available, although perhaps not at the same level as prior to September 11. In the main, then, Third World lobbies will likely continue to try to take advantage of the evolving policy-making environment to affect American foreign policy, albeit with continued limited success.

In short, although lobbies representing interests of the global South are indeed numerous and utilize many traditional methods for seeking influence, they have not had a sustained and continuous impact on the direction of American foreign policy. Instead, their influence either has been sporadic (and usually confined to a narrow set of issues), or it has been limited to affecting the foreign policy agenda. In all, then, the Third World lobbies are more likely to exercise influence through promoting an ethical or moral dimension to foreign policy, inserting new issues on the foreign policy agenda, or maintaining other issues on that agenda, rather than directly shaping American foreign policy. Still, our analysis invites the development of more qualitative and quantitative measures of interest groups in general, and Third World lobbies in particular, and especially in the post–September 11 world.

Notes

Thanks are due to Eugene Wittkopf for his advice on this chapter and to Jürgen Rüland for his excellent shepherding of this chapter and the entire volume.

1. Stephen Zunes and Ben Terrall, "East Timor: Reluctant Support for Self-Determination," in Ralph G. Carter, ed., *Contemporary Cases in U.S. Foreign Policy: From Terrorism to Trade* (Washington, DC: CQ Press, 2002), pp. 11–30. The quote is on p. 27. My earlier work on interest groups and U.S. foreign policy can be found in James M. McCormick, "Interest Groups and the Media in Post–Cold War U.S. Foreign Policy," in James M. Scott, ed., *After the End* (Durham, NC: Duke University Press, 1998), pp. 170–98, and in James M. McCormick, *American Foreign Policy and Process,* 3rd ed. (Itasca, IL: F.E. Peacock, 1998), chap. 11. I draw upon both in developing this research.

2. John J. Judis, *The Paradox of Democracy: Elites, Special Interests, and the Betrayal óf Public Trust* (New York: Pantheon, 2000), p. 3.

3. Ibid., p. 4

4. See Stephen D. Krasner, *Defending the National Interest: Raw Materials Investments and U.S. Foreign Policy* (Princeton, NJ: Princeton University Press, 1978), pp. 56–57.

5. Ibid., p. 70.

6. Ibid., pp. 61–70. The quoted passages are on p. 66.

7. The phrase is from Richard E. Fenno, Jr., *Congressmen in Committees* (Boston: Little, Brown 1973), p. 69, in his characterization of the House Foreign Affairs Committee.

8. See Louis Fisher, *Presidential War Power* (Lawrence: University of Kansas Press, 1995); and Gordon Silverstein, *Imbalance of Powers: Constitutional Interpretation and the Making of Foreign Policy* (New York: Oxford University Press, 1997).

9. See McCormick, *American Foreign Policy and Process,* pp. 72–74.

10. See the decision in the case of *U.S.* v. *Curtiss-Wright Export Corporation et al.* at 299 U.S. 304 (1936).

11. Bernard Cohen, *The Public's Impact on Foreign Policy* (Boston: Little, Brown, 1973).

12. On a typology of foreign policy issues, see James M. Lindsay and Randall B. Ripley, "How Congress Influences Foreign and Defense Policy," in Randall B. Ripley and James M. Lindsay, eds., *Congress Resurgent: Foreign and Defense Policy on Capitol Hill* (Ann Arbor: University of Michigan Press, 1993), pp. 17–35.

13. C. Wright Mills, *The Power Elite* (New York: Oxford University Press, 1956).

14. Aaron Wildavsky, "The Two Presidencies," *Trans-action* 3 (Dec. 1966): 7–14.

15. McCormick, *American Foreign Policy and Process,* p. 303.

16. Arthur Schlesinger, *The Imperial Presidency* (Boston: Houghton Mifflin, 1973).

17. James M. McCormick, "Decision-making in the Foreign Affairs and Foreign Relations Committees," in Ripley and Lindsay, *Congress Resurgent,* pp. 115–53.

18. See, for example, James M. McCormick and Eugene R. Wittkopf, "Bipartisanship, Partisanship, and Ideology in Congressional-Executive Foreign Policy Relations, 1947–1988," in *Journal of Politics* 52 (Nov. 1990): 1077–100; and James M. McCormick, Eugene R. Wittkopf, and David M. Danna, "Politics and Bipartisanship at the Water's Edge: A Note on Bush and Clinton," *Polity* 30 (Fall 1997): 133–49.

19. See Eugene R. Wittkopf, *Faces of Internationalism: Public Opinion and American Foreign Policy* (Durham, NC: Duke University Press, 1990), and "Faces of Internationalism in a Transitional Environment," *Journal of Conflict Resolution* 38 (Sept. 1994): 376–401.

20. Jeremy D. Rosner, *The New Tug-of-War: Congress, the Executive Branch, and National Security* (Washington, DC: Carnegie Endowment for International Peace, 1995).

21. The quoted passages are from Lindsay and Ripley, "How Congress Influences Foreign and Defense Policy," p. 19.

22. These former members were quoted in Miles A. Pomper, "Building Anti-Terrorism Coalition Vaults Ahead of Other Priorities," *CQ Weekly* (Oct. 27, 2001): 2552.

23. See Miles A. Pomper, "Adversity for Ethnic Lobbies," *CQ Weekly* (Oct. 27, 2001): 2558.

24. See Robert Jervis, "An Interim Assessment of September 11: What Has Changed and What Has Not?" *Political Science Quarterly* 117 (2002): 37–54.

25. Ibid., p. 54.

26. Todd S. Purdom and Patrick E. Tyler, "Top Republicans Break with Bush on Iraq Strategy," *The New York Times,* Aug. 16, 2002, available at www.nytimes.com/2002/08/16/international/middleeast/16IRAQ.html?todaysheadlines, accessed Sept. 29, 2002.

27. The estimates come from A. Leroy Bennett and James K. Oliver, *International Organizations: Principles and Issues,* 7th ed. (Upper Saddle River, NJ: Prentice Hall, 2002), p. 282; James A. Paul, *NGOs and Global Policy-Making,* Global Policy Forum at www.globalpolicy.org/ngos/analysis/ana100.htm, accessed Sept. 2, 2002; and Kelly-Kate S. Pease, *International Organizations: Perspectives on Governance in the Twenty-first Century,* 2nd ed. (Upper Saddle River, NJ: Prentice Hall, 2003), p. 34.

28. Paul, *NGOs and Global Policy-Making.* The 400 total a century ago is from this source, too.

29. See http://hallgovernment.com/government/396.shtml, accessed Sept. 2, 2002.

30. See the coalition's web site, *Central and Eastern European Coalition,* available at http://capitolwebservices.com/ceec/about.html, accessed Sept. 6, 2002.

31. Paul Glastris, "Multicultural Foreign Policy in Washington," *U.S. News and World Report* (July 21, 1997): 31, 34, on the success of the Armenian Assembly obtaining aid for Armenia and prohibiting it to Azerbaijan. For the recent earmarks on military and economic aid to Armenia, see table 8.3 in James M. McCormick, American Foreign Policy and Process, 4th ed., Belmont, CA: Thomson/Wadisforth, 2005.

32. Pomper, "Adversity for Ethnic Lobbies," p. 2558.

33. Dick Kirschten, "From the K Street Corridor," *National Journal* (July 17, 1993): 1815.

34. Daniel P. Erickson, "The New Cuba Divide," *National Interest,* no. 67 (Spring 2002): 70.

35. Philip Brenner, Patrick J. Haney, and Walter Vanderbush, "The Confluence of Domestic and International Interests: U.S. Policy Toward Cuba, 1998–2001," *International Studies Perspectives,* no. 3 (May 2002): 197–98.

36. The information about these other lobbying groups on this legislation is from the Association of Concerned Africa Scholars briefing paper, *Africa Growth and Opportunity Act Passes House, Efforts to Oppose Economic Conditionality Defeated, Opponents Focus on Senate,* available at www.prairienet.org/acas/alerts/agoa/ agoabm.htm, accessed Mar. 30, 2000.

37. See Rodolfo O. de la Garza, "U.S. Foreign Policy and the Mexican-American Political Agenda," in Mohammed E. Ahrari, ed., *Ethnic Groups and U.S. Foreign Policy* (New York: Greenwood Press, 1987), pp. 101–14.

38. This total was calculated from the following web site *Congressional Member Organizations—107th Congress,* available at www.house.gov/cha/CMOlist— 107th.htm, accessed July 12, 2004. On congressional caucuses generally, see Susan Webb Hammond, *Congressional Caucuses in National Policy Making* (Baltimore: Johns Hopkins University Press, 1998); and Glastris, "Multicultural Foreign Policy in Washington," more specifically upon which we rely.

39. Glastris, "Multicultural Foreign Policy in Washington," p. 34.

40. A recent ethnic congressional caucus illustrates the range and temporal nature of these ethnic caucuses. The Congressional Caucus on Sri Lanka and Sri-Lankan-Americans was established for the purpose of providing "Sri Lankan representation in Congress." Further, the caucus sought to promote American–Sri Lankan trade and investment and to ban terrorism and to deplore the violence fostered by the Liberation Tigers of Tamil Eelam. This information is from the caucus's web site at www.house.gov/pallone/srilankancaucus.html, "Congressional Caucus on Sri Lanka and Sri-Lankan-Americans, Rep. Frank Pallone, Jr., Co-Chair," accessed July 13, 2004. This caucus did not appear on the congressional listing of these caucus organizations for the 107th Congress, but it does appear on that listing for the 108th Congress. In this sense, some of these caucuses may arise only for a time, disappear, and return just as quickly.

41. The information on these foreign lobbies was gathered from the *Washington Representatives,* for the various years. The years prior to 1999 appeared previously in McCormick, "Interest Groups and the Media in Post–Cold War U.S. Foreign Policy." See the source note in Table 3.1 for more details.

42. For a recent example, see Richard Bernstein and Ross H. Munro, "The New China Lobby," in Eugene R. Wittkopf and James M. McCormick, eds., *The Domestic Sources of American Foreign Policy: Insights and Evidence,* 3rd ed. (Lanham, MD: Rowman & Littlefield, 1999), pp. 71–83, for the various domestic groups coalescing with China over most-favored nation status efforts for that country.

43. These examples are drawn from McCormick, "Interest Groups and the Media in Post–Cold War U.S. Foreign Policy," p. 184.

44. Ibid., pp. 184–85. Also see Richard A. Oppel, Jr., "Democrats Are Fined $243,000 for Fund-Raising Violations," *New York Times* (Sept. 21, 2002): A13; for more recent evidence on the 1996 campaign violations, see David Kocieniewski, "Campaign in Peril, Torricelli Leaves New Jersey Race," *New York Times* (Oct. 1, 2002): A1, A27.

45. See the discussion in Bernstein and Munro, "The New China Lobby."

46. According to Fr. Bryan Hehir, these kinds of interventions have become the key questions for religious groups. See W. John Moore, "Soldier for the Lord?" *National Journal* (Oct. 2, 1993): 2361–65, especially on p. 2363. Also see McCormick, "Interest Groups and the Media in Post–Cold War U.S. Foreign Policy," p. 182.

47. The number of religious lobbies is based upon the listing of such groups in *Washington Representatives 1999* (Washington, DC: Columbia Books, 1999). The lobbying examples and the discussion draw upon essays in Elliott Abrams, ed., *The Influence of Faith: Religious Groups and U.S. Foreign Policy* (Lanham, MD: Rowman & Littlefield, and Ethics and Public Policy Center, 2001), specifically the essays by Mark R. Amstutz and Andrew S. Natsios that are each entitled "Faith-Based NGOs and U.S. Foreign Policy," pp. 175–87 and 189–200, respectively.

48. Natsios, "Faith-Based NGOs and U.S. Foreign Policy," pp. 194–97. All quoted passages are from these pages.

49. See Cynthia J. Arnson and Philip Brenner, "The Limits of Lobbying: Interest Groups, Congress, and Aid to the Contras," paper prepared for the conference on Public Opinion and Policy Toward Central America, Princeton University, May 4–5, 1990.

50. For some of the economic consequences for developing countries from globalization, see Joseph E. Stiglitz, *Globalization and Its Discontents* (New York: W.W. Norton, 2002); in particular, see his extended treatment of the IMF/U.S. Department of Treasury actions during the Asian crisis, at pp. 89–132.

51. See Manfred B. Steger, *Globalism* (Lanham, MD: Rowman & Littlefield, 2002), pp. 111–12 for full descriptions of these groups and their activities. Also see this source on some of the protest demonstrations by anti-globalization groups, especially on pp. 117–34.

52. See Lawrence S. Rothenberg, *Linking Citizens to Government: Interest Group Politics at Common Cause* (Cambridge, UK: Cambridge University Press, 1992), pp. 191–92. Thanks to my colleague, Bob Lowry, for recommending this source.

53. Ibid., pp. 209–22, and especially pp. 213, 215, 221.

54. For a recent attempt to assess the impact of foreign lobbies on foreign aid, see Charles J. Borrero, "Influencing Aid: Interest Groups, Disaster Relief, and U.S. Foreign Assistance," a paper presented at the 2002 annual meeting of the American Political Science Association, Boston, Aug. 29–Sept. 1, 2002.

55. This total was calculated from the Table 8.1 in Amstutz, "Faith-Based NGOs and U.S. Foreign Policy," p. 183.

56. Ibid., p. 175.

57. Ibid., pp. 175–76.

58. Natsios, "Faith-Based NGOs and U.S. Foreign Policy," p. 200.

59. For some evidence of more public interest in international news and events after September 11, 2001, see *Worldviews 2002: American Public Opinion and Foreign Policy* (Chicago: Chicago Council on Foreign Relations, 2002), pp. 12–13.

60. On the decline of foreign news coverage at least prior to September 11, 2001, see Leonard Downie, Jr., and Robert G. Kaiser, *The News About the News: American Journalism in Peril* (New York: Alfred A. Knopf, Jr., 2002), pp. 240–42.

4

American Foreign Policy Toward Latin America in the Post–Cold War Era

A Case of Benign Neglect?

Howard J. Wiarda

Benign neglect? It has a certain logic as a basis for policy, especially in the post–Cold War era. From a realist or national self-interest point of view, the logic is: If the Soviet Union or other hostile outside powers are not interested in Latin America, or in other Third World areas where U.S. interests are limited, then why should the United States bother to pay them serious attention? This logic may be even more compelling now that the United States has committed itself to the war on terrorism as its main and virtually only foreign policy priority.

Moreover, there is a long history of U.S. benign neglect in Latin America and elsewhere in the Third World. As James Reston, the long-time *New York Times* foreign affairs columnist, once put it, "the United States will do anything [aid, investment, political pressure, military intervention] for Latin America except read about it."[1] At many points in U.S. history, benign neglect has alternated with dramatic, desperate, usually not-so-benign interventions, often of the military kind: Guatemala in 1954, Cuba in 1961, the Dominican Republic in 1965, Chile in 1970, Grenada in 1983, Panama in 1989, and Haiti in 1994 and again in 2004. The United States blows both hot and cold on Latin America—often at the same time, depending on which agency or part of the U.S. government is speaking.[2]

Benign neglect is closely in accord with other notable features of U.S. policy in Latin America that have waxed and waned—and often waxed again over the years. Thus, when the Pentagon speaks of "economy of force," it means that Latin America can be handled with a minimum of attention so that U.S. military forces can be concentrated in other, presumably more important, areas: Germany and along the Iron Curtain during the Cold War, Korea and Japan, Vietnam for a time, now Central Asia and the Middle East. The doctrine (of Lyndon B. Johnson) of "no second Cubas" was a means to simplify the complexities of Latin American politics, and U.S. policy there, by ruling out, for the most part, Marxist, to say nothing of Marxist-Leninist, regimes. Similarly, with "the lesser evil doctrine": When faced with a choice between an authoritarian regime (Somoza, Trujillo, Batista, Stroessner, Pinochet, the Brazilian generals, and others) that was also steadfastly anti-communist, and a (usually) wobbly democratic regime that allowed freedom even for communists, the United States almost always opted for the authoritarian. This, too, simplified our policy conundrums.[3]

The literature is vast,[4] so let us briefly simply stipulate some truths, fortunate or unfortunate, about U.S. policy in Latin America:

1. The United States pays little serious attention to Latin America.
2. The region is low on our list of priorities, behind Europe, Asia, the Middle East, Russia, China, maybe even India, and certainly now the war on terrorism.
3. The United States pays attention to the area mainly in times of crisis; seldom have we had a mature, sustained policy in Latin America.
4. Almost no one at high policy levels (cabinet or above) has an interest or extensive experience in Latin America (Jeane Kirkpatrick, who wrote her PhD thesis on Argentina, and George W. Bush, from Texas, are the only two who come to mind).
5. The United States is unwilling to study or read about Latin America or take it seriously or on its own terms.
6. U.S. attitudes tend to be condescending and patronizing; we treat Latin Americans as "little children" who must be educated and "taught" by the United States. As President Woodrow Wilson once put it, "we will teach Latin America how to elect good men"; similarly, in U.S. democracy and economic development programs.

7. Even more basically, the United States (and other societies) harbors deep-seated but usually unspoken prejudices about Latin America as Roman Catholic, a product of Spain and the Inquisition, racially impure, unsuccessful economically and socially, unable to govern itself, "banana republics."

8. U.S. policy in Latin America (and elsewhere) is exceedingly ethnocentric: we will send our brand of democracy, governance, and free markets to Latin America whether they fit or are appropriate, or not. The attitude is: We are superior, you are inferior; therefore, you must learn from us.[5]

9. For diplomats and military officials (Southcom), being assigned to Latin America is usually considered a career ender, a dead end, low priority, so top officials tend to avoid the area.

10. Latin America is sufficiently unimportant—and expendable—that new administrations often feel they can turn it over as a political patronage plum to their more radical, often highly ideological constituencies: the human rights, environmental, Black or Hispanic lobbies in the case of Democratic administrations; the likes of Ollie North or the Cuban-American National Foundation in the case of Republicans.

11. Since it does not count for or matter much, we frequently use Latin America as a guinea pig or experimental research laboratory for social and political programs that we would never dare to try out in our own or other high-priority areas: radical agrarian reform, national family planning, full transparency, pure forms of capitalism, and democracy.

12. Americans and American politicians can frequently say or do stupid, offensive things regarding Latin America, or Hispanics, that they would never say or do about other people or areas (such as Israel or the Middle East) because, until recently, there were no costs for doing so.

13. Because of Latin America's low priority, it is even more subjected to the play of domestic political interests than are other, more critical areas.

14. Latin America is still seen as "our" sphere of influence, our area of responsibility. This means, still, that outside actors (European, Asian) are not particularly welcome in Latin America unless they support U.S. policy, that Latin America should continue to orient itself toward the United States, and that the United

States should be the leader, model, beacon, and director of Latin America's future development. The Monroe Doctrine is not yet dead after all.

Thus, the picture is not a pretty one. The United States often means well for Latin America and occasionally its policies have been more or less enlightened. But given the strong prejudices toward the area historically, the condescension, the ethnocentrism, we should not expect a great deal from U.S. policy. Having battled these strong prejudices and stereotypes and butted our heads against the walls of ignorance and ethnocentrism for nearly half a century by now, few of us see the fundamentals of policy changing anytime soon. My suspicion is that many of these attitudes apply toward Sub-Saharan Africa, the Middle East, and South and Southeast Asia as well—indeed, throughout the developing world.

But as we conclude this introduction, let us introduce three complexities into this otherwise inglorious picture. First, one could make a strong case that Latin America could do worse, even far worse, than a U.S. policy based on benign neglect. If one's hope is for a consistent, enlightened, wise, mature, progressive U.S. policy in Latin America (which I see, given the preceding discussion, as unlikely anytime soon, or even ever), then one is bound to be disappointed with benign neglect. If, on the other hand, the realistic alternatives are military interventions, constant CIA machinations, or U.S. embassies playing a meddling, proconsular role, then benign neglect—letting Latin America, as Frank Sinatra famously put it, do it "their way"—is not such a bad policy. That, after all, is what the so-called Good Neighbor Policy of Franklin Roosevelt was all about in the 1930s and 1940s.

Second, even if U.S. policy in Latin America has often been unenlightened, the facts on the ground in both the United States and Latin America are changing, which will eventually force a change in policy. On the one side, the United States is, through immigration, increasingly becoming a Hispanic country and increasingly interdependent with Latin America on a host of major issues: immigration, investment, trade, oil and natural gas, tourism, banking, water supplies, drugs, labor supplies, the environment, democracy, human rights, and economic reform. At the same time, Latin America is changing radically in ways that will eventually make U.S. relations with it easier and more realistic if not necessarily always more enlightened: more democratic, more developed, more middle class, more integrated into the global economy, with a much better human rights situation. These facts will surely do more to affect U.S. policy in the area, and to draw the United States into a closer relationship with Latin America, than any wishful thinking we may express regarding Latin America.[6]

Third, I am not convinced "benign neglect" is a correct way to describe the policy. While Latin America is currently low on the United States's list of priorities and receives little high-level attention from Washington, at other levels U.S. policy in Latin America is vigorous and activist. First, a great deal of American foreign policy is taking place at lower policy levels, below the White House and cabinet, often out of sight of media and popular attention, within the foreign policy-making bureaucracies at the assistant secretary and country-desk levels, on trade and other critical issues. Arguably, this is the most effective locus of U.S. policy making since there is a great deal of information and expertise at these levels, whereas once an issue or country is at such a crisis condition that it reaches White House or cabinet levels, the most amount of "politics" and least amount of expertise are brought to bear.[7]

Second, much of the policy is carried out at local, county, state, and regional levels, on such important issues as drugs, immigration, water rights, the environment, and so on—what in the literature is called "local foreign policy." Third, despite the lack of high-level attention, U.S. officials at all levels remain committed to and vigorously engaged in pursuing the "golden triad" of the so-called Washington Consensus (more on this below): democracy, free trade, and open markets—itself an activist agenda. Fourth, while official Washington may be paying less attention to Latin America, in the field, in U.S. embassies throughout the region, activist, even "proconsular," often only slightly reduced from Cold War days policies are still being pursued by energetic U.S. officials. And finally, while official Washington may be less engaged in Latin America, the private sector, chiefly U.S. private businesses, capital, and foreign direct investment (FDI), but also including NGOs and civil society actors, have stepped into this vacuum; furthermore, this shift from public to private attention was part of a conscious U.S. strategy and does not signal any decline in U.S. interest in the area, only a shift in means and agencies. Overall, this does not add up to a policy of benign neglect toward Latin America.

The Domestic Background

All American presidents from John F. Kennedy on have proclaimed, shortly after taking office, that they "really care" about Latin America.

At one level, this is a sop to Latin American public opinion, which, among Third World areas, is the most "Western" (albeit reflecting a traditional, premodern Iberian/Southern European variant of the Western developmental model) and, therefore, likes to feel itself, by aspiration if not always reality, closest to the United States and to the developed Western world. At another level, these expressions of interest and brotherhood are often a cover for underlying Cold War/strategic concerns and, presently, for considerable confusion and uncertainty about Latin America's place in U.S. thinking.

President George W. Bush is no exception to this rule. After the hyper activity (in more ways than one) of the Bill Clinton years, Bush was elected as an amiable fellow, a regular guy, marginally less boring than Al Gore, who would return the country to non-activist "normalcy" and presumably concentrate, now that the Soviet Union had been vanquished and the United States as the lone surviving superpower had few serious enemies, on domestic social and economic issues. Mr. Bush had little experience in or knowledge about foreign affairs, had never lived abroad, had traveled only to Mexico and, like many Texans, presumed to know Latin America based on his knowledge of Hispanics in Texas and cross-border excursions into Mexico.

Latin America was touted as the one foreign policy area that Mr. Bush understood and "knew." He speaks Spanish and has Mexican Americans in his family. During the 2000 campaign he promised that Latin America would not be an "afterthought" (benign neglect) of his foreign policy but would constitute a "fundamental commitment." Once inaugurated, he met with a steady procession of Latin American leaders, took his first presidential trip abroad to Mexico, promised support for the Free Trade Agreement of the Americas during the Hemisphere Summit in Quebec City, and entertained Mexican president Vicente Fox at his first White House state dinner.

President Bush's key foreign policy advisers, including the vice president, secretary of state, secretary of defense, national security advisor, and CIA director, did not share his view of the importance of Latin America. First, they tend to come out of the realist school of international relations, which relegates Latin America to a low priority. Second, examining their careers closely reveals that, to a person, their backgrounds and priorities were forged, not on Latin America, but on U.S.-Soviet relations, NATO, Eastern Europe, and the Cold War. Those were all, of course, issues that were at least ten years old by the time

Bush came to power. In addition, no one at high levels in the Bush team had any interest in Latin America or viewed it as important, seeing it rather as a "second order" foreign policy issue, which means it got no attention at all and was often viewed disparagingly. Experienced in foreign policy these advisers were but, by this time, out of date and certainly not a team that could boast of knowledge or experience anywhere in the Third World. Alone among high-level officials, only President Bush had a strong interest in Latin America, and one would have to go to a lower (undersecretary) tier of officials even to find any that had a long-term interest and experience in Asia or the Middle East.

Latin American issues at the "grand policy" level were, therefore, by default, handled by lower-level, often more ideological officials at the National Security Council, the Department of State, the Department of Defense, and the CIA. Recruited mainly from the conservative think tanks, they tended to see Latin America in stark either-or terms left over from the Cold War. Thus, Venezuela's populist President Hugo Chávez had to be opposed and gotten rid of; Fidel Castro was still viewed as evil incarnate and there could be no relaxation of the embargo; while Luiz Ignacio Lula da Silva in Brazil was seen as a potential threat to the entire hemisphere. The rhetoric was overheated and often overwrought, fueled by the fact that of the thirteen-or-so officials handling Latin America at the assistant or deputy assistant secretary level, roughly half came out of the Cuban exile community. Although this ethnicity is not a determining factor in explaining their policy views, it may help us understand some of their policy attitudes. This situation is not necessarily unusual, if nevertheless often destructive, in American politics: as with Sub-Saharan Africa or the Middle East, policy making has been largely turned over to the very ethnic/political group that has a particular vested interest in its outcome.

Another political consideration enters into the equation, and that is the appointment of key Latin America ambassadorships on a political basis. As is well known, President Bush's electoral mandate was less than overwhelming and, as a result, his political advisers in the White House determined not to allow that to happen again in 2004. One of their targets, therefore, became the U.S. Hispanic community, a rising group, now the largest minority voting bloc in the United States, and believed to be within grasp of Republican appeals. Hence, appointments to ambassadorships and other key positions were filled by targeting the Hispanic community hoping thereby to secure their votes in 2004. In short, the White House domestic political advisers headed by Karl Rove began to take a strong role in foreign policy making as well.[8]

But policy making is more nuanced than the preceding analysis suggests. First, at even lower levels in the foreign policy bureaucracies, policy on free trade and numerous other concrete issues continued to be hammered out and advanced by competent, professional civil servants, largely devoid of ideological or high-level political interference. Second, a process was already under way by which professional foreign service officers at the State Department and career officials at the departments of Defense and Treasury, and the CIA, and other agencies gradually "recapture" policy making from the ideologues and political appointees who accompany a new president into office and usually dominate the headlines in a new administration's early months. Third, there is a learning process that occurs in the White House and among appointed high government officials—unfortunately in the American system this on-the-job learning occurs after a new administration is inaugurated—as to what can and cannot reasonably be done in the realm of policy.

Meanwhile, other important shifts in policy were taking place out of sight of the usual media coverage. One of these was the post–Cold War shift away from strategic, political, and diplomatic issues in U.S. relations with Latin America (and elsewhere) and toward economic issues. That also meant a shift in power, resources, and budgets away from the traditional foreign policy bureaucracies (Department of State, Department of Defense, CIA) and increasingly toward such economic agencies as the Treasury Department, Commerce Department, and Office of the Trade Representative. Another related shift involved an evolution away from public foreign aid and toward private FDI, of which Latin America is the largest recipient. This trend had been occurring for much of the last decade and was accelerated, for ideological reasons, by Republican administrations. FDI was viewed as both more effective and cheaper than public foreign aid in a time when aid was decreasing. These trends help explain some of the more fundamental shifts in emphasis in U.S. policy.

The Washington Consensus—In Crisis!

The dominant paradigm in U.S.–Latin American relations in the post–Cold War era has been termed the Washington Consensus. Initially everyone in political Washington shared this consensus, and it enjoys widespread bipartisan support. Business, labor, think tanks, religious groups, human rights lobbies, the media, Republicans, Democrats, all of the foreign affairs bureaucracies—all share in this consensus. Latin America bought into it as well as the United States, albeit not always enthusiastically or unanimously; but since the Americans wanted it so badly and Latin America saw no other options, it went along. Since the consensus is, or was, so widely shared, it will be very difficult politically and bureaucratically to change it.

The Washington Consensus consists of three pillars: (1) free trade, (2) open markets, and (3) democratization. All of these parts are assumed to be closely interrelated. Thus, free trade helps stimulate open markets (and vice versa), which give rise to greater prosperity, a larger middle class, and a more stable democracy. One could argue that the sequence works the other way as well, that democracy gives rise to a desire for greater economic freedom and that free trade helps strengthen both; but generally it has been the economic motor forces that have been seen as driving the dynamic. The Washington Consensus sounds remarkably like the Alliance for Progress of John F. Kennedy in the early 1960s and, intellectually, derives from the same supposedly universal, inevitable, economic determinist school of W.W. Rostow (the Stages of Economic Growth) and the U.S. foreign aid (Agency for International Development–AID) program.[9] One size, one formula fits all. Have we learned nothing over the last forty years?

Before discussing the three main points of the consensus, we should point out that there are two glaring omissions in it. First, there is no mention of foreign aid. For one thing, foreign aid has been declining significantly over the decades—so much so that most Latin American countries now think of it as a relatively small, even insignificant part of their overall national budgets, and it no longer gives the United States much leverage over their policy preferences. For another, as compared with Sub-Saharan Africa and other poor areas, most of Latin America is now "transitional" or "intermediary" on most economic indices, and many of the countries from the region have "graduated" from eligibility for most (except in emergencies) U.S. foreign aid programs. A third reason for the lack of attention in the consensus to foreign aid is that for the last twenty-two years, since the first Reagan administration, all but eight of these under Republican administrations, the sense and ideology have been strong, à la Peter Bauer, that foreign aid does little, keeps countries in a dependent status, prolongs their sense of "victimhood," and fails to help them break out of poverty.[10] Far better, the argument has been, to use direct investment, free markets, and capitalism rather than foreign aid.

Nor does the Washington Consensus talk much about security issues. That has been left to the Pentagon; civilians in Washington tend not to see the subject as important or to shy away from it. Among other things, the Soviet Union had been vanquished; the Cold War was over; the guerrilla movements in Latin America had been diminished or had joined the political process as political parties; the communist parties evidenced little popular support; and the Cuban Revolution had run out of steam and no longer served as a beacon for Latin American revolutionaries. Therefore, until the war on terrorism, there seemed to be little reason to be preoccupied with security issues in Latin America.[11]

The "problems," as distinct from "threats," that did exist—drugs, immigration, border patrol, refugees, "boat people"—appeared to be of a lower-order character than the threat of thousands of Soviet missiles aimed at the United States, and only with some reluctance—and out of fear of its budget being reduced—did the Pentagon come to think of them as security issues. Certain specific countries were also seen as potential dangers, even threats—Haiti, Colombia, perhaps Mexico—but not in any conventional sense, only as countries whose potential for instability and drug exporting would affect the United States domestically. But if there was no real threat from Latin America, why pay attention to the area at all? Why not revert to benign neglect or, strategically, economy of force? Absent the Soviet threat, the post–Cold War logic in the United States was: If "Paraguay" wants to "go communist" at this stage, why should we care? Of course, the United States would care and would not carry this logic to its obvious conclusion, but the point was clear: With the Cold War over, and other than the above-mentioned problem areas, why pay serious attention to Latin America at all?

That left the Washington Consensus and its three pillars of free trade, open markets, and democracy. At first, in the early 1990s, there was widespread agreement on these priorities. The consensus encompassed, for the most part, not only the two major American political parties, the several foreign policy-making bureaucracies, the think tanks, and all of the major interest groups, but also both the United States and Latin America. The Washington Consensus was not forced upon Latin America but was widely seen there, at least by the elites, as constituting, since the bankruptcy of the earlier import substitution industrialization (ISI) model, the only route for the hemisphere to follow.

Governmental and business elites in Latin America saw clearly that, for their countries to survive and thrive in the new globalized economy, they could no longer hide behind protectionist barriers or rely on foreign aid but would have to become competitive in world markets. And that meant democracy, transparency, rule of law, judicial reform, efficiency, streamlining, government reform, economic reform, and an end to corrupt, patronage-dominated politics. In addition (but that would have to be the subject of a separate paper), I am convinced that Latin American intellectuals like Guillermo O'Donnell and his collaborators in the "transitions to democracy" school also led Latin America astray by naively arguing that one could ignore Latin American history, political culture, and sociology and concentrate only on institutional variables because, as the argument went, if you got the institutions right, that is all that mattered, everything else would fall into place, and no other variables would need to be taken into account.[12] Professor O'Donnell has since admitted his interpretation was erroneous, but meantime Latin America had been victimized again by what proved to be a less than successful policy.[13]

More recently, the failures of the policy have been emphasized and the successes given less attention. The 1990s, in fact—and the trend is continuing to today—witnessed a gradual decline in support for the main pillars of the policy. In the area of trade, the movement toward a free trade area of the Americas, first articulated by the father of the current president, has slowed considerably, as much due to protectionist pressures in the United States as to reluctance by Latin America to enter this intensely competitive global environment. The movement toward open markets has been slowed by the fact Latin American history and institutions have been more statist and mercantilist; even today Latin America lacks some of the essential institutions of a market economy. And while nineteen of the twenty countries are at least formally democratic, they are often viewed as limited, partial, incomplete democracies—"democracy with adjectives." Let us review briefly the assumptions on which all three of these pillars are based, not providing a complete analysis but only some key reasons why the so-called consensus seems currently to be breaking down.[14]

First, free trade. While the United States has long been committed to a free trade agenda, in Latin America that commitment found expression recently in the North American Free Trade Area (NAFTA) and the Free Trade Area of the Americas (FTAA). In part, the FTAA was designed to counter the European Union as well as what were perceived to be Japanese efforts in Asia to create its own trade zones restricting U.S. trade, by creating a U.S. free trade zone of its own with our "natural partner" in Latin America. In part also, the FTAA, and especially NAFTA, were aimed at stabilizing Latin America, particularly neighboring Mexico, in a time of crisis, and at shifting responsibility for that high priority from the public to the private sphere. In other words, NAFTA and the FTAA are at least as much about U.S. political and security interests in Latin America as they are about economics and trade.

Though reluctant at first, a number of Latin American countries (Chile is the best example) have embraced the free trade agenda. They have reduced tariffs, opened their markets, and sought to become more competitive. It is fashionable these days to say that, because of political and protectionist pressures, it is the United States that stands in the way of free trade, not Latin America. There is some truth in that assertion but not the whole truth. In fact, quietly, unspectacularly, at low levels, and hopefully without making political waves, the FTAA negotiations continue to go forward, with the United States still leading the way, broadening the agreement, and hoping to draw the other Latin American countries along. Provision for "fast track trade" authority has also been passed by the Congress. Of course, as by far the largest and most dynamic economy in the area, the United States is in the best position to take advantage of a free trade regime; and there are increasing doubts (1) if Latin America can effectively compete with the world's high-flying economies in this arena, and (2) if a commitment to free trade is still viable politically in most Latin American countries whose economics are stagnant and where political pressures against free trade are building.

Second, open markets. Latin America has a long history of statism; its economic model is that of the French physiocrats, mercantilism, most recently expressed as import ISI.[15] ISI was discredited by the economic and political failures of the 1970s and 1980s; hence, despite considerable opposition and skepticism from the defenders of statism, a free market ideology was officially embraced in the 1990s. There is considerable doubt as to just how much in fact Latin America warmed to free markets or if that was mainly a sop to U.S. pressures; nor is it clear that Latin America has sufficiently made the economic reforms— transparency, privatization, efficiency, rule of law accountability—

necessary for a free market system to operate effectively. In addition, the effective functioning of a free market system is based on a large number of assumptions that in most Latin American countries are quite shaky, among them:

- a dynamic, independent entrepreneurial class;
- functioning, dynamic markets not hemmed in by statism;
- banks and credit agencies that actually encourage entrepreneurship and free markets;
- a political, bureaucratic, and cultural infrastructure that is conducive to open markets;
- a social system that allows the benefits of free markets to be widely shared instead of concentrated in the pockets of the elites.

Given these and other weaknesses in the Latin American economies, one needs to think, rather as in Russia, that real economic reform and development will take three to four generations, not three to four years—if it can be accomplished at all.

Third, democracy. Democracy is in trouble in Latin America—and this in a continent that has a long, or path-dependent, history of and aspiration for Western-style republicanism, democracy, and human rights. Throughout the hemisphere support for democracy as a system is at 60 to 65 percent, down 25 to 30 points from a decade ago.[16] Support for democracy's essential institutions and pluralist structures (political parties, parliaments, labor unions) is even lower, often in the 10 to 20 percent range. In some countries support for democracy is below 40 percent and trails behind its great "evil" alternative, "strong government," which suggests an authoritarian "out" or solution. Democracy is widely perceived to be not working very well, to be ineffective, not providing the economic and social advances that people had come to expect from it. Similarly with civil society: instead of a dynamic, pluralist Tocquevillian civil society undergirding democracy, what we are increasingly getting is state regulation, control, manipulation, limits on and cooptation of civil society—in other words, a new form of corporatism or public-private partnerships that are often anti-democratic.

In short, in the political as in the economic sphere in the Washington Consensus, the United States has projected its own preferred values, models, institutions, and preferences (free trade, open markets, democracy) on Latin America, whether those fit or are appropriate or not, and with the support of important sectors within Latin America. In my own writings, I have long advocated that U.S. policy in Latin America needs to come to grips better and more realistically with the realities of the area, which may include compromises with such not so attractive and often non-democratic, non-free market features as corporatism, organicism, elitism, patrimonialism, statism, and often a strong dose of authoritarianism.[17]

In practice, in the cases of such quasi-authoritarians as Alberto Fujimori in Peru, Carlos Menem in Argentina, Joaquín Balaguer in the Dominican Republic, or the Mexican Institutional Revolutionary Party (PRI), the United States regularly makes such pragmatic compromises, even while the three legs of the Washington Consensus remain the official, rhetorical policy. In most cases, the gap between the lofty rhetoric and the more pragmatic practice can be managed quite well, but occasionally the practice becomes too much a prisoner of the rhetoric and then the policy may get in trouble. Meanwhile, there is almost no serious examination of the fundamental assumptions of the policy and whether the full agenda of the Washington Consensus of free trade, open markets, and full, participatory democracy may be, as one Latin American ambassador to the United States put it, a "little too rich" for Latin American palates. The issue is not, therefore, activism or benign neglect, for the United States seems always to be activist albeit at different levels; the question to me is whether it is activist for the correct or most appropriate purposes.

The current President Bush was the heir to these policies rather than the initiator of them. He has largely followed the Washington Consensus even while adding to them such initiatives as the possibilities of new immigration standards, the freer flow of labor, and better relations with a democratic Mexico. However, since there is currently little terrorist threat from Latin America, and since that is presently almost the only focus of the president and his cabinet, most of these issues have been temporarily set aside or dropped, while the policy continues to be carried out mainly at other or lower levels. It remains an activist policy rather than one of benign neglect, but it is activist not at a level where it receives major media attention in Washington or in the rest of the world.

Policy Initiatives

American policy and America's relations with Latin America have become increasingly complex over the decades. At one level is the hemispheric policy—the Washington Consensus—partly for rhetorical purposes but also meant to provide guidelines and purpose to the diverse foreign policy bureaucracies involved. At a second level are bilateral relations—the focus of this section—with all the countries, with some countries obviously more important than others and with bilateral relations increasingly taking priority over a broad but vague hemispheric position. A third level of policy is global, on such issues as the environment, human rights, drugs, sustainable development, human rights, terrorism, and democracy, and where Latin America, or especially Latin America, fits (or does not fit, with terrorism) into those larger policy issues. Still a fourth level involves the proliferation of private-interest lobbies—human rights groups, business groups, democracy groups, ethnic lobbies, varieties of civil society groups—and their place in shaping policy, or even carrying out parts of the policy in the absence, or abdication, of much official U.S. government activity.

Among the bilateral relations, Mexico occupies a special place and has become one of the most important countries in the world from the point of U.S. policy. It is not that Mexico is a security threat in any traditional sense; rather, the issue is one of interdependence and the ability of Mexico to impact the United States at a host of levels: immigration, trade, water supplies, drugs, tourism, investment, labor supplies, pollution and the environment, oil and natural gas, and, not least, the potential for instability. It was the last possibility, either economic or political, and the prospect that even the slightest hint of instability would send millions of Mexicans across the border into the United States, thus putting enormous, inordinate pressure on U.S. schools, housing, social services, and law enforcement, that prompted President Bill Clinton to enact NAFTA and for every recent American president to be sensitive to Mexican issues and to periodically bail out Mexico with massive aid packages. Of course, the Mexicans realize that for purely self-interest reasons the United States cannot afford to let Mexico destabilize, which thereby removes most incentives for cooperation and reform. The United States and Mexico are interdependent at so many levels and on so many issues that it is difficult to see their relations ever being characterized as benign neglect.

Colombia similarly comes close to constituting a threat in the modern, post–Cold War sense through its large-scale export of drugs to the United States. Colombia also has some of the last Marxist and Marxist-Leninist guerrilla movements in Latin America, but with the end of the Cold War and ongoing fears by domestic lobbying groups and some in

Congress of another Vietnam, the United States has been reluctant to get too deeply involved in internal Colombian affairs. However, since the guerrillas have also gone heavily into the drug trade, perhaps as their principal activity, the line between counter-narcotics and counter-guerrilla activities has blurred; hence, Plan Colombia, which garnered considerable bipartisan support and is now official U.S. government policy.

Argentina is unloved by both the United States and the rest of Latin America for a variety of political, historical, and cultural reasons; it is also far from the United States and, therefore, not interdependent in the same way that Mexico is. Hence, Argentina cannot expect either great sympathy from the rest of the Americas in its present depressed condition, or consistent, large-scale bailouts from the United States or the international lending agencies.

Venezuela is a fascinating case because, from the U.S. point of view, it has "everything": strategic importance (oil, location), political importance (a faltering democracy), economic importance (oil again, a major trading partner), and ideological importance (a populist, quasi-Marxist president who befriends Fidel Castro, journeys to pariahs Iraq and Libya, undermines business, and rails against the United States). Traditional and modern security interests thus merge in a particularly volatile mix. Even if the United States did not have a hand in the aborted coup against mercurial Hugo Chávez, some of the more ideological persons in the Bush administration privately cheered his ouster—only to see the coup reversed and Chávez returned to power more boisterous than ever. The United States meanwhile straddles the line between intervention at several levels and allowing the Chávez phenomenon to run its course, meanwhile exhausting itself in the process.

Big, important Brazil has not been a priority for U.S. policy but now with the election of Luiz Ignacio Lula da Silva it is becoming so. Brazil is the fifth largest country in the world, sixth in population, eighth in gross national product, and a candidate for a permanent seat on the Security Council. Its diplomatic and strategic importance should be self-evident. Yet as a faltering democracy in dangerous economic difficulties, and with leftist, populist Lula and his even more radical advisers in the presidency, Brazil, like Venezuela, plays into the ideological orientations of conservatives in the Bush administration as well. Meanwhile, rising nationalism and anti-Americanism in Brazil make the relationship tenser still.

Haiti is the case par excellence in the circum-Caribbean of a failed state. As a predominantly African-American country, it resonates strongly in U.S. domestic politics; there is a long and often tortured history of U.S. involvement, which still carries political consequences for all of the parties; and Haitian boat people frequently arrive, dead or alive, on south Florida beaches inconveniently during the tourist season. However, as long as Haiti is a "democracy" (which means Haitians cannot by definition be political refugees), U.S. law gives immigration authorities the power to return the boat people to Haiti. As a poor, underdeveloped, uninstitutionalized country, without a functioning government, now also a major transshipment point in the drug trade, and with these special connections in U.S. domestic politics, Haiti will continue to be a subject of concern to U.S. policy makers.

Cuba is a fascinating case for all the known reasons and more: the embargo, the last surviving Marxist-Leninist state in the Americas (and one of the last in the world), a country only ninety miles from the United States, the politics of the Cuban exile community, the dismal economic and human rights record of the revolution, still pending claims of nationalized U.S. companies against the regime, anger and hatred on the part of many U.S. officials against Cuba, drug trafficking, aid and/or sanctuary for terrorists. At the same time, Fidel Castro is aging; would-be successors are circling in the water; the Atlantic fleet continuously circumnavigates the island; and the United States will certainly seek to influence and manage the post-Castro transition. Although the United States would clearly prefer a peaceful transition to democracy and free markets, one can also envision future scenarios that include insurrection in some of Cuba's provinces, revolt, conflict, civil war, and U.S. military intervention.

Other countries are also important to the United States for different reasons. Nevertheless, the picture that emerges even from this brief survey is one of active engagement and not of benign neglect. But let us make several points about the kind of active engagement involved.

First, as indicated, it is at relatively low policy and bureaucratic levels. Other than the president himself, presently preoccupied with Iraq, North Korea, and the war on terrorism, no one at high policy levels has expertise or special interest in Latin America.

Second, if one knows the politics of American foreign policy making at high levels, this is not altogether bad. At low levels is where the expertise is; in addition, the policy can often be quite rationally managed without much overt outside political interference from the top.

Third, important policy initiatives are being carried out at these subordinate levels especially dealing with trade, human rights and democratization, border conflicts, drugs, immigration, and such "second tier" reforms as transparency, education, governance, civil society, and judicial reform.

But fourth, without high-level guidance, there is little consistency in the policy, an absence of priorities, little follow-through, absence of sustained effort, and often amateurish or mistaken efforts.

Fifth, and again without high-level direction, there is almost no rethinking of the (perhaps fatally) flawed assumptions of the Washington Consensus. Instead, the policy simply continues as a "given" despite the fact that many aspects of it are not working.

Sixth, as the war on terrorism perhaps begins to wind down or fade from our consciousness, a more balanced, nuanced, and updated policy may begin to emerge. Alternatively, some countries—Columbia, Mexico, Haiti, Paraguay, Cuba—have either become havens of various and usually limited kinds of terrorism, or have learned to manipulate the terrorist issue to attract more attention and/or aid for themselves. But unlike the Middle East and some other areas, Latin America has not become a major terrorist haven, which provides one more reason for benign neglect. Hence, I would anticipate few changes in the basics of the policy, and also that Latin America would continue to be viewed as a low-priority, secondary area in the U.S. rank-ordering of regional geopolitics.

Conclusion

It is too simple to characterize U.S. policy in Latin America as "benign neglect." There may be, because of the war on terrorism, benign neglect at high policy levels but not at lower levels within the bureaucracy, among human rights activists, democracy, and civil society groups; and at local, state, and regional levels where there is a great deal of activity. The policies pursued may be outdated or, in the case of the Washington Consensus, based on flawed assumptions; but benign neglect is not an accurate way to describe it.

Rather, the policy remains one of engagement and activism. As part of this activist approach, U.S. cultural, political, economic, and strategic hegemony in the region will continue. U.S. hegemony has actually increased rather than decreased in the last decade, particularly economically, by the virtual withdrawal of European actors (except Spain) from the area. In turn, Latin America recognizes that it is dependent on the United States, that the United States is "the only game in town."

In these respects, U.S. policy in the present Bush administration is not much different from that of past administrations. That means a low priority accorded to Latin America, minimum attention at high levels, economy of both force and focus. And, with the increasing emphasis on foreign direct investment, the prevailing sentiment is "let the private sector do it."

Meanwhile, the lack of high-level U.S. attention, U.S. arrogance as well as hegemony, the condescension shown, proconsular meddling, as well as the failed promises of the Washington Consensus are leading to rising alienation and anti-Americanism in Latin America. Anti-Americanism is palpable (though seldom violent) and at a level seldom observed before. But at the same time, thoughtful Latin Americans understand that for the foreseeable future no one else will come to their rescue; they have nowhere else to turn beside the United States; they have no choice but to reach their accommodation with the United States.

Meanwhile, the facts "on the ground" keep changing. Hispanics are now the largest U.S. minority; in some areas the United States is becoming a "Latin American country," the United States and Latin America are increasingly interdependent on a whole host of issues—just as is Western Europe and its "near abroad" of Central and Eastern Europe, Southeast Europe (including Turkey), and North Africa. Over time, it is these facts, rather than any wishful thinking on our part, that will slowly, eventually, but inexorably alter the posture and priorities of foreign policy.

Notes

1. The statement was coined by Reston in the early 1960s when writing about John F. Kennedy's Alliance for Progress. It continues to have relevance today.

2. A solid treatment is Michael J. Kryzanek, *U.S.–Latin American Relations* (New York: Praeger, 1996).

3. Karl E. Meyer, "The Lesser Evil Doctrine," *The New Leader* 46 (Oct. 14, 1963): 14.

4. See again Kryzanek as well as my own writings: *The Democratic Revolution in Latin America: History, Politics, and U.S. Policy* (New York: Holmes and Meier, 1990); *American Foreign Policy Toward Latin America in the 80s and 90s* (New York: New York University Press, 1992); *Democracy and its Discontents: Development, Interdependence, and U.S. Policy in Latin America* (Lanham, MD: Rowman & Littlefield, 1995).

5. Howard J. Wiarda, *Ethnocentrism in Foreign Policy: Can We Understand the Third World?* (Washington, DC: American Enterprise Institute for Public Policy Research, 1985).

6. Abraham Lowenthal, *Partners in Conflict: The United States and Latin America* (Baltimore: Johns Hopkins University Press, 1987); Abraham Lowenthal and Gregory F. Treverton, eds., *Latin America in a New World* (Boulder, CO: Westview Press, 1994).

7. For an analysis of the domestic bases of U.S. policy, see Howard J. Wiarda, *American Foreign Policy: Actors and Processes* (New York: Harper Collins, 1996).

8. *New York Times* (Sept. 7, 2002): 1.

9. Walt Rostow, *The Stages of Economic Growth* (Cambridge, UK: Cambridge University Press, 1960).

10. Peter T. Bauer, *Dissent on Development* (London: Weidenfeld & Nicolson, 1971).

11. L. Erik Kjonnerod, ed., *Evolving U.S. Strategy in Latin America* (Washington, DC: National Defense University Press, 1992).

12. Guillermo A. O'Donnell and Philippe C. Schmitter, eds., *Transitions from Authoritarian Rule* (Baltimore: Johns Hopkins University Press, 1986).

13. At the 2000 International Political Science Association meeting in Quebec City, Canada.

14. Howard J. Wiarda, *Cracks in the Consensus: Debating the Democracy Agenda in U.S. Foreign Policy* (Westport, CT: Praeger/CSIS, 1997).

15. William Glade, *The Latin American Economies: A Study of Their Institutional Evolution* (New York: American Book, 1969).

16. The best survey data are from *Latinobarómetro,* as published in *Journal of Democracy.*

17. Howard J. Wiarda, *The Soul of Latin America: The Cultural and Political Tradition* (New Haven, CT: Yale University Press, 2001).

5

American Policy in the Post–Cold War Middle East

William B. Quandt

When the Soviet Union suddenly ceased to exist in the early 1990s, Americans across the political spectrum were able to imagine that their future would be safer and more peaceful than it had been during the generation long struggle of the Cold War. Perhaps now, the shadow of nuclear war that had hung over the world since the end of World War II could be removed. Perhaps now, the major world powers would cooperate to find solutions to international problems, much as the founders of the United Nations had imagined. Perhaps now, the powerful forces of globalization could bring the world closer together, raising poor countries from dire poverty and creating a more integrated and peaceful world.

Little more than a decade into the post–Cold War era, such early optimism about a "new world order" seems misplaced, and instead there is growing concern in much of the world—and among some Americans—with American hegemony. French diplomats, often suspicious of American motives, have even coined the term "hyperpower" to describe how far ahead in sheer military power the United States is compared to all other countries in the world.

To get some perspective on how the United States has crafted its foreign policy in the post–Cold War period, we can look at the Middle East. For it is here that the great debates over how to advance American interests have swirled; it is here that new approaches and doctrines have been tried; and it is here that American lives and dollars have been spent on an unprecedented scale, especially since 2001.

It is important to recall that during the first forty years of American preeminence as a global power, roughly from 1950 to 1990, both political parties in the United States, Democrats and Republicans, had been generally internationalist. There was something of a bipartisan tradition in foreign policy that had carried the United States through the early Cold War period, and had only begun to fray at the edges over Vietnam in the late 1960s and intervention in Nicaragua in the 1980s. On the whole, Middle East issues were not treated in a partisan way. Republicans and Democrats alike supported Israel and the need for active diplomacy to resolve the Arab-Israeli conflict, especially after the 1973 war; both parties were concerned with stability in the Gulf and access to the oil resources of that region; and no one wanted either Soviet domination of the region, or a global war sparked by conflicts there.

To be sure, there were always voices on the margins that questioned the wisdom of deep American involvement in the Middle East. A minority of Americans adhered to a historically rooted isolationism. A few libertarians on the left joined them in this stance. And a somewhat larger group felt that the United States should rely more heavily on the United Nations and other international institutions. But on the whole, the American public went along with the series of peace efforts initiated by the Nixon, Ford, Carter, Reagan, Bush I, and Clinton administrations; and they supported the general outlines of policy toward the Gulf region, although here the bottom line concern was more the impact of Gulf stability on oil prices than any altruistic commitment to peace in the region. Apart from the very special commitment of some Americans to Israel, no state in the region could count on very deep support in American public opinion as a matter of principle.

When the Cold War came to an end, it was clear that American foreign policy and security priorities would be reassessed, including in the Middle East. The United States was clearly the most powerful country in the world, but it was not committed to a neo-imperial vocation. Choices would have to be made, priorities established. Some parts of the world would no longer be the focus of much concern. Others would remain central to American interests. On the whole, the Middle East seemed likely to retain its priority because of Israel and oil.

One school of thought began to argue that in the new global circumstances the United States would be able to pursue its interests through "soft power"—a reliance on technology, culture, economics, trade, investment—rather than raw military power. This same liberal view saw possibilities for international institutions—the United Nations, the World Trade Organization, the World Bank—that had been blocked by U.S.-Soviet rivalry during the Cold War.

Throughout the 1990s, something of a contest took place between the advocates of this liberal vision—many of them in the Clinton administration—and those who were convinced that the United States should use its military preeminence to establish a kind of dominance in world affairs that would be unprecedented. Many of the proponents of this muscular policy came from a traditional realist background—an emphasis on power politics and national interest—but they also carried with them a streak of very typical American Wilsonianism, a belief that American power should be deployed on behalf of universal principles such as democracy and human rights. The label "neoconservative" was applied by many to this new breed of crusading hardliners. Largely relegated to the margins of the foreign policy debate in the 1990s, they came into their own with the election of George W. Bush in 2000. Their views became the basis of policies in many parts of the world, but nowhere more so than in the Middle East after the terror attacks on the World Trade Center and the Pentagon on September 11, 2001.

The result of Bush II's adoption of many of the ideas of the neoconservatives has been a shift in Middle East policies of a most dramatic nature. The priority accorded to the peace process has dropped markedly; and deterrence and containment in the Gulf region has been replaced by a policy of military intervention and aggressive nation-building. For a conservative administration, these policies represent remarkably radical departures. Let us try to understand how this took place.

Post–Cold War Policies: The Experience of the 1990s

The end of the Cold War in the early 1990s coincided with a moment of unquestioned American supremacy in the Middle East. Saddam Hussein's invasion of Kuwait was reversed in a matter of weeks by an American-led coalition of over 500,000 troops; the United States persuaded the UN Security Council to take a series of decisions that imposed harsh restrictions on Iraq and called for the elimination of all of its weapons of mass destruction; and by fall 1991, the United States had successfully brought together Israel with all of its immediate neighbors at a peace conference in Madrid. Never had Washington been so close to calling the shots in the Middle East—or so it seemed.

But the end of the Cold War also carried a second message for many Americans. Maybe now the country could turn to addressing some of its own internal problems—education, race relations, income disparities, health care—and could spend less on defense and foreign aid. One should never forget that a strong theme in American history has been the desire to isolate America from the untidy affairs of the rest of the world. Some actively sought a less committed role for the United States abroad, while others feared its consequences. But no one could assume that the extraordinary level of American influence in the Middle East as of 1991 would be sustained for an indefinite period.

Now that more than a decade has passed since the last Gulf War, we can conclude that the United States certainly did not turn its back on the region and return to a posture of benign neglect. Aid levels to Egypt and Israel remain high—as of early 2003, Israel had requested additional aid on top of its usual $3 billion, as well as some $10 billion in loan guarantees. More to the point, nearly 200,000 American troops were in occupation of Iraq, having intervened to depose the Saddam Hussein regime in March 2003. Just as after the first Gulf War, the United States enjoyed a moment of unparalleled influence but also of enormous challenges. The ambitious goals of the George W. Bush administration to rid the region of radical regimes having weapons of mass destruction and to eliminate the threat of terrorism went well beyond the traditional purposes of American foreign policy and reflected the near messianic zeal with which some in the Bush entourage sought to redesign the Middle East.

The key to understanding the intensity of the American commitment to transforming the Middle East lies with the terror attacks on the World Trade Center and the Pentagon on September 11, 2001. The president who had been determined to conduct a low-profile "humble" foreign policy, who had turned his back on Israeli-Palestinian peacemaking, and who had mocked the idea of engaging in "nation-building" was suddenly converted to displaying strong American leadership in the Middle East. Although other presidents had also been deeply engaged in the region, now the premises of policy had shifted dramatically and by early 2003 the Bush administration was well on its way to forging a new strategic doctrine for the Middle East, with war in Iraq as its first manifestation.

How did American foreign policy in the Middle East evolve from the multilateral strategy of containment and peacemaking under Bush I in 1991 to one of unilateralist assertions of "dominance" and "preemption" as underlying policy impulses under Bush, Jr.? And why, in particular, did Iraq become the prime target? Part of the answer, of course, resides in the reaction to the terror attacks of September 11, 2001. Indicative of the new mood was a comment by Secretary of Defense Donald Rumsfeld in September 2002. When asked what had changed in the past year or so that made it so urgent to act militarily against Iraq, he responded that 3,000 Americans had been killed in a single day.[1] No one bothered to underscore the fact that Saddam Hussein seemed to have no involvement in September 11. It was enough that his kind of regime might some day cooperate with a movement such as Al-Qaeda to make him a legitimate target.

Evolving American National Interests in the Region

Throughout most of the Cold War era, American policy makers had little trouble listing the top three interests of the United States in the Middle East. First was the prevention of Soviet domination of this region; second, access to the region's oil resources for America and its allies; and third, the security and well being of Israel. Each administration weighed the priority of these interests, sometimes reacting to events, but every president acknowledged that these three concerns trumped all others in the region.

The problem for American leaders, of course, was that these interests did not all lead in a common direction. To contain Soviet influence, for example, did it make more sense to court Nasser's Egypt or to back Israel? And while containing Soviet influence was a widely shared goal, so was the avoidance of nuclear confrontation. So efforts needed to be made to manage the rivalry with Moscow, as well as to challenge Soviet inroads.

And then there was the question of oil. The United States has historically been a major producer and major importer of oil, especially in recent decades. This has meant that American companies have not always had common interests with respect to oil. Some wanted to keep "cheap" Middle East oil out of the United States; others made most of their profits on overseas production. Throughout the 1950s and 1960s, a formula was found that kept Middle East oil relatively inexpensive and domestic oil was protected at higher prices by quotas or tariffs. This structure began to fall apart in the early 1970s, and soon the United States was worried more about expensive Middle East oil and its impact on the world economy. By the late 1980s, after experiencing and learning from two "oil shocks," American policy makers seemed to have come to a conclusion that their key interest was in relative stability and predictability of oil prices—somewhere in the $15 to $25 per barrel range. The 1990–91 crisis was in significant measure about oil—had Saddam managed to control Kuwaiti and Saudi production, he would have been able to set prices at a high level and he would have enjoyed an enormous flow of petrodollars to fuel his military ambitions. For American leaders, it was far better to maintain a system in which several large producers controlled the oil reserves of the Gulf region rather than just one.

The U.S. interest in Israel was always a bit of a puzzle, both for Americans and for others. At the time of Israel's independence in 1948, many in the U.S. government—including Secretary of State George Marshall and Secretary of Defense James Forrestal—were opposed to recognizing the Jewish state. They feared that to do so would alienate the Arab countries and provide openings for Soviet influence in the region. President Harry Truman, however, immediately recognized the new state (though he did not agree to send arms to it, even after Arab states declared war). This initial phase was one in which the basis of American support for Israel seemed anchored in history, shared democratic values, and domestic American politics. Few would have seen Israel as a strategic asset. If anything, Israel was more often thought of in the State Department as a strategic liability.

This perception of Israel began to change after 1967. Israel had proved its military potency—it defeated two Soviet clients in a matter of days. Before long, the United States became the primary supplier of weapons to the Jewish state, as well as offering substantial economic aid. The Jordan crisis of 1970 reinforced the view that Israel could act as a strategic partner of the United States. But the 1973 war was a reminder that the United States could not achieve stability in the region simply by pouring arms into Israel. Egypt was also an important player, and Nixon and Kissinger adroitly moved to draw Sadat into the American camp. Carter solidified this relationship at Camp David, and ever after the United States has considered Egypt a junior strategic partner, just behind Israel, and given it the second largest amount of American military and economic aid.

With the end of the Cold War, this traditional list of American interests changed significantly. No longer did Washington worry much about Moscow or about any other major power outside the region. The new challenges were from within—radical regimes like those of Saddam Hussein; Islamic extremism, with Khomeini's Iran at the head of the list; and after September 11, the general phenomenon of terrorism. One theme that quickly seemed to emerge was that the United States could best serve its interests in Gulf security and in protecting its relations with Israel and Egypt by actively promoting Arab-Israeli peace. Just as the Camp David accords had been a prerequisite for the development of a strong U.S.-Egyptian relationship, so now it was thought that a more comprehensive Arab-Israeli settlement would help to secure American interests in the region. And now that the Cold War rivalry with Moscow was over, it might be easier to deal with these issues in a regional, rather than global, context.

Let us see how the three American administrations since the end of the Cold War have managed to balance the concerns with the new threats, Israel's security, relations with friendly Arab states like Egypt and Saudi Arabia, and access to oil.

Bush, Sr., and "The New World Order": 1990–92

It is striking to look back at the Gulf crisis of 1990–91 and see how genuinely multilateral the diplomacy of the Bush I administration was then compared to now. The president was in touch with many world leaders within days of the Iraqi invasion of Kuwait; he immediately went to the United Nations to get condemnation of the attack; he enlisted support from key Arab countries, most importantly Egypt, Saudi Arabia, and Syria; and when the use of force was finally decided on in January 1991, armies and air forces from several countries were involved. Although the bulk of the effort was American, many others made contributions as well. In fact, most of the financial costs of the war were borne by others.[2]

The Bush administration pointed to its management of this crisis as the harbinger of a "new world order," one in which the major powers would cooperate to maintain international peace and where the United Nations might work as originally intended. Skeptics, however, saw the crisis in another light and spoke of a "new world disorder." Shortly after the war with Iraq had ended, Secretary of State James Baker launched a new round of diplomacy designed to bring Israel and its Arab neighbors to the bargaining table. A Middle East peace conference was finally held in Madrid in fall 1991 under the co-chairmanship of the United States and the Soviet Union, with the participation of Israel, Syria, Jordan, Lebanon, and the Palestinians, and the Europeans, the United Nations, Saudi Arabia, and Egypt as observers.[3]

The Madrid conference had an ambitious goal of promoting several parallel tracks of negotiations—Israel-Syria, Israel-Jordan, Israel-Jordan-Palestinian, Israel-Lebanon—plus a number of multilateral tracks dealing with arms control, environment, water, refugees, and economic cooperation. Needless to say, progress was not possible in all of these channels, but for the next two years a great deal of activity took place, contacts were made, and some of the hard substantive issues in the negotiations were discussed.

At the core of these initiatives was a belief on the part of the Bush administration—with the intellectual contribution of National Security Adviser Brent Scowcroft and Secretary of State James Baker—that American power could be used most effectively within a broad international framework. Bush was intrigued with the possibility of developing good working relationships among all of the major powers—Europe, Russia, China, and Japan—and developments in Europe, especially Germany's reunification and the peaceful end of the Soviet empire, gave great impetus to the inclination to cooperate with former rivals.[4]

Clinton Takes Charge: 1993–2001

Clinton came to the presidency with much less international experience than President George H.W. Bush. Nonetheless, he did share the basic internationalist views of his predecessor, and there was no dramatic change in policy toward the Middle East when he took charge. In fact, the key Middle East foreign policy adviser to Bush and Baker, Dennis Ross, stayed on as adviser to Clinton and his new secretary of state, Warren Christopher.

Like most newly elected presidents, Clinton spent the first several months learning about issues and meeting many foreign leaders, including those from the Middle East. By all accounts, he was deeply impressed by Israel's Yitzhak Rabin, and his strong inclination was to let Rabin take the lead in setting the direction and pace of Arab-Israeli peace-making. Clinton saw his role as a "facilitator," a supporter of initiatives that should be taken by the local parties. He was not sure enough of his own instincts in this area to take a strong position of leadership.

Rabin was convinced that he could not politically afford to move on more than one negotiating front at a time. It would either be the Syrians or the Palestinians with whom he took the first step. Since the issues on the Syrian front were much simpler to deal with than those involving the Palestinians, and since the U.S. role was essential in dealing with Syria's president Hafiz al-Asad, Rabin asked Clinton to focus on the Syrian track. The result was a number of trips by Secretary Christopher to the Middle East in 1993. It quickly became clear that the territorial issue would be crucial in determining whether a deal could be struck. Asad had always insisted on Israeli withdrawal from every inch of Syrian territory. Without such a commitment, Asad was simply not prepared to put any of his cards on the table.

In August 1993, Rabin met with Christopher and told him in fairly explicit terms that Asad could be reassured that in the context of peace and security he would get the Golan Heights back. Christopher rushed off to Damascus with the good news, only to be asked by the excessively cautious Asad if this meant Israeli withdrawal to the June 4, 1967, lines (his preference) or to the old international border (Israel's preference). When Christopher reported this conversation back to Rabin, the Israeli leader concluded that Asad was not bargaining in good faith and decided to shift his attention to the Palestinian track. As far as we know, Clinton and Christopher did not try to persuade him to keep negotiating with Asad.[5]

Rabin's interest in the Palestinian track had probably been prompted by developments in a secret diplomatic channel that had been set up with the help of the Norwegians. The formal channel for Israeli-Palestinian negotiations in Washington had produced little more than mutual recriminations. But in parallel, a second channel had emerged in early 1993 that seemed more promising. Rabin had gradually shown interest in it, even though it meant dealing directly with the long demonized Palestine Liberation Organization (PLO). Over a number of months, an outline of a preliminary agreement had been reached, but then the talks had faltered. Now, in August, Rabin turned his attention to this front and within a short period a deal was struck, including an agreement on mutual Israeli-PLO recognition. This was the famous Oslo Accord, signed with much fanfare in Washington on September 13, 1993.[6]

Clinton had made little contribution to Oslo, but he was more than willing to embrace it and become its major sponsor. In many ways, the breakthrough in the secret channel seemed to vindicate the views of some of his advisers like Ross who had always argued that the parties themselves should bear the main responsibility for negotiation and that the United States might make things worse by getting involved in substance prematurely. For Ross, the American role should be primarily procedural, one of nurturing, helping to build trust, offering reassurances and payoffs, but not getting very far out ahead of the parties themselves.[7] Still, with the signing of the Oslo Accords in Washington, and with Clinton presiding over a historic handshake between Arafat and Rabin, the United States found itself deeply involved in the "Oslo process," as it soon came to be called.

While he sympathized with Israel and admired Rabin in particular, Clinton set out to build a relationship with the now-respectable PLO leader Yasir Arafat. Clinton prided himself on being able to befriend people on both sides of any dispute; he possessed a strong personality, great self-confidence, and boundless energy. He seemed to think that he could help forge an agreement between these two long-time adversaries.

Oslo proved to be a complex negotiation. The Americans got deeply involved, but usually by pressing the parties to agree on next steps, not by clarifying the ultimate destination. A so-called interim period of five years finally began in May 1994, with agreement that "final status" issues would be tackled beginning in the third year of the transition. And in fact, by October 1995, top-level Israeli and Palestinian negotiators were beginning to flesh out the contours of a final status agreement (the Beilin–Abu Mazin proposals).[8] Within days, however, Rabin was assassinated by a fanatic Israeli, bringing this phase of the peace process to a close.

During the remainder of Clinton's presidency, Israeli-Palestinian peacemaking went through two quite different phases. While Benjamin Netanyahu was prime minister of Israel (1996–99), the Clinton team worked to keep the Oslo process alive. This meant pushing ahead with incremental agreements (Hebron and Wye) and making a serious effort to cultivate a relationship with Yasir Arafat.

During the mid-1990s, Clinton had to adjust his approach to Israeli-Palestinian peacemaking and to Gulf security. Early in his administration, Clinton and his national Security Adviser Tony Lake had enunciated a doctrine of dual containment. In essence, this was a rejection of the notion that Gulf security could be maintained by some kind of balance-of-power game among Iran, Iraq, and Saudi Arabia. That had been tried in the 1980s and had failed. Clinton would be tough with both Iran and Iraq, seeking to contain these two regional powers simultaneously.

Critics of his policy, and there were many, immediately noted that Iran and Iraq were hardly in the same situation. Iraq was subject to UN sanctions; its imports were carefully monitored; it was obliged to eliminate its weapons of mass destruction; and it could not export its oil without permission. By contrast, Iran was recognized as a legitimate government by most of the world, was free to sell its oil on the world market, engaged in normal trade relations with Europe, Japan, and other countries, and was even buying nuclear reactors from Russia. How could one contain Iran in the same way as Iraq? By refusing to trade with, or invest in, Iran the United States might make a symbolic point, but it would make little real difference for the Iranian economy. By implying a kind of identity of policy toward Iran and Iraq, dual containment seemed off the mark. Soon the administration began to talk of "differentiated containment," but even that had few supporters.

In 1997, Iranian politics took an interesting turn with the overwhelming election of Mohammad Khatami as president. Khatami spoke of a "dialogue of civilizations," instead of the much vaunted "clash" that seemed to pit Islam versus the West. He seemed to be a man of moderation, with democratic inclinations. The Clinton administration took note and began to respond with small gestures. By the end of the Clinton administration, one could detect a distinct warming of U.S.-Iranian relations, although both sides were still wary of opening an official dialogue. One of the issues that continued to irritate the relationship was the ongoing Arab-Israeli conflict, an issue on which Iran took a particularly hard-line policy of calling for Israel's destruction. But even on this issue, Iran made it clear that if Palestinians and Syrians wanted to make peace with Israel, Iran would not stand in the way.

The ostensible end of the five-year transitional period envisaged in the Oslo Accords coincided with Israeli elections. Netanyahu was decisively defeated by Ehud Barak, a man who seemed to be much like Yitzhak Rabin (although much less experienced politically). Clinton, who seemed eager to throw himself into peacemaking again after his own traumatic encounter with impeachment, immediately set to work with Barak on reviving negotiations. Barak had promised his electorate that Israeli troops would be withdrawn from Lebanon within one year, and thus he decided to seek a deal with Syria before engaging with the more complex issues of final status with the Palestinians.

Much of Barak's first year was spent in a futile effort to find an agreement with Asad. Clinton even went to Damascus to try to persuade the aging dictator to accept Barak's offer of almost full withdrawal, but Asad was not prepared to budge from his long-standing position and the talks came to a sudden end in late spring 2000. Barak proceeded to withdraw his troops from Lebanon even without an agreement, which in some quarters was interpreted as a victory for Hizbollah, the Lebanese Shiite radical party.[9]

By mid-2000, time was running out for all the key protagonists. Barak was losing support domestically; Clinton had only six more months left in his mandate; and Arafat was showing signs of age and dwindling popularity. The circumstances were not propitious for a breakthrough. At the same time, there was a real fear that without diplomatic progress, an eruption of violence was inevitable. Palestinians were frustrated that Oslo had produced so little for them and that deadlines had come and gone with no results.

In this setting, Barak and Clinton decided to go for broke with a summit meeting. Arafat was reluctant to agree, but finally acquiesced. In July 2000, the three leaders met at Camp David for a frustrating and ultimately unsuccessful round of talks. Some headway was made on sensitive issues such as Jerusalem and borders, but the gap between the two sides remained large. Clinton, who had invested a great deal in the summit, was angered by Arafat's unwillingness to engage in substantive negotiations, and made it clear that he felt that Arafat was responsible for the failure.

Still, negotiations continued even after the failure of the summit, even after the outbreak of the so-called second Intifada in late September 2000. Finally, just one month before leaving office, Clinton unveiled a specific set of proposals for resolving the conflict. The terms were relatively balanced and both sides could find elements in the proposal that met their core concerns as well as others that were difficult to accept. Barak, now in deep political trouble at home, announced his conditional acceptance of the proposals; Arafat was less overt in embracing the Clinton ideas, but his negotiators did respond with a series of sensible questions. Negotiations continued right up until early February 2001, when finally the overwhelming electoral victory of Ariel Sharon brought the whole process to an end. By then, of course, Clinton had also been replaced by George W. Bush.[10]

Bush, Jr.: Not Just His Father's Son

Many Americans, and some in the Arab world as well it seems, expected George W. Bush to resemble his father in his conduct of foreign policy. Some even imagined that James Baker might return as secretary of state. Others from Bush I's team, after all, were in key positions, most importantly Colin Powell as secretary of state and Richard Cheney as vice president. But Baker stayed on the sidelines, and others of a different disposition, some veterans of the Reagan administration, made their appearance. At the Pentagon were Secretary of Defense Donald Rumsfeld and his deputies Paul Wolfowitz and Douglas Feith.[11]

Almost immediately, it became clear that the Bush administration would not simply continue the policies of its predecessors. For example, on Israeli-Palestinian peacemaking, the president made clear that he had little to suggest. The parties had tried and failed, Clinton had invested enormous time and energy, and it had all come to naught. Unlike both his father and Clinton, President George W. Bush was not initially inclined to involve himself deeply in the "peace process." Nor was he likely to follow through with Clinton's hesitant opening toward Iran, since Iran was seen as a sponsor of terrorism in both Lebanon and Palestine.

Bush was also much less of a multilateralist than his predecessors. He showed little regard for the United Nations; he was eager to disengage from multilateral agreements that seemed to restrain the United States, whether on the environment, arms control, or the new International Criminal Court. The Bush team was hardly isolationist, but they did not want American power to be fettered by multilateral commitments. The "thinkers" in this administration had been toying with a new doctrine of "dominance" ever since the Cold War had come to an end, but it had not caught on during the 1990s. Many Americans were uneasy about the imperialist overtones of such a doctrine, and Clinton was too fond of leading by persuasion to turn to the raw use of power to establish American hegemony. Even within the administration, Colin Powell and his colleagues at the State Department were wedded to a more conventional approach to diplomacy. One of Powell's deputies had written a book with the title *Reluctant Sheriff*.[12] At the Pentagon, there were few signs of such reluctance.

While President Bush seemed hesitant to resolve some of these underlying tensions within his own administration, events forced him into a more assertive leadership role on September 11, 2001. Now, in the words of the president, the United States was at war with terrorism and the axis of evil (Iraq, Iran, and North Korea) that supported terror and sought weapons of mass destruction.[13]

Despite the harsh rhetoric, the initial moves of the Bush administration to destroy Al-Qaeda, the group held responsible for the terror attacks on New York and Washington, were surprisingly multilateral. Bush sought congressional and UN support; he tried to negotiate with the Taliban in Afghanistan to get them to turn over Usama Bin Laden and his followers; and when that failed, he took military action that seemed relatively precise and effective. Within a matter of weeks the Taliban regime had collapsed and Bin Laden was on the run. A new regime came to power in Afghanistan that seemed acceptable to a fairly broad spectrum of society, as well as to Afghanistan's immediate neighbors to the west, north, and east. A large number of countries pledged aid to the new government and several countries, including Turkey and Germany, agreed to send peacekeeping contingents. On the whole, this seemed to be a relatively successful example of U.S.-led multilateralism, rather like the Gulf War in 1991. As time went by, it became apparent to many observers that the process of rebuilding Afghanistan was not going particularly well, but by then most Americans had lost interest. Afghanistan, unlike the rest of the Middle East, might well suffer from neglect by official circles of Washington.

By spring 2002, a new phase in Bush's Middle East policy opened. The trigger was a wave of Palestinian suicide bombings against Israeli targets. Hundreds of Israelis were killed and wounded in a period of several weeks. Arafat was either unwilling or incapable of stopping the bombings. Sharon declared that Israel's war against terror was identical to that of America, and after a few hesitations, George Bush seemed to agree. By summer 2002, he had signaled that Sharon had a green light to deal with the Palestinians pretty much as he chose, as long as Arafat was not physically eliminated. Bush and his colleagues made clear that they thought Arafat had to be replaced and refused to have any further direct dealings with him. Anti-American sentiment in the Arab world rose in response to what was seen as an arrogant and one-sided position, especially after Bush referred to Sharon as "a man of peace." Bush also proclaimed that he had a "vision" of a Palestinian democratic state side by side with Israel, but since he provided no credible road map to that destination, his words fell on deaf ears.[14]

As Israeli-Palestinian peacemaking faded from the Bush agenda, Iraq came to the fore. During summer 2002, the hawks in the Bush administration began to build the case for invading Iraq and destroying Saddam Hussein's regime and its weapons of mass destruction. The rationale for this action shifted from week to week, but the basic elements of the argument were the following: Saddam was a particularly cruel and ruthless ruler; he had chemical and biological weapons and was trying to get nuclear ones; he supported terrorism and might have been involved in some way with Al-Qaeda; he was hostile to Arab-Israeli peace and gave support to radical Palestinian elements; he had flagrantly violated UN Security Council resolutions.[15]

Alongside this familiar list of charges could be detected a more radical strand of thinking, one that envisaged a totally new approach to the Middle East. In this view, terrorism in the Middle East was not so much the product of frustrations born of the Arab-Israeli conflict or of concrete socioeconomic conditions in countries like Egypt or Pakistan. Instead, there was a civilizational component—illegitimate regimes such as those in Saudi Arabia or even Egypt would foment anti-American and anti-Israeli propaganda, allowing a fundamentalist version of Islam to rule the public discourse as long as it did not question the existing domestic order. To put an end to terrorism, this line of argument went, the Arab Middle East, and perhaps Iran as well, needed a thorough housecleaning—new educational institutions, respect for women's rights, and above all democratization. In short, the Arab-Islamic world had to be modernized. Only then would it be possible to root out extremism and promote Arab-Israeli peace. To say the least, this was an ambitious vision, but it was strongly held by a number of neoconservative advisers to the Bush administration and began to gain currency among some mainstream commentators as well. A certain irony could be found in conservatives preaching such a radical doctrine, while old-style liberals lamented the parlous state of the Middle East but were much more reluctant to rock the boat.

Bush easily won congressional support for his war against Iraq in fall 2002, and then proceeded to work for a UN resolution to provide some justification for military action in the event that Saddam refused to cooperate with weapons inspections. Unlike the Gulf crisis in 1990–91, this time the United States had few allies, except for Britain's Tony Blair.

While a number of Arab regimes quietly endorsed Bush's plans and offered some cooperation, few were willing to offer public support.

Saddam responded by playing for time and allowed UN inspections without blatant restrictions. By March 2003, Bush was showing intense frustration with Saddam, the inspections, and the lack of allied support. War was imminent. Finally, on March 19, 2003, Bush ordered a strike designed, it seems, to kill Saddam Hussein. Within days, large numbers of American troops poured into Iraq from nearby Kuwait. The troops were supported by remarkably accurate airpower, and in a matter of weeks they were in downtown Baghdad, having encountered little in the way of serious resistance from Saddam's infamous Republican Guards. The regime not only collapsed; it disappeared. Saddam and his sons were nowhere to be found, at least in the initial period after the fall of Baghdad. Iraq now "belonged" to the United States. The question arose immediately of what the Bush administration would do with it. Preliminary thoughts of a quick turnover of power to grateful Iraqis were soon dispelled as Americans realized the complexities of the Iraqi political scene and the enormous task of providing basic security and reviving the economy.

By the end of 2003, the occupation of Iraq did not seem to be working out very well for the American and British forces. True, Saddam Hussein was captured in December 2003, but attacks on American forces continued at a steady pace. Each day there were clashes with Iraqis, often resulting in casualties—with a total of about 500 Americans killed and well over 10,000 wounded since the beginning of the war in March. While many Iraqis had welcomed the demise of the Saddam regime, they quickly began to express their distaste for foreign occupation. But even if the Americans wanted to leave quickly, many feared what the consequences of a sudden departure might be. One way or another, America was slipping into its first overt imperial adventure in the Middle East, with unforeseeable consequences.

In an attempt to stem the tide of anti-American feeling that had been unleashed by the war in Iraq, the Bush II administration, much like that of Bush I, turned its attention back to the Israeli-Palestinian conflict. An effort had been under way for some time, in cooperation with the European Union, Russia, and the UN secretary general, to sketch out a Road Map that might help Israelis and Palestinians get back to the negotiating table.[16] One key element, from the American standpoint, was the naming of a new Palestinian prime minister, Mahmud Abbas. With Arafat now seemingly less central to Palestinian political life, the Bush administration put its weight behind the Road Map and in early June 2003 the president went to the Middle East to show his support for the new initiative. Within weeks, the parties were beginning to talk about a cessation of hostilities and some initial withdrawals of Israeli forces. But the distance between these first steps and the announced goal of a viable Palestinian state by 2005 seemed enormous. Still, the Bush administration was once again asserting the role of leadership that in the past had always been critical to success in Arab-Israeli peace efforts.

This is not the time or place to try to predict the future. It is enough to say that the United States, which has long seen the Middle East as an important region, but one that required a fairly nuanced policy, is in the midst of trying a fundamentally new approach to dealing with this area. The new concepts are regime change, anti-terrorism, democratization, development, and modernization. The old vocabulary of "peace process," negotiations, confidence building, stability, UN resolutions, containment, and deterrence will be heard less often if the hardliners win the internal debate. As the presidential election campaign got under way early in 2004, foreign policy issues were high on the agenda and Americans seemed almost evenly divided between those who strongly supported President Bush and those who strongly opposed him for both domestic and foreign policy reasons.

Within the United States, public opinion, which had been supportive of the war with Iraq, was beginning to sour on the idea of a large military presence in Iraq for years to come, especially if casualties and costs continued to rise. A great deal is at stake here. One way or the other, the Bush administration seems determined to try a new approach in the Middle East. By the time we are able to assess the Bush administration's approach to the Middle East with some objectivity, we may wish that American policy had involved a bit more "benign neglect," the theme of this volume. But for the moment, that is as far from reality as one can imagine.

Notes

The author is particularly grateful to Carol Huang for research assistance in preparing the final draft of this chapter.

1. Transcript of Secretary of Defense Donald Rumsfeld's interview on CBS's *Face the Nation*, Sept. 8, 2002, available at www.usis.it/file2002_09/alia/ a2090601.htm, accessed July 7, 2004. Rumsfeld is quoted as saying: "If you go

back to September 11th, we lost three thousand innocent men, women and children. Well, if—if you think that's a problem, imagine—imagine a September 11th with weapons of mass destruction. . . . It's not three thousand, it's tens of thousands of innocent men, women and children." The suggestion is that Saddam Hussein might in the future supply weapons of mass destruction to a group like Al-Qaeda. To prevent such a possibility, war might be necessary.

2. For a good review of the war, see Michael Gordon and Bernard E. Trainor, *The Generals' War: The Inside Story of the Conflict in the Gulf* (Boston: Brown & Company, 1995).

3. William B. Quandt, *Peace Process: American Diplomacy and the Arab-Israeli Conflict Since 1967* (Washington DC: Brookings Institution Press, 2001), p. 310.

4. George H.W. Bush and Brent Scowcroft, *A World Transformed* (New York: Knopf, 1998), p. 491.

5. Helena Cobban, *The Israeli-Syrian Peace Talks: 1991–96 and Beyond* (Washington, DC: United States Institute of Peace, 1999), p. 57.

6. Uri Savir, *The Process: 1,100 Days that Changed the Middle East* (New York: Random House, 1998).

7. For an influential statement of the "ripening" thesis, supported by many, including Dennis Ross, who went on to play important roles in the Bush and Clinton administrations, see Washington Institute for Near East Policy, *Building for Peace: An American Strategy for the Middle East* (Washington, DC: 1988).

8. For text, see William B. Quandt, *Peace Process: American Diplomacy and the Arab-Israeli Conflict Since 1967,* available at www.brookings.edu/dybdocroot/press/appendix/appen_t.htm, accessed July 7, 2004.

9. Ibid., pp. 357–62.

10. Ibid., p. 372; Charles Enderlin, *Shattered Dreams: The Failure of the Peace Process in the Middle East,* 1995–2002 (New York: Other Press, 2003), p. 377.

11. On the influence of the neoconservatives, see Jim Mann, *The Rise of the Vulcans: The History of Bush's War Cabinet* (New York: Viking Press, 2004); and more generally, Ivo Daalder and James Lindsay, *America Unbound: The Bush Revolution in Foreign Policy* (Washington, DC: Brookings Institution, 2003).

12. Richard Haass, *The Reluctant Sheriff: The United States After the Cold War* (New York: Council on Foreign Relations, 1997).

13. For text, see White House, *President Delivers State of the Union Address,* available at www.whitehouse.gov/news/releases/2002/01/20020129–11.html, accessed July 7, 2004.

14. For text, see White House, *President Bush Calls for New Palestinian Leadership,* available at www.whitehouse.gov/news/releases/2002/06/20020624–3.html, accessed July 7, 2004.

15. For an influential argument for war by a source outside the Bush administration, see Kenneth M. Pollack, *The Threatening Storm: The Case for Invading Iraq* (New York: Random House, 2002).

16. For the text of the Road Map, see BBC News, *The Roadmap: Full Text,* available at /news.bbc.co.uk/2/hi/middle_east/2989783.stm, accessed July 7, 2004.

6

Southeast Asia and the United States After September 11, 2001

Amitav Acharya

In Southeast Asia, the post–Cold War era began with plenty of uncertainty about the U.S. policy objectives and engagement in the region. Well before the Cold War ended, Southeast Asia had a marginal place in U.S. strategy. As Catharin Dalpino and Bridget Welsh point out: "U.S. attention to the region evaporated after 1973, when American troops were withdrawn from South Vietnam. For the past three decades, officials and analysts have viewed the region as marginal to security in Asia, focusing instead on threats in the Taiwan Strait and on the Korean Peninsula."[1] But the end of the Cold War further contributed to the erosion of U.S. interest in the region. This was indicated in three ways. First, domestic pressure in the Philippines resulted in the removal of U.S. military bases from the country in 1991. The loss of these bases was partially offset by Singapore's offer of military facilities to U.S. naval and air forces, but this could hardly replace the gigantic Subic Bay naval base and Clark Field air base in the Philippines. Moreover, Singapore's offer was within the framework of "places, not bases," and its lack of space precluded any large-scale American military presence that might have offset the loss of the huge bases in the Philippines. Despite repeated U.S. assurances of continued strategic engagement and the "revitalization" of the U.S.-Japan alliance, Southeast Asia remained secondary to other theaters, while U.S. involvement in regional security organizations, though not insignificant, was secondary to its bilateral commitments and defense linkages in the region.[2]

Second, the settlement of the Cambodia conflict meant that the U.S. policy framework of assisting its Third World allies to roll back communist influence in the Third World, the so-called Reagan Doctrine, was no longer relevant.[3] Third, the scaling down and eventual withdrawal of Soviet naval forces from Cam Ranh Bay and the general retreat of the Soviet navy from East Asian waters deprived the United States of a rationale for strengthening its naval presence in the region.

America's economic engagement with Southeast Asia remained robust, but much of it has been driven by market forces. The volume of trade between the Association of Southeast Asian Nations (ASEAN) and the United States increased almost fourfold from $23 billion in 1980 to $80 billion in 1996. ASEAN became the fourth largest trading partner of the United States after Canada, Japan, and Mexico.[4] U.S. investment in ASEAN rose from $11.7 billion in 1990 to $53.0 billion in 2001, although according to one source, this figure "significantly understates the actual level of U.S. investment in the region."[5] For the United States, ASEAN has been one of the fastest growing export markets, growing at an average annual rate of 14.1 percent between 1990 and 1994.[6] In contrast, Southeast Asia has received little U.S. development assistance.[7] Moreover, in 1992, Congress restricted U.S. military aid to Indonesia through the U.S. International Military Education and Training (IMET) program because of the military's poor human rights record. While the United States continued to sell arms to Indonesia (until 1999), Singapore, Malaysia, and Thailand, and conducted military exercises with Thailand, there was no combined exercise with the Philippines between 1995 and 2000.

Although the post–Cold War U.S. grand strategy sought to replace containment of communism with "enlargement" of democracy and human rights, it would be an exaggeration to suggest this policy was seriously applied in Southeast Asia. The United States continued to support the authoritarian Suharto regime and played a minimal role in the post-conflict peace-building process in Cambodia, which involved the country's transition to democracy. The Philippines enjoyed greater stability under the Ramos government, and hence did not require any robust U.S. assistance in democratic consolidation, which, if forthcoming, would have been most likely counterproductive. The only exception to this passive U.S. stance in promoting democracy in Southeast Asia was Burma. Here, the Clinton administration opposed ASEAN's policy of "constructive engagement" of the military junta in Burma, and pressed for the release of its jailed opposition leader Aung San Suu Kyi. But this was hardly a vigorous campaign, especially compared to the European Union's (EU) far stronger stance that involved postponing an economic agreement with ASEAN because of its decision to grant membership to Burma. American scholars and policy makers occasionally indulged in debating the relativist conceptions of human rights and democracy advanced by the proponents of the "Asian values" school in Singapore and Malaysia, but American strategic and economic engagement in the region continued to respect the "performance legitimacy" of the ASEAN governments that refused to move away from soft authoritarianism. Most studies of the prospects for democratization in Southeast Asia stressed the agency role of internal factors, such as the role of the middle class, rather than that of external actors, such as the United States.[8] Even after the regional economic crisis swept the Suharto regime out of office in 1998, the U.S. role in encouraging democratic transition and consolidation in Indonesia was limited.

The neglect of Southeast Asia in U.S. strategy was also determined by its relatively benign security climate compared to Northeast Asia, South Asia, and the Middle East. Southeast Asia had no weapons of mass destruction, nor was there an enduring rivalry threatening international stability and U.S. interests like that between North and South Korea, China and Taiwan, Israel and the Arab states, and India and Pakistan. Despite Southeast Asia's problems with diffuse transnational dangers such as drug trafficking, illegal migration, and piracy, these were not considered to be significant threats to U.S. national security comparable to the problem of terrorism a decade later. ASEAN had reached accommodation with its longtime ideological rival Vietnam, marking an end to the most serious intraregional fault line in Southeast Asia. And due to a combination of strong authoritarianism and rapid economic growth, Southeast Asia did not seem to be going the way of failed states in Africa. The United States had much more reason to worry about instability in other parts of the world—the Balkans, Central Africa, the Middle East, Northeast Asia, and South Asia—than Southeast Asia, where a regional organization was seemingly well placed to address regional security concerns. In fact, this contributed to a fear that a U.S. disengagement from the region could be in the offing, a concern that dominated strategic discourses in the region for much of the early post–Cold War period, despite the fact the rise of China was causing the United States to consider a counterbalancing strategy that would have required some engagement with Southeast Asia. But even then, this balancing strategy was tempered by the development of a new multilateralism in the region spearheaded by ASEAN and resulting in the ASEAN Regional Forum (ARF), with the objective of engaging both China and the United States.

Against this backdrop, the September 11 terrorist attacks on the United States have affected its policy toward Southeast Asia in important ways. Terrorism has emerged as a major determinant of U.S. strategic policy toward Southeast Asia. It has brought about the "reengagement" of the United States in Southeast Asian security. As one analyst puts it, ASEAN, established in 1967 at the height of the Vietnam War and being for so long a time Asia's only major regional organization, now has a "more prominent place in U.S. foreign policy than at any time since the end of the Cold War."[9] Second, the U.S. commitment to regional cooperation in Southeast Asia appears to have diminished, partly reflecting the Bush administration's general lack of support for multilateral approaches at the global level. Moreover, the new strategic links with Southeast Asia have been undertaken mostly outside the scope of existing multilateral institutions.

Like the Middle East and other parts of Asia, Southeast Asia has seen a marked rise in anti-U.S. sentiments. The resentment against specific aspects of the war on terror and the war in Iraq has aggravated the lingering sense of resentment against the United States for its perceived lack of support for Southeast Asian states when a severe currency crisis hit the region in mid-1997. The U.S. failure to join the international rescue package for Thailand was partly responsible for this. International economic bodies that played a key role in the handling of the financial crisis, the International Monetary Fund (IMF) and the World Bank, were seen as pliant instruments of American hegemony.

The war on terror waged by the United States in Southeast Asia has implications for our understanding of the U.S. security role in Asia. In the past, U.S. hegemony, espousing a liberal institutionalist international order, was conducive to international, including regional, cooperation. Indeed, as John Ruggie points out, "multilateralism was less the product of an American *hegemony,* than of American hegemony."[10] While Southeast Asia lacked a directly American-sponsored multilateral security institution, with the exception of the weak and relatively short-lived Southeast Asia Treaty Organization (SEATO), U.S. strategic dominance and its bilateral security alliances served as a collective public good and compensated for the absence of a formal multilateral alliance. But the war on terror, while affirming U.S. hegemony as a military power, is undercutting American legitimacy as a hegemonic leader. The liberal international order that many saw as the organizing framework for U.S. policy has been sidelined by a more realpolitik approach. There is a possibility that the increased security push by the United States undertaken in the name of the war on terror will have a polarizing impact on the region, because of a disjunction between U.S. strategic objectives and the domestic political imperatives and national (read regime) security objectives of Southeast Asian governments. This, combined with the perceived unilateralism of the United States at the global level, undermines security cooperation at the regional level.

Southeast Asian Responses to September 11, 2001

There is a major difference between attitudes of Southeast Asian peoples toward the United States after September 11 and their response to the U.S. invasion of Iraq.[11] Moreover, official attitudes in Southeast Asia toward the United States differ from popular sentiments. As governments are willing to work with the United States and, out of pragmatic reasons such as consideration of U.S. aid, support its "war on terror," anti-Americanism is a rising trend in many Southeast Asian societies. Southeast Asian governments and elite circles responded to the September 11 attacks on the United States with considerable empathy. They also recognized the vulnerability of the world's sole superpower in the face of the new, postmodern threat of transnational terrorism. Even Burma, a target of U.S. sanctions for its flagrant violations of human rights, the use of forced labor, and lack for democratic reform, has pledged to "stand side by side" with the United States in fighting terrorism. But at the popular level, there was a general understanding that the U.S. support for Israel has been a "root cause" of the terrorist menace. In Muslim-majority countries such as Malaysia and Indonesia, there has been especially strong popular resentment against the United States for what is seen as its arrogant and unjust treatment of the Palestinian people.[12]

Nonetheless, the perception of the sources or root causes of terrorism among Southeast Asian countries differed in important ways from that of the Bush administration. In Islamic Southeast Asia, societies showed less sympathy and support for the United States than did their own governments. Some of this popular anger was directed against their own governments, especially those that had sided with the United States or had not been sufficiently forthcoming in condemning the U.S. military action in Afghanistan. Popular resentment of American support for Israel made it difficult, though not impossible, for Southeast Asian governments, except for Singapore and the Philippines, to show understanding and support for the United States. Soon after September 11, President Megawati of Indonesia made a much publicized visit to the White House to show solidarity with the United States. But domestic disapproval of this stance soon forced her to criticize the U.S. attack on Afghanistan. Domestic pressures also explain why Prime Minister Mahathir of Malaysia, after making it difficult for his own citizens to travel to Afghanistan to fight with the Taliban, also attacked the U.S. military campaign in Afghanistan.

Domestic politics is an important factor in shaping Southeast Asian countries' perception of September 11 and the threat of terrorism. This was perhaps most salient in the case of Indonesia and Malaysia. As the world's largest Muslim nation, Indonesia is an attractive ally for the United States in its eagerness to prevent the perception of its war against terror as a war against Islam. This was evident during Megawati's visit to the White House (she being the first leader of a Muslim-majority nation to pay a visit in the aftermath of September 11), when George W. Bush received her warmly and offered increased economic aid. But upon returning home, the Indonesian president found her domestic situation sufficiently difficult as to distance herself from the U.S. attack on the Taliban. Domestic opposition has since prevented her from taking strong action against suspected terrorists in Indonesia linked to Al-Qaeda. Jakarta brushed aside American (and Singaporean) accusations of turning itself into a safe haven for Al-Qaeda elements. Even in the wake of the horrific Bali attacks, Jakarta faced, and continues to face, domestic pressure in taking action against suspected terrorists. While it passed new internal security regulations, the arrest of Abu Bakar Bashir, the alleged spiritual leader of the shadowy terrorist network Jemaah Islamiyah, was criticized even by moderate political leaders as a capitulation to U.S. demands.

Given the wide differences in domestic political circumstances and strategic perceptions, there can be no uniform Southeast Asian perception of, and response to, the U.S. war on terror, and in most cases, the supposed economic and security benefits of siding with the United

States have all-important political downsides, which are especially driven by domestic factors.

For many regional governments, support for the U.S.-led war on terror can be a double-edged sword. While it allows countries to gain access to U.S. resources, military and economic, and helps them to conduct their own war on terror, it is also risky and costly on the domestic front, where the U.S. role as a world power is viewed with increasing misgivings. Southeast Asian governments have to maintain a delicate balance in supporting the United States while preserving domestic cohesion. In a multiethnic milieu, Southeast Asian governments risk domestic friction and backlash unless they maintain a careful distance from the excesses of U.S. unilateralism and its pro-Israeli stance. Most of all, both public and elite opinion throughout Southeast Asia, in both Muslim and non-Muslim segments (although it is more pronounced in the former) continue to identify the U.S. support for Israel as the "root cause" of terrorism. Malaysian deputy prime minister Badawi told a conference in Kuala Lumpur in June 2002 that "Muslim anger is . . . fueled by the impunity with which Israel ignores and flouts UN resolutions and the protection it receives in the world body from friends that prevent any enforceable sanctions being imposed upon [it]." He said that "international terrorism . . . cannot be quelled without resolving the Palestinian-Israeli issue."[13]

ASEAN–United States Counter-Terrorism Cooperation

In the post–post Cold War era that emerged from the ashes of the World Trade Center, Southeast Asia's place in U.S. strategic policy has changed dramatically. The September 11 attacks prompted a rethinking of the relative strategic importance of regional theaters for U.S. grand strategy. While the importance of the Middle East as part of America's sphere of vital interests was expectedly confirmed, South Asia now would have a higher profile in U.S. grand strategy than was the case for some time. Moreover, American strategic engagement in Southeast Asia has been strengthened. Apart from being regarded as the second front in the war against terrorism, Southeast Asia has also become important to the United States for overflight and access rights for its military deployments to the Gulf. During the war against the Taliban in 2001, the United States found it easier to secure overflight rights through Southeast Asia than through Europe. And Southeast Asian worries about U.S. withdrawal have given way to mounting concerns about U.S. unilateralism.[14]

These perceptions were strengthened by the revelation that some perpetrators of the September 11 attacks had used Southeast Asia as a planning base and transit point. They had discussed their plans at a meeting in Kuala Lumpur in January 2000, which had been noted and communicated to U.S. intelligence authorities by Malaysian intelligence. In fact, Malaysia was described in some U.S. media sources as a "major staging area" for the terrorist attacks, and the U.S. State Department in December 2001 labeled Malaysia, the Philippines, and Indonesia as "potentially Al-Qaeda hubs."[15]

The United States has recognized Southeast Asia as a second front in the war on terror.[16] This view rests on the belief that with its defeat in Afghanistan, Al-Qaeda has shifted its attention to Southeast Asia. Southeast Asians who trained in Afghanistan have returned home (with one analyst, Rohan Gunaratna, estimating the number of trained terror operatives at 400, out of which only 100 have been apprehended), where they could respond to the Al-Qaeda leadership's periodic call for terrorist strikes (both low- and high-impact) against targets, especially entertainment spots frequented by Western tourists. In this view, Southeast Asia offers an attractive home to international terrorism, thanks to a combination of factors: multiethnic societies, weak and corrupt regimes with a tenuous hold over peripheral areas, ongoing separatist insurgencies that lend themselves to exploitation by foreign elements, governments in general weakened by the financial crisis, and newly created democratic space in some of its larger polities such as Indonesia and the Philippines, which have found it difficult to mobilize public support for security regulations to ensure preventive suppression of terrorist elements.[17]

The extent of the U.S. engagement in Southeast Asia should not be overstated. Critics note that while the United States has clearly recognized Southeast Asia's potential as a safe haven for Al-Qaeda fugitives and homegrown terrorists, its strategic priorities remain firmly focused elsewhere, including the Middle East, South and Central Asia, and Northeast Asia. The offer of economic assistance to Indonesia, an information-sharing agreement with Malaysia, and the conduct of joint "training" operations with the Philippines, do not make for full-scale strategic engagement. Although Southeast Asia enjoys a higher profile in U.S. strategy, this is not comparable to the more recent U.S. engagement with India and Pakistan or in Central Asia.

Although the U.S. response to the threat of terrorism affects the region as a whole, its most visible impact is felt in the maritime domain of Southeast Asia, where the dangers seem most apparent. This domain comprises Malaysia, the Philippines, Singapore, and Indonesia. Among ASEAN countries, Singapore is most clear in appreciating the U.S. response to the threat of transnational terrorism in Southeast Asia as a catalyst for a more favorable regional balance of power. This accords with Singapore's traditional preference for U.S. military predominance in the region as the regional balancer. Singapore has maintained significant military links with the United States, including as a major logistics hub for U.S. naval forces operating in the region—this relationship, of course, predates September 11—and as a provider of facilities for U.S. operations against Iraq.

U.S. counter-terrorism cooperation with Southeast Asian countries has taken two main forms: bilateral and regional.[18] The latter has been the more important of the two. The following sections examine these relationships in some detail.

The Philippines has developed close military links with the United States since September 2001. Visiting Washington in November 2001, President Arroyo issued a strong statement of support for U.S. actions, declaring that "the American and Filipino people stand together in the global campaign against terrorism."[19] This was followed by a flow of U.S. military assistance totaling more than $100 million to Manila, including equipment such as a C-130 transport plane, eight UH-1 helicopters, several fast patrol boats, trucks, and more than 30,000 M-16 rifles.[20] Later, in early 2003, the United States offered another $78 million to train and equip Philippine troops.[21] Manila also received trade benefits such as trade credits, tariff reductions, and debt write-offs, potentially worth more than $1 billion.[22] The signing of a Mutual Logistics Support Agreement (MLSA) in November 2002, allowing the United States the right to stockpile essential equipment and supplies in the country, represented another major milestone in the evolving security ties between the two countries.

A key highlight of U.S.-Philippines counter-terrorism cooperation is the conducting of joint exercises between their troops against the Abu Sayyaf group. After being designated as a target suitable for immediate retaliation against the terrorist network responsible for September 11, 2001, the United States moved in January 2002 to deploy a joint task force of some 1,200 troops, including 160 U.S. Special Forces' advisers, to the southern Philippines, backed by aircraft and surveillance technology for the Armed Forces of the Philippines (AFP) to be used against the Abu Sayyaf group.[23] Though described as "training exercises," the operation actively involved U.S. Special Forces in anti–Abu Sayyaf combat operations in June 2002.[24] In February 2003, the Bush administration announced its intention to deploy 3,000 combat troops (as opposed to trainers) to the Philippines, sparking a major controversy in the Philippines and forcing a backdown by the United States, which moved to clarify that training will remain the sole purpose of the new deployment.

U.S.-Philippines military cooperation is driven by several factors. For the Philippines, increased American presence and strategic links with the United States not only helps its resource-starved military gain access to vital U.S. equipment, it also mitigates Manila's immediate and long-term concerns about the rise of Chinese power. This is especially evident since a new logistics agreement with the United States negotiated in the context of the war on terror could also be a strategic asset to Manila in countering future Chinese encroachments in the territories that it disputes with China in the South China Sea.

For Malaysia, the war on terror presented an opportunity to gain U.S. recognition for its role in regional affairs. U.S.-Malaysian ties had dipped to historic lows in the late 1990s, with Mahathir's regular criticisms of U.S. strategic hegemony and U.S.-led globalization. In the wake of the Asian economic crisis in 1997, Mahathir had openly and loudly criticized international financial institutions such as the IMF and the World Bank for acting as a tool of U.S. hegemony, and challenged the Washington Consensus, a framework of economic liberalization that is supposed to reflect American economic imperatives and approaches. Following September 11, however, U.S.-Malaysian ties have improved considerably. Malaysia has sought and earned American sympathy and support as well as praise as the model of a progressive and moderate Muslim nation. The leaders of the two countries met at the leaders meeting of the Asia-Pacific Economic Cooperation (APEC) in Shanghai in November 2001. Mahathir was warmly received in the White House in May 2002, in what was described as an American "thank you to a respected leader for his very stirring response in the global campaign against terror."[25] The United States and Malaysia have signed a bilateral agreement on information-sharing and other forms of cooperation against terrorism. Even more striking is the American attorney general's endorsement of Malaysia's Internal Security Act (ISA), which is viewed now by the United States less as a threat to civil liberties and more as a vital instrument to fight terror.[26] This is especially helpful to Kuala Lumpur at a time when the Mahathir government has been seen by its critics as having used the terrorist threat to outmaneuver its domestic political opposition, especially the Islamic Party (PAS). Malaysia's response to September 11 also won Malaysia recognition from the United States as a progressive and moderate Islamic state.[27] Its support would enable the Bush administration to demonstrate that the war on terror is not a war against Islam.

Military and intelligence cooperation between the two countries has increased dramatically since September 11, although Kuala Lumpur downplays this.[28] In a significant move, the United States proposed that Kuala Lumpur host a regional training center to counter terrorism in Southeast Asia.[29] In May 2002, Defense Minister Najib Tun Abdul Razak revealed that U.S. military aircraft averaged more than 1,000 overflights annually (adding that since September 11, 2001, that number grew significantly). Moreover, Malaysia hosted more than seventy-five military ship visits in the previous two and a half years, while the United States conducted training exercises with the Royal Malaysian Air Force and Malaysia's Navy SEALs (Sea Air Land) twice a year.

But subsequently, the relationship soured as Malaysia refused to endorse the U.S. attack on Iraq. Moreover, Mahathir stepped up his vocal criticism of U.S. unilateralism and interventionism. Malaysia refused to grant the United States overflight rights in support of its attack on Iraq. According to Mahathir, "this is no longer just a war against terrorism. It is in fact a war to dominate the world."[30]

Indonesia's response to the U.S. war on terror is heavily influenced by its domestic politics.[31] Being the most populous Muslim nation in the world, Indonesia is an especially attractive ally for the United States. When President Megawati visited the United States on September 19, 2001 (which was prearranged), she condemned the attacks as "barbaric," and offered support for the U.S. war on terror. Jakarta granted overflight rights for U.S. military support aircraft, while in return the Bush administration offered some $150 million in economic assistance for Jakarta.[32] But, as previously mentioned, domestic reaction to her support for the United States was quite hostile, which made her retreat somewhat from her earlier support for the United States. The United States for its part viewed with exasperation Indonesia's lack of firm action in cracking down on its domestic terrorists, which the United States claimed had developed close links with Al-Qaeda. The Indonesian cleric Abu Bakar Bashir was named by the United States and Singapore as the spiritual head of the Jemaah Islamiyah regional terrorist network seeking to establish a Islamic super-state in Southeast Asia. The United States accused Jakarta of being in denial over its domestic problem of terrorism.[33] Jakarta rejected accusations that Indonesia was a safe haven for Al-Qaeda elements. While firm action to arrest Jemaah Islamiyah elements (with significant Australian support) followed the Bali bombings in October 2002, Indonesia still remains inhibited by domestic pressures from closely identifying with the U.S. counter-terrorism effort.[34]

This, in turn, has thwarted efforts to revive military-to-military ties, suspended in the wake of violence in East Timor in 1999, which was blamed partly on the Indonesian military. The United States offered funding for the TNI (Tentara Nasional Indonesia) through the suspended IMET program worth $400,000 after September 11, along with about $12 million for counter-terrorism activities inside Indonesia. It has also offered an additional $60 million in counter-terrorism assistance, to be used for strengthening the police, combating terrorist financing and money laundering, and financing regional counter-terrorism fellowships designed to train the armed forces (TNI) in counter-terrorism "and related issues."[35]

Singapore's close security ties with the United States predate September 11, 2001. But the latter gave it an added emphasis. Indeed, Singapore has always regarded a U.S. military presence as "vital to the stability and peace in the region," and has constantly sought to keep the United States strategically engaged in the region. This has given rise to "longstanding and close defence relations" between the two countries, as one Singapore analyst notes.[36] Although Singapore does not consider itself an American ally, choosing instead to be a "strategic friend," its bilateral security relations with the United States are perhaps its "most substantive and extensive."[37] Former U.S. secretary of state William Cohen confirmed this view by calling Singapore "a very steady partner and ally."[38]

This relationship is embodied in various cooperative initiatives that involve Singapore and American armed forces. In November 1990, the two sides signed a memorandum of understanding. This and an accompanying addendum grant the United States access to the Sembawang port, the Paya Lebar air base, and the new Changi naval base. The first foreign warships to berth were three U.S. naval vessels, including an aircraft carrier, in March 2001.[39] When the Subic Bay naval base in the Philippines closed, Singapore invited the United States to establish a small logistical presence in the country.

Following September 11 and the subsequent war in Afghanistan, Singapore provided logistics and support facilities for a number of transits by U.S. military aircraft and naval vessels. Singapore has also benefited from its close relations with the United States. In 2000, its observer status was converted into full-fledged participant status in the U.S.-Thai Cobra Gold exercises that increasingly focus on peace enforcement and counter-terrorism. It also maintains an annual trilateral air exercise with the United States and Thailand, coded Exercise Cope Tiger. There have also been naval exercises—CARAT (cooperation afloat readiness and training)—with the U.S. Navy, which are parallel to those that the United States conducts with Indonesia, Malaysia, the Philippines, and Thailand. Finally, there are roughly 120 Singapore air force personnel based and training in the United States. In April 2003, Singapore's Apache squadron in Arizona was inaugurated.[40] The eight Apache helicopters stationed there form the Peace Vanguard; a delivery for twelve more of these attack helicopters is anticipated for 2005.[41]

Singapore has also been cautious about the domestic and regional fallout of its close ties with the United States, including a realization that such ties make Singapore a terrorist target. But such concerns were outweighed by the benefits of partnership with the United States. Singapore officially listed itself as a member of the coalition of the willing in the Iraq War. It justified this decision by citing the threat posed by Saddam's development of weapons of mass destruction. Moreover, it also cited Iraqi violations of UN resolutions. Another argument concerned U.S. credibility—a retreat from military confrontation at a late stage would have undermined U.S. credibility and encouraged other dictators to challenge U.S. power and international order. Since Singapore signed a free trade agreement (FTA) with the United States soon after the Saddam regime was toppled, this led to speculation that Singapore's support for the United States was partly a way of ensuring that the FTA was not disrupted. The Singapore government, however, has denied such a link.

The increased U.S. military presence does not mean the United States has secured or sought permanent military bases in the region. Even in the Philippines, where the United States had until the early 1990s large military bases, negotiations for long-term access have been stymied by

Philippine domestic sensitivities, as well as U.S. reluctance to link its presence there with Manila's dispute with China over the Spratly Islands. Thailand has offered its facilities (Utapao air base) to the U.S. air force in the war against the Taliban and Iraq, but it refused to join the coalition of the willing assembled by the United States against Iraq out of deference to the sensitivities of its Muslim population.[42]

There continue to be important divergences between the strategic perceptions and priorities of the United States and those of its closest regional partners in Southeast Asia. There is a widespread perception that the U.S. approach to the threat of terrorism in Southeast Asia is overwhelmingly strategic.[43] Its military assistance, economic aid, and security agreements have not been backed by efforts to address what is perceived in Southeast Asia as a fundamental root cause of contemporary Islamic radicalism—the issue of Palestine.

Although bilateral linkages have proven to be more important than multilateral efforts in U.S.–Southeast Asia security relations after September 11, the United States has used regional institutions to advance its counter-terrorism agenda. The main example of this is the U.S.–ASEAN Joint Declaration for Cooperation to Combat International Terrorism, which provides for intelligence sharing, capacity building, and improved border controls.[44] The United States also pushed the ARF to devote its attention to combating terror, especially at the 2002 ministerial meeting in Brunei. Here, the United States's push was mainly responsible for the adoption of an ARF statement on measures against terrorist financing. The United States also strongly encouraged APEC to take a strong stand against terrorism at its 2002 summit meeting at Los Cabos.

But many of these measures consist mainly of statements of principles and aims, and lack operational significance. At the operational level, U.S.-ASEAN multilateral security cooperation is proving difficult to realize. A key example is the U.S. proposal for a Regional Maritime Security Initiative (RMSI) aimed at enhancing security in the Straits of Malacca and preventing terrorist and piracy activities there.[45] As part of the RMSI, mooted first by Admiral Thomas Fargo, the U.S. military commander in the Pacific, the United States sought to use its own naval forces to intercept suspected vessels in the straits. This idea drew support from Singapore and Thailand, but provoked immediate rejection from Malaysia and Indonesia, which want the United States to offer technical support and engage in information sharing. Malaysia would like the security of the straits to be the primary responsibility of the littoral states, while Indonesia wants to institutionalize regional maritime security cooperation within the framework of an ASEAN security community, which Singapore, America's closest Southeast Asian ally in the war on terror, is reluctant to endorse out of concern that this might come at the expense of a direct U.S. security role. The regional response to the RMSI shows how the U.S. war on terror can undermine prospects of regional security cooperation in Southeast Asia.[46]

The Bush Doctrine and the War on Iraq

Indeed, this divisive impact of the U.S. war on terror in Southeast Asia becomes clearer when one discusses the second major development affecting U.S.–Southeast Asian relations: the new American strategic doctrine of "preemptive" strikes enunciated one year after September 11.[47] Like past presidential doctrines that have signaled major shifts in U.S. strategic policy—such as the Nixon Doctrine, which announced the United States's disengagement from mainland Asia, and the Reagan Doctrine, which announced the U.S. determination to roll back Soviet geopolitical advances in the Third World, including those made through its allies, like Vietnam in Cambodia—this underscored the new dangers and outlined new strategies for coping with them.

The Bush Doctrine's core premise is that the United States will use force, preemptively if necessary, to deal with regimes that pose a threat to U.S. strategic interests, especially by sponsoring terrorism or acquiring weapons of mass destruction.

Southeast Asia itself is not a direct target of the Bush Doctrine. No country in Southeast Asian meets the threefold criteria laid down by the doctrine to qualify as a target: possession or development of weapons of mass destruction, tyranny, and state-sponsored terrorism. However Southeast Asian critics, especially Malaysia's former prime minister Mahathir, have viewed the Bush Doctrine as dangerous. The doctrine, its critics argue, gives Washington a blank check to strike any regime deemed unfriendly to the United States, and which can be linked to terrorism or some other pretext. The doctrine would lead to hasty military action, without exhausting all possible diplomatic means. Also important is its flouting of the sovereignty principle. Furthermore, critics see the doctrine as a clear example of the U.S. turn toward unilateralism, giving America the right to use force without authorization by the UN Security

Council. It is seen against the backdrop of a long and growing list of U.S. actions against multilateral institutions, including the International Criminal Court, the Kyoto Protocol, and the Anti-Ballistic Missile (ABM) Treaty. Moreover, critics see the doctrine as a pretext for the United States to pursue its other strategic and economic interests through military force. For example, an occupation of Iraq, ostensibly to eliminate weapons of mass destruction and human rights abuses, has also put under American control one of the world's largest proven reserves of oil.

While the United States itself has not made any Southeast Asian state a target of preemption, its closest ally, Australia, which under the Howard government has proclaimed itself as a deputy sheriff to the United States, has not been so reticent. Australia has announced its own preemptive strategy, the Howard corollary. Australia's prime minister, John Howard, has warned that he will strike preemptively if necessary against terrorists and their bases in Southeast Asia if an attack on Australia is deemed imminent. In some ways, the Howard corollary actually went a step further than Bush's preemptive strategy. The latter targets rogue states accused of developing weapons of mass destruction and exporting terror. Howard's targets are Southeast Asian states that have no plans for such weapons and that are not willing exporters of terror to Australia or elsewhere.

While the Howard policy has to be seen against the backdrop of the terrorist attacks in Bali, which killed about 100 Australians, thereby making preemptive regional strikes a way of calming a domestic audience questioning the government's preparedness against terror, Howard's pro–U.S. stance meant that it was seen to some extent as an extension of the Bush Doctrine to Southeast Asia. The United States helped to further this perception by openly endorsing the Australian prime minister.

The United States strike on Iraq brought out some of the reservations held by Southeast Asian states regarding the Bush Doctrine in particular and the U.S. war on terror in general. There were major public demonstrations against the war in Malaysia and Indonesia. While Singapore, Thailand, and the Philippines joined the coalition of the willing, Indonesia and Malaysia opposed the war and remained unconvinced of the rationale for a U.S. strike on Iraq.[48] The Bush administration's claim that war was necessary to rid the world of a regime that threatened U.S. and global security, by quietly but surely building up an arsenal of deadly weapons of mass destruction, was viewed with widespread skepticism in the region. Many Southeast Asian analysts sensed other motives. Some saw the war as a personal family vendetta. Others viewed it as a ploy to secure firm U.S. control over the vast oil resources of the Middle East.

It would have been politically easier for Southeast Asian countries to support the United States had Washington secured the Security Council's formal authorization for a strike on Iraq after the submission of the report of the UN inspectors. In the absence of this, the strike on Iraq heightened perceptions in Southeast Asia of U.S. unilateralism and arrogance. Southeast Asian governments faced the possibility of a popular Muslim backlash if they were to support the war against Iraq. Moreover, given that no credible evidence linking the Saddam Hussein regime with Al-Qaeda was forthcoming from the United States, Southeast Asian countries viewed the Iraqi issue as a huge distraction from the war on terrorism, which for them is a much more urgent and important challenge. When North Korea disclosed its secret nuclear weapons program, Southeast Asian critics of the war against Iraq, especially Malaysian leaders, accused the United States of double standards. North Korea's nuclear program is more advanced than Iraq's. Since the main reason for going to war against Saddam was his program of weapons of mass destruction, critics of the Bush Doctrine asked whether the same logic should not apply to North Korea. And the demonstrated U.S. failure to find any weapons of mass destruction in Iraq, its failure to pacify Iraq, the revelations of torture at the Abu Ghraib prison, and the U.S. 9/11 Commission's finding suggesting no evidence of a link between Iraq and Al-Qaeda has led to more popular distrust of the U.S. handling of terrorism, although here, too, the governments of Singapore, Thailand, and the Philippines have maintained a more pro-U.S. stance than that of Indonesia and Malaysia.

Conclusion

In conclusion, let me highlight some of the deeper reasons behind the ambivalent attitude of Southeast Asian states toward the United States since September 11. First, the post–September 11 debates about terrorism in Southeast Asia clearly focused on U.S. arrogance and its staunchly pro-Israeli stance as the root causes of terror. Second, the U.S. response to terrorism was seen as being biased in favor of the military instrument. Third, the Bush administration's decision to go to war against Iraq despite the lack of authorization from the UN Security Council was seen as decisive proof of growing U.S. unilateralism and lack of respect for the rule of law in international affairs. Finally, many Southeast Asian critics of the war against Iraq were upset by what they saw as the U.S. failure to secure law and order in Iraq after its quick and decisive victory. This was seen as further evidence of an uncaring and imperial U.S. policy that could threaten the interests of weaker developing countries.

Throughout the region, domestic politics served to aggravate the lack of trust between the United States and regional governments. In the Philippines, nationalist forces, including Vice President Teofisto Guingona, were angered by the presence of U.S. advisors and the signing of new security agreements between the two countries.[49] Washington and Manila differed on the status of some militant groups, most notably the Moro Islamic Liberation Front (MILF), especially whether to place the MILF on the State Department's list of foreign terrorist organizations alongside Abu Sayyaf and the communist New People's Army (NPA). In Malaysia, the government was responsive to world Islamic opinion as it criticized the U.S. military attacks against Afghanistan in October 2001. Fear of a domestic political backlash was responsible for Malaysia's opposition to U.S. troop deployments in the region.[50] Similarly, Indonesia, despite its need for U.S. military and economic assistance, opposed the attack on Iraq and distanced itself from some of the military-strategic aspects of the U.S. war on terror.

Southeast Asia's response to the U.S.-sponsored war on terror has been marked by some ironies. While the post–September 11 milieu has seen a dramatic increase in American hard power, there has been a noticeable erosion of American soft power. Many U.S. actions on the world stage related to Iraq, the ABM treaty, Kyoto Protocol, the international war crimes tribunal, and so on have created a perception of U.S. heavy-handedness. Southeast Asian countries are now less worried about a U.S. military retreat (as they were in the early 1990s), but more concerned about its assertive primacy and unilateralism. Moreover, differences over the conduct of the war on terror by the United States are complicating regional efforts at counter-terrorism. While governments in the region have, out of pragmatic concerns, shown acceptance of the U.S. policy (despite differences especially among Singapore, Malaysia, and Indonesia), America's declining legitimacy as a world leader in the eyes of the general public in Southeast Asia has made it difficult for governments to fully and publicly identify with U.S. strategic goals and approaches in the region.

Notes

Parts of this chapter draw from some of the author's previously published work, including: Amitav Acharya, *Southeast Asian Security After September 11*, Foreign Policy Dialogue Series, 2003-8 (Vancouver: Asia Pacific Foundation of Canada, 2003); David Capie and Amitav Acharya, "A Fine Balance: U.S. Relations With Southeast Asia Since 9/11," paper presented to the Colloquium on "United States–Asia Relations Today: A New World Order?," Paris, Centre d'Études et de Recherches Internationales, 2–4 December 2002; and Amitav Acharya, *Age of Fear: Power Versus Principle in the War On Terror* (Singapore: Marshall Cavendish and New Delhi: Rupa & Co, 2004).

1. These analysts add: "Policy has been ad hoc and event-driven, with brief bursts of attention to single countries—Burma after the 1990 elections and the political exile of Daw Aung Sang Suu Kyi, Cambodia immediately after the 1991 peace accords, and Indonesia after the fall of President Suharto. This patchwork approach has allowed other countries (China, Japan, and Australia) to take the lead in the region. Relations suffered another downturn when several Southeast Asian nations were hit hard by the 1997–98 economic crisis. In their eyes the American response was lackluster and remote. Catharin Dalpino and Bridget Welsh, "Southeast Asia Needs More Attention," *International Herald Tribune* (Feb. 14, 2002).

2. For background to U.S.–Southeast Asian relations, see J. Robert Kerrey and Robert A. Manning, *The United States and Southeast Asia: A Policy Agenda for the New Administration* (New York: Council on Foreign Relations Press, 2001); Rizal Sukma, "U.S.–Southeast Asia Relations After the Crisis: The Security Dimension," background paper prepared for the Asia Foundation's Workshop on America's Role in Asia (Bangkok, Mar. 22–24, 2000).

3. Amitav Acharya, "The Reagan Doctrine and International Security," *Peace Research: The Canadian Journal of Peace Studies* 20, no. 2 (May 1988): 23–31.

4. ASEAN Secretariat, *ASEAN-US Dialogue,* Bangkok, ASEAN Secretariat, available at www.aseansec.org/7728.htm, accessed July 13, 2004. The upward trend in trade continues. Two-way trade in goods was over $120 billion in 2002, and U.S. direct investment in ASEAN was over $50 billion, five times as much as in China, slightly higher than that in Mexico. Source: Committee on International Relations, U.S. House of Representatives, *U.S. Trade Policy with Southeast Asia and Oceania: Testimony of Ralph F. Ives, Assistant U.S. Trade Representative for Asia-Pacific and APEC Affairs* (Washington, DC: June 25, 2003), available at wwwa.house.gov/international_relations/108/ive0625.htm, accessed July 13, 2004.

5. There has been an increasing diversification of U.S. investment in the region, from a concentration in the oil and gas sector (which in the early and mid-1980s accounted for more than half of the total U.S. investment in the region) to investment in manufacturing and services, which now accounts for the largest share of U.S. investment activity in ASEAN. In 1999, 36 percent of U.S. investment in the region was concentrated in the manufacturing sector; see U.S.–ASEAN Business Council, *U.S. Investment in ASEAN and China, 1990–2002,* available at www.us-asean.org/statistics/US_investment.htm, accessed July 20, 2004.

6. ASEAN Secretariat, *ASEAN–US Dialogue,* available at http://202.154.12.3/5928.htm, accessed July 13, 2004.

7. In 1993, the United States announced that its assistance to ASEAN would be

provided only through the Private Investment and Trade Opportunities (PITO) project and the Environment Improvement Project (EIP). The PITO project, which lasted until 1995, "aimed at enhancing the development of ASEAN and providing benefits to U.S. firms through increased trade and investment activities in the region." ASEAN Secretariat, *ASEAN–US Dialogue*, available at http://202.154.12.3/5928.htm, accessed July 13, 2004.

8. Amitav Acharya, "Southeast Asia's Democratic Moment?" *Asian Survey* (May/June 1999): 418–32.

9. John Gershman, "Is Southeast Asia the Second Front?" *Foreign Affairs* 81, no. 4 (July/Aug. 2002): 60–74.

10. John Gerard Ruggie, "Multilateralism: The Anatomy of an Institution," in John Gerard Ruggie, ed., *Multilateralism Matters: The Theory and Praxis of an Institutional Form* (New York: Columbia University Press, 1993), p. 8.

11. This section draws from David Capie and Amitav Acharya, "A Fine Balance: U.S. Relations with Southeast Asia Since 9/11," paper presented to the Colloquium on United States–Asia Relations Today: A New "New World Order?" organized by Sciences Po, Paris, Dec. 2–4, 2002, available at www.ceri-sciencespo.com/archive/jan03/artca.pdf, accessed July 13, 2004. The author would like to thank David Capie for sharing his research.

12. Amitav Acharya, "State Society Relations: Asian and World Order After September 11," in Ken Booth and Tim Dunne, eds., *Worlds in Collision: Terror and the Future of Global Order* (London: Palgrave, 2002), pp. 194–204.

13. Abdullah Badawi, keynote address to the Asia-Pacific Roundtable Conference (Kuala Lumpur: June 3, 2002).

14. See for example, Kumar Ramakrishna, "9/11, American Praetorian Unilateralism, and the Impact on State-Society Relations in Southeast Asia," Working Paper no. 26 (Singapore: Institute of Defence and Strategic Studies, 2002).

15. "Suspect Calls Malaysia a Staging Area for Terror Attacks," *New York Times* (Jan. 30, 2002); "Southeast Asia Bars Help of U.S. Troops," *International Herald Tribune* (Dec. 4, 2001).

16. "U.S. May Turn Attention to Far East Terror Groups," *Guardian* (Oct. 11, 2001).

17. For an overview of Southeast Asian reaction to September 11, see Angel M. Rabasa, *Southeast Asia after 9/11: Regional Trends and U.S. Interests,* testimony to the Subcommittee on East Asia and the Pacific House of Representatives Committee on International Relations (Washington, DC: Dec. 12, 2001).

18. "ASEAN Countries Benefit From Anti-terror Pact," *Straits Times* (Aug. 3, 2002).

19. White House, *Joint Statement Between the United States of America and the Republic of the Philippines,* Nov. 20, 2001, available at www.whitehouse.gov/news/releases/2001/11/20011120–13.html, accessed July 13, 2004.

20. Federation of American Scientists, 2002, *War on Terrorism: Security Assistance Tables,* available at http://fas.org/terrorism/at/docs/WaronTerroraid.html, accessed July 20, 2004.

21. Oliver Teves, "Manila: U.S. Set Rules on Military Exercise," *Washington Post* (Feb. 14, 2003).

22. "U.S. Trip Yields $4.6B Investments, Trade, Aid," *Philippines Daily Inquirer* (Nov. 22, 2001).

23. "The Bush Administration's New Strategy in the War Against Terrorism,"

New Yorker (Dec. 23, 2002): 66; "Philippine Troops Eagerly Await U.S. Help and Arms," *New York Times* (Feb. 12, 2002).

24. *U.S. Mission in Philippines Too Little?* MSNBC News Online, 2002, available at www.msnbc.com/news/720731.asp?cp1=1, accessed Aug. 18, 2004.

25. James Kelly, transcript of press conference, U.S. embassy, Kuala Lumpur, Apr. 15, 2002.

26. "Malaysia Minister Says U.S. Endorses Detention Law," Deutsche-Presse Agentur (May 12, 2002).

27. "U.S. Pragmatic Toward Malaysia," *Far Eastern Economic Review* (June 6, 2002): 10.

28. Najib bin Tun Abdul Razak, "U.S.-Malaysia Defense Cooperation: A Solid Success Story," lecture to the Heritage Foundation (Washington, DC: May 3, 2002).

29. "Anti-terrorism Centre: U.S. Offers Services, Assistance," *New Straits Times* (Jan. 4, 2003).

30. Dato Seri Mohamed Mahathir, speech at the opening session of the XIII Summit Meeting of the Non-Aligned Movement at Putra World Trade Centre, Kuala Lumpur, Malaysia, Feb. 24, 2003, available at www.nam.gov.za/media/030225na.htm, accessed July 13, 2004.

31. Donald K. Emmerson, "Southeast Asia and the United States Since September 11th," statement prepared for a hearing on "Southeast Asia After 9/11: Regional Trends and U.S. Interests," organized by the Subcommittee on East Asia and the Pacific, Committee on International Relations, U.S. House of Representatives, Washington, DC, Dec. 12, 2001.

32. White House, *U.S. and Indonesia Pledge Cooperation: Joint Statement Between the United States of America and the Republic of Indonesia as Leaders of the World's Second and Third Largest Democracies* (Washington, DC: White House, Sept. 19, 2001), available at www.whitehouse.gov/news/releases/2001/09/20010919–3.html, accessed July 13, 2004.

33. "Megawati's Silence Irks Americans," *Far Eastern Economic Review* (Oct. 18, 2001).

34. Barry Desker, "Islam and Society in Southeast Asia After September 11," Working Paper no. 33 (Singapore: Institute of Defence and Strategic Studies, 2002).

35. "White House Seeks to Resume Aiding Indonesia's Army," *New York Times* (June 29, 2002); Raymond Bonner and Jane Perlez, "Whose Eleventh? Indonesia and America Since September 11," *Brown Journal of World Affairs* 9, no. 3 (Spring 2002).

36. "Singapore Defence Minister Visits U.S.," Deutsche-Presse Agentur (Apr. 6, 2003).

37. Kin Wah Chin, "Singapore's Perspective in the Regional Security Architecture," paper presented at Evolving Approaches to Security in the Asia-Pacific Conference, organized by Institute of Defence and Strategic Studies (Singapore: Dec. 9–11, 2002).

38. "U.S. Aircraft Carriers to Get Access to Changi Base," *Straits Times* (Jan. 16, 1998).

39. Within a year, five American carriers and around 100 other naval vessels berthed at the base. Chin Kin Wah, "Singapore's Perspective in the Regional Security Architecture."

40. "SAF Marks Milestone in Attack Helicopter Capabilities with Apache Inauguration," *Channel NewsAsia* (Apr. 10, 2003).

41. Ibid.

42. Raymond Bonner, "Thais Give U.S. Secret Help in War on Terror," *International Herald Tribune* (June 9, 2003): 6.

43. Barry Desker and Kumar Ramakrishna, "Forging an Indirect Strategy in Southeast Asia," *Washington Quarterly* 25, no. 2 (Spring 2002): 161–76.

44. The text of the U.S–ASEAN Joint Declaration on Combating Terrorism can be found online on the Bureau of Public Affairs, U.S. Department of State web site at www.state.gov/p/eap/rls/ot/12428.htm, accessed July 13, 2004.

45. Rungrawee C. Pinyora, "Bangkok Backs U.S. in Straits Initiative," *Nation* (June 25, 2004).

46. Felix Soh, "No More Lone Ranger, But U.S. Still Ready to Ride Alone If Need Be," *Straits Times* (June 9, 2004); Richard Hubbard, "Malaysia Rejects Use of Outside Forces in SE Asia," Reuters (June 6, 2004).

47. White House, *The National Security Strategy of the United States of America* (Washington, DC: White House, 2002), available at www.whitehouse.gov/nsc/nss.pdf, accessed July 13, 2004.

48. "No Case for War Against Iraq, Say Asians," *Straits Times* (Sept. 30, 2002).

49. "Troop Presence Splits Philippine Opinion," *Washington Times* (Jan. 29, 2002).

50. "War on Terror Fuels Political Feuds in Malaysia," *New York Times* (Oct. 19, 2001).

7

U.S. Policy Interests in South Asia

Continuities and Disjunctures

Sumit Ganguly and Brian Shoup

South Asia continues to remain a limited priority in the scheme of American foreign policy interests. It is a region with which the United States has few cultural or historical ties, it is marked by endemic poverty, and apart from being a sanctuary for certain terrorist groups, it poses no significant security threat to the United States. Consequently, American policy interests in and attention to the region remain circumscribed and occupy only a moderately high priority. After the current preoccupation with the terrorist menace from South Asia, particularly from Pakistan and Afghanistan, comes to a close, American policy toward the region will, in considerable measure, depend upon its ties to the principal power in region, India.

This chapter assesses the recent history of American diplomacy toward the region. In so doing, it adopts an implicitly neorealist orientation.[1] Its central argument is that South Asia's relative economic and military insignificance has led American policy makers to accord the region a limited priority. Only when other, global security concerns have meshed with the region has the United States devoted significant military and diplomatic resources to the region.

The Historical Palimpsest

Apart from specific periods during the Cold War, South Asia did not figure prominently in American foreign or security policy concerns. Indeed, apart from a sporadic American involvement in the region during

145

the Soviet invasion and occupation of Afghanistan, after the mid-1960s the United States devoted only limited attention to the region. The relative neglect of South Asia in the calculus of U.S. foreign policy interests is easily explicable. None of the nations of the region posed a significant security threat to the United States or its allies, none was an important destination for American exports, and few had strong cultural or historical ties with the United States.[2]

Accordingly, during much of the Cold War the United States's goals were limited to sporadically supporting democratic regimes in the region, initially containing Chinese, and more consistently, Soviet influence in the region, limiting the spread of weapons of mass destruction, providing humanitarian assistance, and aiding economic development. At the end of the Cold War, American interests in the region did not change dramatically. Obviously, the preoccupation with containing Soviet power and influence in the region no longer had any significance. The other goals, however, mostly remained in place.

Some important shifts in the pursuit of these goals did ensue in the aftermath of the Cold War. The two Clinton administrations attached considerable significance to rolling back the nuclear and missile programs of India and Pakistan. In the end, despite considerable effort, they met with little success in this endeavor. They also paid renewed attention to India after it embarked upon a program of economic liberalization following an acute economic crisis in 1991.[3] The success of India's economic reforms was of significant interest to American policy makers because they could open a hitherto sheltered Indian market to American firms.

The Bush administration, shortly after assuming office, dramatically altered American priorities in South Asia. It not only dispensed with the harsh and mostly unyielding rhetoric of nonproliferation, but also sharply altered existing policies in that arena. It moved with some dispatch to remove the raft of punitive sanctions that the Clinton administration had imposed on both India and Pakistan in the wake of their nuclear tests of May 1998. It also chose to accord a far greater priority to its relations with India while initially downgrading the significance of Pakistan. Its decision to bolster relations with India, at least in part, stemmed from the view of some key players within the administration, including Deputy Secretary of Defense Paul Wolfowitz and National Security Advisor Condoleezza Rice, that India could serve as a possible bulwark against a recalcitrant China in Asia. Separately, the administration took a harsh view of Pakistan's involvement with the Taliban regime in Afghanistan.[4]

Security Issues in South Asia

American interests in South Asia were dramatically redefined following the terrorist attacks on the United States on September 11, 2001. The Bush administration, which had initially ostracized Pakistan, now needed to elicit its cooperation to unseat the Taliban regime and to eviscerate Al-Qaeda. Accordingly, Pakistan assumed renewed significance to American foreign and security policy interests. Given Pakistan's new role as a U.S. ally in the war on terror, the Bush administration dropped nonproliferation and democracy-related sanctions, thereby clearing the way for the United States to provide a number of aid programs to Islamabad in exchange for its political and military support. In June 2003 the United States announced a five-year, $3 billion aid package for Pakistan to begin in October 2004. The aid package included funds earmarked for social services and human development, but approximately $300 million per year was to be spent on programs aimed at military financing and training. Beyond this, the United States dropped important sanctions that prevented the sale of improved military technologies to Pakistan, a consequence of both army chief Gen. Pervaiz Musharraf's coup and Pakistan's development of nuclear weapons. A further $400 million was approved by the U.S. Congress in January 2004 as part of a plan to reschedule or forgive Pakistan's crushing multilateral external debts.

However, unlike in the past, the Bush administration sought to ensure that the renewal of a security nexus with Pakistan would not lead to a dramatic decline in its carefully and newly forged relationship with India. Some key American policy makers in the Bush administration remained convinced that despite the importance of courting Pakistan to achieve certain policy goals in the region, India's long-term significance in the region should not be overlooked. They emphasized India's growing economy, its newfound willingness to expand defense contacts with the United States, and its ability to serve as a potential counterweight to future Chinese revanchism in Asia. Consequently, policy makers in Washington sought to fashion a policy that would enhance American interests in both states.

U.S. Strategic Interests in South Asia

Pakistan's role as an American ally varied during the Cold War. Especially during the last decade of the Cold War, Pakistan's strategic significance to the United States was considerable because of the latter's role in supporting the mujahidin in Afghanistan. As a reward for its willingness to advance American strategic goals in Afghanistan, Pakistan became the renewed recipient of substantial amounts of American economic and military assistance. Following the ouster of the Soviet Union from Afghanistan, Pakistan's utility to the United States dwindled and its continuing pursuit of nuclear weapons despite American admonitions led to a fundamental rift in U.S.-Pakistan relations.

Such a rupture in U.S. relations with Pakistan had no appreciable impact on Indo-U.S. relations. India, unlike Pakistan, as is well known had initially pursued a strategy of nonalignment and subsequently had tacitly allied itself with the Soviet Union from about the early 1970s.

The Exigencies of Indo-Pakistani Tensions

A policy of "dual engagement," if successfully implemented, would best serve American interests in the region.[5] However, formulating and implementing such a policy was neither easy nor simple. Given that in Indian perceptions, most American involvement in Pakistan had redounded to India's disadvantage, this policy was met with some skepticism in New Delhi. Policy makers in New Delhi feared that in its quest to court Pakistan's support for actions against the Taliban and Al-Qaeda, the United States might again adopt a pro-Pakistani stance in the conflict over the contested territory of Kashmir, which had led to three Indo-Pakistani wars, in 1947, 1965, and 1971.[6]

The Bush administration, cognizant of these fears, sought to allay India's misgivings through a series of high-level visits. Apart from allaying India's concerns about a new American alignment with Pakistan, the administration, of course, had its own interests in addressing India's concerns. A deteriorating India-Pakistan relationship would divert Pakistan's attention away from and undermine its ability to cooperate with the United States in the "war on terrorism."

It was only in the waning days of the Cold War that the Reagan administration made a deft and concerted effort to woo India away from its military-technological dependence on the Soviet Union. To this end it offered India various forms of complex military technology that theretofore had been off limits. Among other items were the GE-404 engines for use in India's quest to develop an indigenous Light Combat Aircraft (LCA). During the Bush administration this momentum continued. In 1991, General Claude M. Kicklighter visited India and proposed a range of military-to-military contacts. The "Kicklighter proposals" as they came to be called, laid the foundations for the steady expansion of military contacts and joint exercises. India's willingness to expand these contacts stemmed in considerable measure from the demise of the robust Indo-Soviet military relationship with the collapse of the Soviet Union. Consequently, it made eminent sense for Indian political and military decision makers to develop a better diplomatic and military relationship with the United States, the emergent global power without parallel.

The incipient military-to-military relationship initially stalled under the Clinton administration for a variety of reasons. The new administration laid renewed emphasis on the nonproliferation question and failed to promptly appoint a new ambassador to New Delhi. In addition, the new assistant secretary of state for South Asia, Robin Raphael, caused more than a diplomatic contretemps when she publicly, if inadvertently, called into question the legality of Kashmir's accession to India. After these initial pitfalls the relationship started to obtain some traction. In April 1994, Prime Minister Narasimha Rao visited the United States and discussions about defense cooperation despite continuing differences on the nonproliferation question were resumed. Subsequently, Defense Secretary William Perry, who had developed a good working relationship with the Indian ambassador to the United States, Siddhartha Shanker Ray, took an active interest in defense cooperation with India. To this end, he visited India in January 1995. During this visit he and the Indian minister of defense, S.B. Chavan, signed an Agreed Minute on Defense Relations, which provided a more substantial basis for defense cooperation. As a consequence, limited defense cooperation got under way, especially in the realm of naval exercises.[7] Also, at an institutional level, the Agreed Minute contributed to the creation of the joint Defense Policy Group, a civilian-to-civilian, high-level group, which would meet at periodic intervals to discuss defense cooperation.

The Indian and subsequent Pakistani nuclear tests ruptured the growing defense ties between India and the United States. Invoking the Glenn Amendment, President Clinton cut off most forms of assistance to India and also cancelled all defense cooperation in an attempt to induce India to abandon its nuclear weapons program. He also deputed the deputy secretary of state, Strobe Talbott, to conduct extensive discussions with both Pakistan and India, in an effort to curtail their nuclear and ballistic missile programs and reduce ongoing bilateral tensions. To this end, for the remainder of Clinton's term in office, Talbott held extensive discussions with his Indian and also Pakistani counterparts. While these discussions did dramatically improve the political climate of Indo-U.S. relations, they did little to move India to abandon its nuclear and ballistic missile programs. In turn, the administration let most of the Glenn sanctions remain in place even after a hugely successful visit to India in March 2000. The meeting, however, dramatically improved the overall political context of bilateral relations and led to other important agreements. Such a successful meeting, in part, could be attributed to the already changed atmosphere in Indo-U.S. relations. In July 1999, the United States had unequivocally supported the Indian position in brokering an end to the Kargil war. The war, as is well known, had ensued when Pakistani forces had crossed the Line of Control in the disputed state of Jammu and Kashmir in early May 1999. The unstinting American support of the sanctity of the Line of Control had done much to endear the United States to significant segments of the Indian attentive public.

The new Bush administration accorded much greater priority to expanding defense ties with India. It also sought to downplay the differences on the nonproliferation question. Not surprisingly, a significant spurt ensued in military-to-military ties. The full scope and extent of these meetings, contacts, and exercises have been discussed elsewhere.[8] Suffice it to say that the most substantive exercises have been in the naval sphere as army and air force exercises are more complex and involve greater costs. Also, during 2004 two exercises of some note have taken place. In the summer of 2002 Indian para-commandos conducted an exercise in the historic city of Agra with American Special Forces and have also held joint exercises in Alaska.[9]

It is important to underscore that many of the recent developments in Indo-American military ties took place against the backdrop of sharply deteriorating Indo-Pakistani relations. These tensions, while not ending the growth of a new Indo-U.S. defense relationship, have nevertheless had an adverse impact on their steady evolution. A brief discussion of Indo-Pakistani tensions and their influence on the course of Indo-U.S relations is in order.

Indo-Pakistani Tensions and the United States

In the aftermath of a terrorist attack on the Indian parliament on December 13, 2001, the Bush administration's worst fears about a dramatic downturn in the Indo-Pakistani relationship almost materialized. Two Pakistan-based and aided groups, the Lashkar-e-Taiba and the Jaish-e-Mohammed, were implicated in these attacks. The Indian government was confronted with a limited array of choices to end Pakistani support for these insurgent groups. Pakistan's possession of nuclear weapons effectively neutralized India's own nuclear capabilities. India could ill afford to resort to war with Pakistan for fear of provoking a larger, wider conflict with the potential for escalation to the nuclear level. Additionally, Indian decision makers were aware that an attack on Pakistan could inadvertently result in the deaths of American military and civilian personnel who had been deployed there in significant numbers since September 11, 2001.

Faced with these constraints, India resorted to a strategy of "forceful persuasion": To this end, New Delhi recalled its ambassador from Pakistan, cut all road and rail links, stopped Pakistani civilian overflights across Indian territory, and deployed close to 750,000 troops along the Indo-Pakistani border.[10] More to the point, it placed significant other military assets along the border in a state of high alert. These diplomatic and military pressures had a dual purpose. At one level they were designed to induce Pakistan to reconsider its strategy of supporting the Kashmiri insurgents. At another level, they were also directed at the United States. Indian decision makers anticipated that such a massive display of firepower along the volatile border would inevitably lead Pakistan to divert significant military capabilities to its side of the border. Such a shift of military forces would degrade its ability to assist the United States in its pursuit of the remnants of Al-Qaeda and the Taliban. Moreover, the presence of over a million troops along this border would also arouse Washington's fears of a possible Indo-Pakistani war.

Accordingly, in early 2002, as Indo-Pakistani relations continued a steady downward slide, the Bush administration devoted considerable time and attention to prevent yet another Indo-Pakistani conflagration. This strategy involved sending a series of high-level officials to both India and Pakistan to induce the two sides to alter aspects of their political and military strategies to diminish the prospects of war. Administration officials urged the Pakistanis to desist from supporting the Kashmiri insurgents and counseled the Indians to exercise military restraint along the border. This delicate diplomatic minuet paid important dividends and despite a long stretch of tensions, war was effectively forestalled. The problem of Pakistani support for the insurgents still remains. By the same token, India remains frustrated by its inability to directly coerce Pakistan or to persuade the United States to alter Pakistan's continued support of the insurgents.

The U.S. willingness to address India's concerns will, for the present, remain confined to efforts geared to the prevention of war between India and Pakistan. To this end, the United States will also continue to urge India to open a diplomatic dialogue with Pakistan. India, in turn, will seek to resist these pressures until Pakistan curbs its support of terror in Kashmir. Despite this basic disjuncture, as long as India evinces a willingness to cooperate with the United States in the security arena, the U.S. military presence in South Asia will expand, albeit incrementally. The long legacy of mutual distrust and recrimination, the bureaucratic inertia within the Indian political system, and the existence of other, more compelling American security priorities elsewhere in the world, will limit a rapid expansion of security ties with India.

The expansion of the Indo-U.S. security relationship may stall further in the aftermath of the Bush administration's decision to grant Pakistan the status of a "major, non-NATO ally" in March 2004.[11] The United States chose to grant Pakistan this status in its quest to elicit Pakistan's continuing and possibly expanded cooperation in the hunt for Usama Bin Laden and his key associates.[12] Given the recent revelations of Pakistan's deep involvement in transferring nuclear weapons technology to Iran, Iraq, and North Korea, the American decision to grant Pakistan this new dispensation, normally reserved for key strategic relationships, was seen in India as hypocritical, disingenuous, and potentially damaging to Indian security interests.[13]

Economic Ties With South Asia

As with security ties to South Asia, the expansion of economic contacts within the region also hinges on some key developments. Unless India, the principal country in the region, can provide some serious impetus to its limited economic reform program, American economic interests in the region will remain limited, at best. American economic involvement in South Asia will also depend upon the future of Pakistan's political stability and on Sri Lanka's ability to bring an end to its fratricidal civil war, one that has sapped much of the energies of this otherwise moderately prosperous island nation.

Historically, South Asia has not been a significant destination for American trade or investment. The poverty of the region, the absence of natural resources critical to the well-being of the American economy, and India's policy of import-substituting industrialization, which effectively closed its markets to foreign investment, inhibited American investment. Consequently, the region's significance in the calculus of American economic interests was minimal. Since 1991, American economic involvement in South Asia, especially in India, has expanded considerably. Yet, as a percentage of total American foreign direct investment the region still lags significantly behind most other areas of the world.

The South Asian states also do not constitute significant American trading partners. The 1999–2000 trade figures with the principal states in the region are revealing. Bangladesh's exports to the United States amounted to a mere $1.9 billion and its imports to $429 million. Pakistan imported some $576 million from the United States and exported $2 billion. Sri Lanka's import figures for this period are unavailable. However, it exported about $2 billion worth of goods to the United States. Finally, India, the principal state in the region, imported $5.5 billion worth of goods and exported $9.5 billion.[14] These trade figures underscore the current economic insignificance of South Asia to the overall well being of the American economy, which has a gross national product of over $12 trillion.

American investment in South Asia is also limited. In fact, American investment in Bangladesh, Sri Lanka, and Pakistan is mostly negligible since India embarked upon its strategy of economic liberalization in 1991. As the labyrinthine set of controls, regulations, and barriers to foreign investment were dismantled, American firms started to invest in India. However, even today India receives a small fraction of American foreign direct investment in comparison with such states as the People's Republic of China. Some comparisons are instructive. According to the United States Department of Commerce, in fiscal year 2000 India received $118 million of U.S. foreign direct investment while China received $1.6 billion. In 2001, India attracted $289 million while China drew in $1.2 billion.[15] These figures demonstrate that despite the adoption of a strategy of economic liberalization, India still seriously lags behind China.

The reasons for this discrepancy are not that difficult to adduce. First, China embarked on a strategy of economic reform at least a decade prior to India. Second, thanks to India's fractious democratic polity, liberalization has proceeded in fits and starts. The result has been policy uncertainties, which has inhibited foreign investors. Third, India has yet to adequately address at least three infrastructural bottlenecks: power, transportation, and telecommunications. Unless and until India successfully tackles these three critical problems its ability to attract significant amounts of foreign investment will be hobbled.

American economic assistance to the region has also dwindled over the last several decades. During a significant span of the Cold War years Pakistan and also India were significant recipients of American foreign assistance. Much of this assistance was closely tied to the anticommunist impulse in American foreign policy. It was also based upon the premise that economic development would contribute to political liberalization in the Third World and that "all good things go together."[16] Apart from the renewed largess to Pakistan for its cooperation in the "war on terrorism," the bulk of American overseas assistance in South Asia is directed to Bangladesh.

Today American overseas development assistance to India is mostly negligible. The total American assistance to India for fiscal year 2002 was about $182 million. It was directed toward several key areas, including access to reproductive health, providing food and health services for the poor, fostering energy efficiency, improving environmental conditions in urban areas, improving the capacity of financial markets, and reducing suffering associated with natural disasters. Laudable as these goals are, the sums allocated for these purposes will at best only have demonstration effects in an economy and society as large as India's. Today the significance of American economic assistance to India lies more in the symbolic rather than the substantive realm.

The American aid program to Pakistan is far more substantial and is likely to expand in the foreseeable future. In 2005 alone the United States spends some $625 million in Pakistan. Some of this assistance is a direct consequence of Pakistan's willingness to cooperate with the United States in the "war on terrorism." Much of the spending is directed toward the revitalization of Pakistan's educational system, especially at the primary and secondary school levels, both of which are in a state of considerable disarray.

American assistance to Sri Lanka is far more modest. The total allocation for Sri Lanka in fiscal year 2002 was about $8.5 million. Assuming congressional approval, it was expected to increase to about $10 million in 2003. The assistance is targeted to improve Sri Lanka's global competitiveness, creating and expanding social opportunities, and promoting peace and human rights. Finally, the United States spent about $83 million in economic assistance in Bangladesh in fiscal year 2002. The bulk of American assistance to Bangladesh is directed toward agribusiness and small business development, the promotion of food security, and disaster preparedness and the conservation of water resources and tropical forests.[17]

Support for Democratization and Civil Society

Despite a professed commitment to the spread of democracy on a global basis and in the region, in fact American support for democratization in South Asia has been distinctly fitful. A variety of American administrations have evinced little difficulty in accommodating themselves to military regimes in South Asia, especially in Pakistan.[18] The exigencies of pursuing other, seemingly more compelling interests, has repeatedly led American policy makers to attach lesser significance to the promotion of democracy than to the pursuit of seemingly more compelling interests.[19] During much of the Cold War the anticommunist enterprise took precedence over the promotion of democracy in South Asia. This pattern has been alarmingly demonstrated in Pakistan where short-term regional interests have consistently overridden any professed interest by the United States in democratic reform. For example, in the aftermath of the Soviet invasion and occupation of Afghanistan, the United States bolstered the military regime of General Zia-ul-Haq. The need to elicit Pakistani support to prosecute a covert war against the Soviet occupation of Afghanistan overrode the imperative of promoting democracy in Pakistan. In a markedly similar fashion, the United States is once again overlooking the many shortcomings of General Musharraf's regime in Pakistan in the aftermath of September 11, 2001. The necessity of pursuing the remnants of Al-Qaeda and the Taliban through Pakistan has led the Bush administration to mostly ignore the steady dismantling of Pakistan's already weakened constitutional order at the hands of General Musharraf.

It might be an unfortunate coincidence that Pakistan's relevance to U.S. geopolitical interests has tended to be correlated with periods of military rule. Yet the historical pattern of U.S. involvement with Pakistan suggests that military regimes in Islamabad have benefited greatly from a fairly myopic vision of U.S. policy makers. Even at their absolute nadir in 1977, when angry crowds attacked the U.S. embassy, relations with Pakistan were quickly accorded high priority owing to U.S. interests in Afghanistan. In many ways, U.S. policy makers have viewed the Pakistani military as a necessity, albeit a feeble and corrupt necessity. Ironically, U.S. interest in developing more credible democratic institutions in Afghanistan has almost necessitated ignoring Pakistan's shortcomings on the democratic reform front.

The administration has also proffered the most anodyne criticisms of the recent assaults on one of the most significant pillars of Indian democracy, namely secularism, under the Bharatiya Janata Party–led regime. For example, even in the aftermath of the vicious pogrom directed against significant segments of the Muslim community in the western Indian state of Gujarat, the Bush administration rebuked India in very mild terms.

In this connection, it should be underscored that U.S. support for human rights in South Asia has also been selective and fitful. The Bureau of Human Rights and Democracy in the U.S. Department of State has historically documented, cataloged, and condemned human rights violations across South Asia. Yet this reporting and documentation, to no particular surprise, has been subjected to political considerations. For example, during much of the early years of the Kashmir insurgency, when the overall state of Indo-U.S. relations was not felicitous, the failure of Indian security forces to uphold the human rights of the insurgents received considerable attention and discussion. No systematic attempt, however, was made to bring into relief the shocking human rights violations that were the stock in trade of the vast majority of the insurgent groups.

Cultural Relations

American cultural ties with South Asia are extremely limited. The reasons are fairly straightforward. Most of the states of South Asian emerged from the British colonial experience. Consequently, in the immediate postwar era the cultural ties with the colonial power endured, especially at the elite level. Subsequently, elements of American popular culture did make inroads into South Asia but this was confined mostly to the urban, educated, and middle to upper classes. Mass poverty, concomitantly low levels of literacy, and the inherent conservatism of many of these societies limited the penetration of American popular culture. Additionally, in the aftermath of the Cold War, American governmental funding for the promotion of cultural diplomacy has dramatically declined. Consequently, a range of cultural programs, including cinema to modern dance to musical performances, has now become a fading memory.

The Role of Domestic Organizations

South Asia still does not loom large in the various domestic institutions shaping American foreign policy. Until 1992, for example, South Asia did not merit a separate regional bureau in the U.S. Department of State. It was only because of the efforts of former congressman Stephen Solarz of Brooklyn that a separate bureau was created in 1992. The post of assistant secretary, however, was not filled until the next year. In the U.S. Department of Defense and in the apex National Security Council, South Asia remains folded in with the Middle East.

Congressional interest in South Asia, while growing, still remains mostly confined to India. In 1993, two congressmen, Frank Pallone, a Democrat from New Jersey, and Bill McCollum, a Republican from Florida, helped create the India Caucus in the U.S. House of Representatives. The caucus was created largely as a consequence of constituency pressures and today it counts as many as 175 members of Congress in its ranks. Its influence on legislation, nevertheless, remains limited.

In the waning days of the last decade, largely as a consequence of the Indian nuclear tests and also because of India's growing economic prowess, a number of Washington, DC–based think tanks started to create South Asia programs. Among the more prominent of these include the Brookings Institution, the Center for Strategic and International Studies, and the Henry L. Stimson Center. It is hard to ascertain what influence, if any, these organizations and their programmatic activities have on the United States policy-making process toward South Asia. What is evident, however, is that policy makers frequently use these organizations as sounding boards when embarking upon new policy initiatives.

Conclusion

American interests in South Asia still remain limited despite the present preoccupation of the Bush administration with the "war on terrorism." Several factors will shape the future of American interests in South Asia. The most important of these are as follows: First, significant and steady economic growth in India could lead to a substantial expansion of American attention to the region. There is no gainsaying India's potential to achieve significantly higher levels of economic growth than it has currently achieved. Whether India will succeed in bringing about such an economic breakthrough still remains an open question. Ideological and structural opposition to further and speedy implementation of economic reforms still dogs the Indian polity. Second, U.S. involvement in the region will also depend upon its success or lack thereof in eviscerating the remnants of Al-Qaeda and the Taliban in Pakistan. A quick end to this campaign may well lead to a significant contraction of the current American presence in Afghanistan. Third and finally, American involvement in South Asia will also depend upon India's willingness to pursue a broader, more robust military relationship with the United States. Despite the growth in U.S.-Indian military contacts and cooperation at the end of the Cold War, the two sides still approach each other warily. Residual anti-Americanism still pervades many segments of India's foreign and security policy bureaucracies. More to the point, important policy differences still characterize the relationship. At a general level, key Indian decision makers remain wary about the overweening sweep of American political, economic, and diplomatic power. Also at a more specific level, they have important disagreements with the United States about Pakistan's reliability as an ally in the "war on terrorism." Not surprisingly, American decision makers also remain hesitant about seeking any dramatic breakthroughs in Indo-U.S. security relations. Consequently, it is doubtful that India and South Asia will assume a significantly greater weight in the calculus of U.S. foreign and security policy interests in the foreseeable future.

Notes

1. For the standard discussions of neorealist premises, see Kenneth Waltz, *The Theory of International Politics* (New York: Random House, 1979); for an impor-

tant and more recent statement, see John J. Mearsheimer, *The Tragedy of Great Power Politics* (New York: W.W. Norton, 2001).

2. For an early discussion of American interests and involvement in South Asia, see William J. Barnds, *India, Pakistan and the Great Powers* (New York: Praeger, 1972); for two important diplomatic histories of American foreign policy toward South Asia, see Dennis Kux, *Estranged Democracies: India and the United States, 1947–1991* (Washington, DC: National Defense University Press, 1993), and *Disenchanted Allies: The United States and Pakistan, 1947–2000* (Washington, DC: Woodrow Wilson Center Press, 2001).

3. For a thoughtful discussion of the forces that contributed to India's economic crisis and the subsequent efforts at economic reform, see Jagdish N. Bhagwati, *India in Transition: Freeing the Economy* (Oxford: Clarendon Press, 1993).

4. Much of this is discussed in Sumit Ganguly, "The Start of a Beautiful Friendship? The United States and India," *World Policy Journal* 10, no. 1 (Spring 2003).

5. I am grateful to my friend and colleague Professor Michael Mastanduno, of Dartmouth College, for suggesting this term.

6. For a detailed analysis of the Kashmir dispute since its inception to the present day, see Sumit Ganguly, *Conflict Unending: India-Pakistan Tensions Since 1947* (New York: Columbia University Press, and Washington, DC: Woodrow Wilson Center Press, 2001).

7. Much of the evidence presented here has been drawn from Ravi Tomar, *India-U.S. Relations in a Changing Strategic Environment,* Research Paper no. 20, 2001–02 (Canberra: Department of the Parliamentary Library, 2002).

8. See Colonel Steven B. Sboto, "India and U.S. Military Cooperation and Collaboration: Problems, Prospects and Implications," unpublished thesis (New Delhi: National Defense College, 2001).

9. Personal communication with Colonel Jack Gill, National Defense University, Washington, DC.

10. For a discussion of the concept of "forceful persuasion," see Alexander L. George, *Coercive Diplomacy: An Alternative to War* (Washington, DC: United States Institute of Peace, 1991).

11. V. Sudarshan, "Uncle Sam's Sly Sally," *Outlook* (Apr. 5, 2004): 44–45.

12. John Cherian, "A Shock from the West," *Frontline* 21, no. 8, available at www.frontlineonnet.com/fl2108/stories/20040423003803600.htm, accessed July 8, 2004.

13. Sumit Ganguly, "The Other Rogue Nation," *Current History* (Apr. 2004): 147–50.

14. Figures derived from Central Intelligence Agency sources.

15. U.S. Department of Commerce, *International Investment Data: U.S. Direct Investment Abroad: Capital Outflows,* available at www.commerce.gov, accessed May 2003.

16. For a discussion of the premise that "all good things go together" as a cardinal principle shaping American doctrines of foreign assistance and modernization, see Robert Packenham, *Liberal America and the Third World* (Princeton, NJ: Princeton University Press, 1973).

17. Much of this information has been derived from www.usaid.gov/locations/asia_near_east/, accessed May 2003.

18. See the discussion in Husain Haqqani, "America's New Alliance with Pakistan: Avoiding the Traps of the Past," *Policy Brief* (Washington, DC: Carnegie Endowment for International Peace, Oct. 19, 2002).

19. On this point, see Sumit Ganguly, "Pakistan's Slide into Misery: Explaining Half a Century of Misrule," *Foreign Affairs* 81, no. 6 (Nov./Dec. 2002).

8

The Revival of Geopolitics

U.S. Policies in Afghanistan and Central Asia

Conrad Schetter and Bernd Kuzmits

The terrorist attacks on the World Trade Center and the Pentagon on September 11, 2001, triggered a radical reassessment of the regional priorities of U.S. foreign policy. Afghanistan and its Taliban regime, which had disappeared almost completely from the international agenda in the 1990s, were suddenly identified as the most pressing security threats to the United States. Moreover, the Central Asian states in the north—Kazakhstan, Kyrgyzstan, Tajikistan, Turkmenistan, and Uzbekistan—were comprehended as a region, rather than a distant part of the Eurasian landmass. For Washington, much of this region was *terra incognita*: Whereas the United States had been involved in Afghanistan since the 1950s, relations between Washington and the Central Asian successors to the Soviet Union dated back only to the 1990s.

The drastic increase in the U.S. military presence in the region testifies to the importance Washington now attaches to Afghanistan and Central Asia. The Taliban, sheltering Usama Bin Laden and providing a safe haven for Al-Qaeda, was the first American target in the "war on terror" declared by U.S. president Bush soon after the September 11 attacks. "Enduring Freedom," the military intervention spearheaded by the United States in autumn 2002, drove the Taliban from power and paved the way for the deployment of 10,000 to 20,000 troops in the country to combat the remnants of Al-Qaeda and the Taliban. Simultaneously, Washington intensified its military presence and its political involvement in the post–Soviet Central Asian states. One important consequence of the events since September 11 is the shift in political perceptions of Afghanistan. Situated between the Middle East and South and Central Asia, Afghanistan is now generally perceived as part of Central Asia largely because Pakistan to the south and the east, which assisted the Taliban, has little influence on the new Afghan government, and Iran, which the U.S. still treats as a pariah state, acts as a barrier to the west.

While some justify U.S. involvement in this region by the need for security and to fight international terrorism, others argue that Washington used this argument as a pretext for securing longterm economic and geopolitical interests. Taking these contradictory assessments as a starting point, this chapter analyzes the motivations behind U.S. policies in the region. Are American policies inspired mainly by concerns about international terrorism and drug production and trafficking, or by the attraction of the region's large oil and gas deposits? What role does Central Asia's geopolitical location play as a pivot between Russia, China, Iran, and Pakistan—all politically significant countries for the United States? Finally, the chapter looks at the question of the compatibility between these interests and the normative objectives of U.S. foreign policy, such as the promotion of democracy and good governance.

To determine the effect of the terrorist attacks of September 11 on the quality and scope of U.S. policies toward Afghanistan and Central Asia we shall focus on the period between the early 1990s and 2004. While Operation Enduring Freedom was a watershed in recent Afghan history, the U.S. military presence in Central Asia only accelerated processes already underway. For this reason, we will examine different phases of American policy toward Afghanistan, focusing especially on September 11. By contrast, the analysis of U.S. policies in the Central Asian states will be broken down by policy field, such as security, energy, and development assistance. Before we explore recent American policies toward Afghanistan and Central Asia in greater detail, we shall briefly review the significance of the region for U.S. policy in the past.

The U.S. Presence in Afghanistan and Central Asia Before 1990

In the nineteenth century the region between the Indus and Syr Darya rivers was the theater of what became known as the "great game," the fierce rivalry between Russia and Britain for control of this region. This contest facilitated not only the geopolitical partition of one of the last white spots on the globe, but also the incorporation of this region into the international system. The region north of the Amu Darya was gradually annexed by Russia between 1861 and 1900, whereas to the south the state of Afghanistan evolved out of two Anglo-Afghan wars of 1838–42 and 1879 and agreements between British India and Russia in 1887 and 1893.[1] Afghanistan eventually gained its independence from British India after a third Anglo-Afghan war in 1921.

There were major shifts in the balance of power in the region in the first half of the twentieth century. In the decades following the 1917 Russian Revolution, rapid modernization strengthened the Soviet position in Central Asia.[2] In the second half of the twentieth century, the Iron Curtain cordoned off Central Asia from foreign influence until the collapse of the Soviet Union in 1991.

Another, scarcely less decisive change was the post–World War II decline of the British empire, reflected in the creation of the states of Pakistan and India in 1947 and ultimately the end of direct British influence in South and Central Asia. In Afghanistan the United States half-heartedly filled this gap from the late 1940s. During the Cold War, Washington courted the states along the southern fringe of the Soviet Union (Turkey, Iran, and Pakistan) in order to prevent Soviet expansion in the direction of the Indian Ocean. This coincided with American interests in shielding the oil-rich region of the Persian Gulf from Soviet influence. By the late 1970s, nearly 40 percent of the petroleum imports of the United States and an even greater proportion of those of Washington's European and East Asian allies came from the Gulf region.[3]

By ignoring the significance of Central Asia, the United States missed the chance to win Afghanistan as an ally in the late 1940s. American reluctance to provide military aid to Afghanistan was instrumental in Kabul's refusal to join the U.S.-engineered Baghdad Pact in 1955 and its decision to strengthen relations with the Soviet Union. However, by the late 1950s the United States had recognized Afghanistan's geostrategic importance and since then cooperated with the country in numerous ways.[4] Officially neutral, for two decades Afghanistan became one of the few countries in the world to receive substantial amounts of development aid from both the United States and the Soviet Union. American aid ended with the Soviet invasion of Afghanistan in 1979.[5]

The coup d'état of the People's Democratic Party of Afghanistan (PDPA) in 1978 and the Soviet military intervention in Afghanistan in late December 1979 placed the country at the forefront of world events. The Soviet occupation marked the end of the superpower détente of the 1970s and inaugurated a new phase in the arms race, which peaked in the Strategic Defense Initiative (SDI) of the Reagan administration in the 1980s.

In 1979, another cornerstone of U.S. security policy in the Middle East collapsed when the shah of Iran was overthrown in the Islamic revolution led by the Ayatollah Khomeini. In addition, relations with Pakistan had cooled after General Zia-ul-Haq's coup d'état in 1977. By 1980, there was a serious possibility that the United States would be forced to abandon its geopolitical priorities in the region, particularly its oil interests.[6]

In response to this dilemma, the Reagan administration devised a dual strategy: It sought to build up resistance against the Soviet forces and to destabilize the Soviet system by supporting religious radicalism in Central Asia.[7] This included mending ties with Pakistan, which emerged as the key ally of the United States in the region in the 1980s. By using Pakistan's military infrastructure, especially the Inter-Services Intelligence (ISI), Washington was able to counter Soviet influence by building up a proxy in the shape of Islamic guerrilla militias, the so-called mujahidin, who were regarded as highly motivated and believed to be fundamentally opposed to communism. In doing so, Washington unwittingly supported precisely those militant Islamists (including Usama Bin Laden and Gulbuddin Hikmatyar) identified today as the most serious security threat to the United States and the main obstacle to political reconstruction in Afghanistan.[8] Between 1980 and 1989, the United States channeled about $2 billion in money and weapons to the mujahidin; the same amount of support was provided by Saudi Arabia, a U.S. ally.[9] The United States also supplied the mujahidin with heavy military equipment, such as Stinger rockets, that they denied even to close allies.[10] For a while, U.S. support for the mujahidin appeared highly successful: the mujahidin not only denied the Soviets control of Afghanistan, they also tied down approximately 100,000 Soviet troops, thereby reducing the military presence of the Red Army in other strategic zones, such as Eastern Europe. Moreover, the protracted and expensive war in Afghanistan hastened the economic decline of the Soviet Union and contributed to discontent with the regime among the Soviet population.[11]

The major shortcoming of U.S. policy toward Afghanistan was

Washington's loss of interest in the country once its strategic and ideo-logical goals were achieved. After the withdrawal of the Soviet Army in 1988 and the breakup of the Soviet empire in 1989–90, the United States missed the opportunity to pressure the warring factions in Afghanistan to hold peace talks.[12] In the early 1990s, the Afghan War grew into a regional conflict driven largely by the interests of neighboring coun-tries, especially Iran and Pakistan.[13] The factional fighting destroyed the last vestiges of a functioning state and eventually led to the complete collapse of state structures.[14]

U.S. Policies in Afghanistan: Economic Interests, Human Rights, and Security Concerns

A review of U.S. policies in Afghanistan since the mid-1990s reveals several changes during the past decade. Up to 1996, Afghanistan fig-ured as one of the least important regions for the State Department, as reflected in the low profile the first Clinton administration assigned to the Taliban regime. This changed between 1996 and 2001, when Wash-ington launched actions of varying intensity. Finally, the military inter-vention in the aftermath of September 11 catapulted Afghanistan to the top of the U.S. foreign policy agenda. In the past decade U.S. policies toward Afghanistan have been driven by diverse interests and influ-enced by a variety of domestic pressure groups, including oil compa-nies, women's groups, and human rights advocates.

Favoring the Taliban

The reformulation of U.S. policy toward Afghanistan was pushed pri-marily by the U.S. oil industry, in particular Unocal Corporation, fol-lowing the discovery of sizeable gas fields near Daulatabad, south of Turkmenistan, in the early 1990s. Turkmenistan, which was completely dependent on the heavily used Russian pipeline system to export its natural gas, had been looking at alternative pipeline routes since the beginning of the 1990s. The most economical solution was to extend the Iranian pipeline system to the Turkmen gas fields. This option set alarm bells ringing in Washington, as since the 1980s one political priority of the United States in the region was to maintain the economic isolation of the Iranian regime. The United States made it clear to Turkmenistan that linking up with the Iranian pipeline system would provoke strong reactions. Aside from alternative routes, such as a pipeline via Baku to Ceyhan in Turkey (projected to be completed in 2005) and one via Kazakhstan to China, there was also a proposal for a pipeline through western and southern Afghanistan to the port of Gwadar in Pakistan.[15] In 1994, the Argentine Bridas company attempted to persuade the Taliban to build this pipeline, and in 1995 a consortium of Unocal and Delta Oil, a Saudi Arabian company, followed suit. Although Unocal had contacts with the Northern Alliance—a coalition of various political parties and warlords opposed to the Taliban—the company reportedly did not conceal its sympathies for the Taliban.[16] To win the support of the Taliban, Unocal allegedly spent between $15 and $20 million in the 1990s, including technical and office equipment, the erection of a vocational center to train Afghans in pipeline construction, and an invitation to Taliban leaders to visit the United States in November 1997.[17]

Aside from the involvement of American companies, the U.S. government itself showed considerable interest in the Taliban right from the time this movement was founded in late summer 1994. American diplomats frequently traveled to Kandahar to hold talks with Taliban leaders.[18] Nevertheless, it is difficult to establish the extent to which the United States supported the formation and rise of the Taliban. At the very least, Washington allowed its allies Pakistan and Saudi Arabia to provide the Taliban with logistic and financial support, and it tolerated the Taliban's rapid advance in Afghanistan and its entry into Kabul in September 1996. Immediately after the Taliban took Kabul, the State Department announced it was establishing diplomatic relations with the new government. The acting State Department spokesman Glyn Davies allegedly stated that the United States could see "nothing objectionable" in the version of Islamic law that the Taliban had imposed.[19] Two months later, Robin L. Raphael, the assistant secretary of state for South Asian affairs, conceded that there were international "misgivings" about the Taliban, but insisted on acknowledging the Taliban as an "indigenous" movement that had fought legitimately to "stay in power."[20]

Washington had several reasons to tolerate the rise of the Taliban in the Afghan struggle. It hoped the Taliban would restore order and stability to a fragmented, disordered, and conflict-riven country. The improvement in security was a prerequisite for the construction of the gas pipeline and the reduction in opium cultivation.[21] Opium production had increased dramatically since the beginning of the 1990s. By the mid-1990s,

Afghanistan was already the second largest producer of opium in the world.[22] The terrorist attack on the World Trade Center in 1993 and the ambushing of U.S. diplomats in Saudi Arabia and Pakistan in 1995 had caused the Pentagon to realize for the first time that Islamic terrorists were taking advantage of the power vacuum in Afghanistan to build up an infrastructure and training camps. Although the United States should have been suspicious of the proximity between the orthodox ideology of the Taliban and the Islamic radicalism of anti-American groups, it was precisely the religious beliefs of the Taliban that attracted the United States: The Sunni credo of the Taliban was seen as a counterweight to the Shiite revolutionary zeal of the Islamic Republic of Iran.[23]

Although the rise of the Taliban appeared to be in America's interest, Afghanistan was not a priority for the State Department. Worse perhaps, an overall strategy to pursue U.S. interests in the region was lacking.[24] Nor did the then U.S. secretary of state, Warren Christopher, mention Afghanistan in his speeches. In other words, the U.S. administration tacitly approved of the rise of the Taliban, but avoided any proactive moves.

Demonizing the Taliban

In 1997, several developments led to a marked deterioration in U.S. relations with the Taliban—a shift that has been described as turning "from unconditionally accepting the Taliban to unconditionally rejecting them."[25]

An important reason for the change in American attitudes toward the Taliban was U.S. domestic politics. From the mid-1990s onward, there was growing public condemnation of the Taliban in the United States. More than 300 women's rights groups, human rights groups, and labor groups critical of Taliban rule succeeded in making the public aware of the relationship between the State Department and the Taliban.[26] By mid-1996, Congress had placed the Taliban on its agenda. The Senate eventually passed a resolution that assigned top priority to the resolution of the Afghan War.[27]

In 1997, after Madeleine Albright took over from Warren Christopher as secretary of state, the State Department also abandoned its erstwhile pro-Taliban course. Many analysts believe that the biography of Madeleine Albright, who fled from the Nazis as well as the communists as a child, had an impact on the increasingly negative attitude of the

State Department toward the Taliban.[28] In August 1997 the State Department ordered the closure of the Afghan embassy in Washington and a few months later, in November 1997, Mrs. Albright unequivocally rejected the Taliban during a visit to an Afghan refugee camp in Pakistan: "I think it is very clear why we are opposed to the Taliban. Because of their approach to human rights, their despicable treatment of women and children, and their general lack of respect for human dignity . . . that is more reminiscent of the past than of the future."[29]

Besides the human rights violations of the Taliban, other developments in the region also influenced the new Afghanistan policies of the United States. One was the temporary improvement in relations between the United States and Iran following Mohammad Khatami's victory in the Iranian presidential elections in May 1997. Another was the realization that—contrary to initial expectations—under Taliban rule opium production had increased drastically and Afghanistan had become a haven for militant Islamists from all over the world.[30] Finally, the rout of the Taliban in Mazar-i Sharif in late May 1997 convinced political analysts that the Taliban was incapable of bringing the whole country under its control. This insight also gained ground within Unocal. In addition, owing to the Taliban's repression of women, not only feminist organizations but also Unocal shareholders pressured the company to give up its pipeline project.[31] However, it was not until December 1998 that Unocal withdrew from the pipeline project, a decision it took after the terrorist attacks on the U.S. embassies in Dar es Salaam and Nairobi, which prompted the U.S. government to launch missile attacks against training camps of Usama Bin Laden in eastern Afghanistan in August 1998.

The terrorist attacks spurred another radical change in U.S. policy toward Afghanistan. Hitherto, the United States had attempted to promote peace talks between the Taliban and the Northern Alliance.[32] The terrorist attacks not only caused the United States to abandon attempts to mediate in the Afghan conflict, but also to place Afghanistan at top of its list of so-called rogue states and to make the surrender of Usama Bin Laden a top priority.[33] The U.S. government imposed unilateral sanctions against the Taliban in July 1999 and got the UN to pass a resolution on October 15, 1999, calling on the Taliban to hand over Usama Bin Laden. UN Resolution 1333 of December 19, 2000, called for the complete isolation of the Taliban regime. Apart from these diplomatic endeavors to put pressure on the Taliban, the United States sought to negotiate the extradition of Usama Bin Laden with the Taliban.

War on Terror

The terrorist attacks of September 11, 2001, catapulted Afghanistan to the forefront of international politics. Immediately after the attacks the United States organized under its leadership a broad coalition against terrorism, including the European Union, Russia, and Pakistan. First, the United States made several attempts to persuade the Taliban regime to extradite Usama Bin Laden and other suspected terrorists hiding in the country. The uncooperative attitude of the Taliban and its disregard of the U.S. ultimatum of September 20, 2001, provoked the UN Security Council into authorizing a military "war on terror." The Security Council ruling enabled the United States to legitimize military intervention in Afghanistan by stressing the right to "self-defense" laid down in Article 2, paragraph 2, of the UN Charter. The UN thus provided the "collective legitimacy" for a war that otherwise could be interpreted as a unilateral U.S. military intervention.[34] The United States, assisted by coalition forces, began its military operation Enduring Freedom in Afghanistan on October 7, 2001, and expelled the Taliban from Kabul on November 12. The last Taliban stronghold, Kandahar, fell barely a month later.[35]

To minimize U.S. casualties, the U.S. army restricted its military operations to air raids and certain missions by Special Forces and agents of the Central Intelligence Agency (CIA).[36] The war on the ground was executed by the so-called Northern Alliance, a coalition of Afghan anti-Taliban militias that received financial, military, and logistic support from the United States and Great Britain.[37] This proved to be a double-edged strategy: After the collapse of the Taliban regime precisely the same warlords that were responsible for civil war and atrocities in the first half of the 1990s divided up the country into petty dominions and impeded any attempt at state-building.[38] To date, the warlords control the bulk of the country, while the governance capacity of the Afghan Transition Administration (ATA) hardly runs beyond Kabul.[39] Even though U.S. secretary of defense Donald Rumsfeld declared on May 1, 2003, that the war in Afghanistan was all but over, U.S. military operations involving between 5,000 and 10,000 Special Forces continue the search for remnants of the Taliban and Al-Qaeda in southern and eastern Afghanistan.[40] The U.S. strategy of deploying a network of small, mixed civilian and military provincial reconstruction teams (PRTs) in Afghanistan, especially in the southern and eastern regions, indicates that the

U.S. government is aware that the "war on terror" will be protracted and that military operations in Afghanistan will continue for a number of years.[41]

Contrary to the UN and most member states of the European Union, the United States understands its involvement in Afghanistan primarily as a contribution to an ongoing "war on terror." Donald Rumsfeld made this clear in a speech on August 16, 2002, stating that "it is up to other countries to do more" and that "nation-building is something that Washington is not prepared to undertake."[42] Nonetheless, the United States has made substantial efforts in connection with the reconstruction of Afghanistan. By doing so, it aims to demonstrate to global public opinion, especially in the Islamic world, that the "war on terror" goes hand in hand with the economic and political reconstruction of Afghanistan and works to alleviate poverty in that country.[43] Moreover, to satisfy U.S. domestic pressure groups such as women's rights and human rights groups the intervention needs to make clear that the general situation of the Afghan people, and particularly of women, has improved and that human rights and democracy remain priorities in Afghanistan. The Afghanistan Freedom Support Act of the U.S. Congress underlines the commitment of the United States to stability, security, reconstruction, and democratic development in Afghanistan. This commitment is also reflected in the fact that the United States provided approximately half of the total $4.4 billion in reconstruction assistance for Afghanistan between 2001 and 2005. This makes the United States the largest donor for Afghanistan. Support and commitment were also demonstrated by several invitations from the White House to Afghan president Hamid Karzai in the past three years and his attendance at President Bush's State of the Union speech on January 29, 2002.

Besides humanitarian assistance and infrastructure projects, the United States has concentrated on certain strategic fields of reconstruction. In order to transfer anti-terrorist military operations to the Afghan army while retaining control over security matters, the United States gives high priority to rebuilding and training the security forces, particularly the Afghan army.[44] In the political domain, Washington was keen to install Afghans with strong pro-American sentiments as key ministers of the ATA, which assumed power on December 22, 2001. Several ministers of the first Afghan government were U.S. citizens. The United States also provided nearly every ministry with a U.S. Afghan as political adviser. The recruitment of political personnel focused on Afghans, mainly Pashtuns, who had studied at American universities or worked for U.S. companies, notably Unocal.[45] Whereas initially former leaders of the Northern Alliance (e.g., Mohammad Fahim, Yunis Qanuni) were largely responsible for formulating Afghan government policies, the appointment of U.S.-backed experts to key positions in the Afghan government has enabled American Afghans to increasingly assume this role since mid-2003.

Similarly, the Afghan government's policy agenda was strongly influenced by the United States. Thus, on the initiative of the UN and the United States, Hamid Karzai was accepted as president of the ATA at the Bonn peace talks in November–December 2003, although the delegation of the royalist Rome group, with which Karzai was officially affiliated, refused to accept him as a candidate.[46] Furthermore, the schedule of the Afghan peace process mapped out at the Bonn talks was influenced by domestic U.S. politics: President George Bush has pressed for the Afghan presidential election to be held before the American presidential elections in November 2004, since the Bush administration needs success to justify the "war on terror," which events in Iraq increasingly call into question. By contrast, nearly all political advisers agreed that the Afghan elections would hardly be fair and free, and involve the risk of destabilizing Afghanistan.[47] Another event that clearly demonstrated American influence was the Emergency Loya Jirga held in June 2002. During the meeting, Zalmay Khalilzad, the special presidential envoy and ambassador to Afghanistan, persuaded Zahir Shah, the former king, not to stand for the presidency but to endorse Hamid Karzai.[48] Although the United States has exercised a strong influence on the process of political reconstruction, it remains to be seen whether it has a genuine interest in nation-building and in establishing a fully functioning state or whether it is satisfied with the rule of U.S.-allied warlords and the maintenance of a weak central state.[49]

American involvement in Afghanistan is also an acknowledgement of the geostrategic importance of the country. Iran in particular, one of the states of the "axis of evil," faces the problem of being sandwiched between pro-American governments in Afghanistan and Iraq. Pakistan, which many experts view as a time bomb owing to its high potential for conflict (e.g., nuclear weapons, militant Islamists, and the Kashmir conflict) is within reach of U.S. troops based in Afghanistan. The American military presence in Afghanistan may even prove a long-term asset in the containment of China. Thus, even if the "war on terror" should lose its relevance, it is unlikely that the United States will willingly with-draw its troops from Afghanistan.[50] Especially the air base at Bagram, north of Kabul, is an ideal command center for military operations throughout the region.

Finally, it should be mentioned that renewed interest by Unocal has revived the project of a pipeline through Afghanistan. Not surprisingly, Hamid Karzai visited Turkmenistan and Pakistan in the early months of his presidency to initiate a new round of talks.[51] In December 2002, Afghanistan, Turkmenistan, and Pakistan signed a framework agree-ment for a $3.2 billion gas pipeline project, which is supposed to be built by Unocal.

U.S. Involvement in Post–Soviet Central Asia

September 11 was also a crucial date in the short history of U.S. rela-tions with the post-Soviet states of Central Asia. But it is debatable whether the military entry of the United States on the Central Asian stage was a turning point in this history or merely a logical consequence of an ongoing process. According to some observers, U.S. interest in the new Central Asian states was fairly marginal in the immediate after-math of the collapse of the Soviet Union.[52] Although by mid-March 1992 the United States had become the first country to establish embassies in all five newly independent states, the first Clinton administration in par-ticular hesitated to promote collaboration for fear of alienating Russia by operating in its sphere of interest known as the "near abroad." The United States abandoned such reservations in the wake of September 11, the shock waves of which placed Central Asia firmly on America's map of the world.[53]

Other observers believe that the region may have changed less after the attacks in New York and Washington, DC, than a cursory glance suggests. First, even before the attacks Russia's influence in the region was gradually but steadily weakening, while America's was on the rise.[54] Second, there was a U.S. military presence in the region before Septem-ber 11, albeit in the form of the NATO Partnership for Peace Program (PfP).[55] However, the fundamental shift in the geopolitical landscape in the aftermath of September 11 caused the United States to redefine its strategic priorities, which meant for most Central Asian states closer cooperation both qualitatively and quantitatively—predominantly in military affairs. As Assistant Secretary of Defense J.D. Crouch stated in testimony in June 2002, the military relationships with each Central Asian nation "have matured on a scale not imaginable prior to September 11."[56] Uzbekistan, and to a lesser degree Kyrgyzstan, Tajikistan, and Kazakhstan emerged as key frontline partners in America's war on terrorism and served as crucial military platforms for Operation Enduring Freedom. It is the military necessities of the war in Afghanistan and the geostrategic position of Central Asia that have contributed most to making the region a security priority for the United States. Moreover, it has given the United States the opportunity to leave a footprint in the region that will be visible for a long time.

For the moment, Uzbekistan is America's main military partner in Central Asia. The United States has about 1,000 troops in Uzbekistan, primarily at the former Soviet Khanabad air base near the town of Kharshi. Another 700 personnel are based at Manas, Kyrgyzstan. Officially, there are no U.S. troops in Tajikistan, but the government has guaranteed overflight rights to the United States. The same applies to Kazakhstan, which also provides territorial access for logistical transfers.[57] Turkmenistan, the state with the largest and most strategically positioned facility in Central Asia—the former Soviet air base at Mary— is the only Central Asian state to have adopted a policy of neutrality and officially avoided becoming a member of the Enduring Freedom coalition.[58] While providing overflight rights for humanitarian missions, the Turkmen leadership has refrained from offering any form of combat support to the United States and the coalition forces.

U.S. involvement in Central Asia before September 11 was motivated by security issues such as nuclear proliferation and energy security and— to a lesser extent—the promotion of regional stability through development aid and fostering democratization. A more discreet objective of U.S. involvement should not be neglected: the prevention of Russian or Chinese hegemony in the region.

Security Concerns

In the immediate aftermath of the Soviet breakup, U.S. policies toward Central Asia centered on security relations with Kazakhstan largely as a result of concerns about the country's nuclear arsenal. In December 1993, the United States and Kazakhstan signed a cooperative threat reduction (CTR) agreement to dismantle and destroy 104 SS-18 missiles. In 1995, the last of about 1,040 nuclear warheads had been removed from the missiles and transferred to Russia. Kazakhstan announced that it was free of nuclear weapons. In 1995, the U.S.-Kazakh defense relationship was expanded to deepen cooperation on nuclear security and defense conversion. The potential proliferation of raw material for the production of weapons of mass destruction posed another crucial security concern that shaped U.S. policy and led to the signing of a CTR agreement with Uzbekistan in 1999.[59] Core objectives of CTR funding included the dismantling and decontamination of arms production facilities, and the retraining of scientists and their employment in peaceful research.[60]

Security cooperation between the United States and the Central Asian republics was gradually extended during the 1990s. By mid-1994, all Central Asian states except Tajikistan had joined NATO's PfP. Tajikistan decided to join well before September 11, but signed accords on admission only in February 2002. Since 1995, Central Asian officers and troops have participated in exercises in the United States within the framework of PfP, and U.S. troops have participated in joint exercises in Central Asia since 1997. In the same year, the Pentagon allocated Central Asia as an area of responsibility to the Central Command (CENTCOM)—a significant shift in contingency planning that was viewed with concern in Moscow.[61] Reportedly, pre–September 11 ties included Uzbek permission for secret U.S. operations against Al-Qaeda in Afghanistan.[62] In 2000, Uzbekistan also became the first recipient of a sizeable transfer of military equipment under the Foreign Military Financing (FMF) program.[63] This measure was taken against the background of, and probably influenced by, reports that insurgents were gaining ground in the Fergana Valley and bomb attacks in Tashkent in 1999, allegedly carried out by the Islamic Movement of Uzbekistan (IMU). Both events raised fears of an Islamist threat to political stability.

The attacks of September 11 focused attention on the dangers inherent in the region's longterm susceptibility to Islamic fundamentalist movements and the possibility that one or more of the Central Asian states might fragment or fail and become the "next Afghanistan." By referring to both the Islamic Movement in Uzbekistan and Al-Qaeda in his address to Congress on September 20, 2001, President Bush made it clear that Central Asia's primary relevance to U.S. security planning lay in its dual utility as a possible haven for terrorists as well as a launching pad for anti-terrorist operations.[64]

Drug money supposedly makes up the lion's share of the income of Islamist and terrorist groups.[65] While Afghanistan is the world's largest

Table 8.1

Proven and Potential Reserves of Oil and Natural Gas in the Caspian Basin and in Saudi Arabia (respectively, the Persian Gulf)

	Caspian Basin		Saudi Arabia	
	Proven	Potential	Proven	Potential
Oil (billion barrels)	32	186	264	Up to 1 trillion
Gas (trillion cubic feet)	232	560	224.7[a]	Persian Gulf 1.923[b]

Sources: United States Energy Information Administration. Caspian Sea: Key Oil and Gas Statistics, August 2003, available at www.eia.doe.gov/emeu/cabs/caspstats.html; Saudi Arabia Country Analysis Brief, December 2003, available at www.eia.doe.gov/emeu/cabs/saudi.html, accessed July 3, 2004.

[a]Ranking fourth in the world (after Russia, Iran, and Qatar).
[b]Includes Iran and Qatar (s. 1).

producer of opium, the five Central Asian states are heavily involved in the shipment of drugs.[66] Destroying opium crops in Afghanistan and blocking smuggling routes will likely take higher priority in the medium term, as the United States looks beyond immediate stability operations and the pursuit of leading terrorists.

Energy Security

During the 1990s, Washington's primary interest in greater Central Asia apart from nuclear non-proliferation concerned energy security. However, the energy potential of the Caspian region was greatly exaggerated.[67] These misperceptions together with unresolved conflicts over the status of the Caspian Sea and the routing of pipelines have revived the geopolitical myth of the "great game."[68] Recent figures and estimates of the U.S. Energy Information Administration (EIA) on the proven and potential reserves of oil and gas in the Caspian Basin show that although it may become an important source of natural gas, it does not have the potential to alter the prominence of the gulf states in oil exports (Table 8.1).[69]

Nevertheless, it is U.S. policy to diversify sources of oil, not only for itself but also for other oil importers, as U.S. policy toward the Taliban and Unocal's involvement in Afghanistan prior to 1997 made clear. Reducing dependency on any one particular region decreases the possibility that political upheaval in one country or region will significantly affect oil supplies and trigger a global economic crisis. The switch to exporters outside the Organization of Petroleum Exporting Countries (OPEC) could weaken OPEC's monopoly, thereby enhancing influence on oil-pricing policies and ultimately contributing to lower oil prices. Moreover, American firms are among the world's largest oil producers, and their interests in developing and exporting Caspian energy resources coincide with the U.S. desire to increase the world's sources of oil.

The terrorist strikes against the World Trade Center and the Pentagon confirmed the view that the Caspian Basin contained fewer security risks than other parts of Eurasia. However, missing differentiations persist, as illustrated by the failure to distinguish properly between the Caucasus and Central Asia—both the State Department and the Office of the Secretary of Defense continue to lump Central Asia and the Caucasus together under a single deputy assistant secretary and office director, respectively.[70] But the prominent role played by Uzbekistan—a state marginal to considerations of Caspian energy wealth—in the wake of September 11 underscored the decreasing relevance of energy as a security issue and the eastward shift of the focal point of Eurasian security dynamics. Similarly, development aid to stabilize the Central Asian states and to prevent a "second Afghanistan" also gained in importance.

Development Assistance

U.S. assistance to the Central Asian states is regulated by the Freedom Support Act (FSA) of 1992, the Silk Road Strategy Act of 1999, and bilateral agreements.[71] While the FSA initially focused on humanitarian aid, and promoted nuclear demilitarization, market reforms, and democratization in the successor states of the Soviet Union, the Silk Road Strategy Act sought to provide additional aid for conflict resolution, border controls, and economic and civil society development in the Caucasus and Central Asia. In other words, U.S. politicians were concerned about security threats emanating from "Eurasia's volatile South" well before September 11.[72] However, the scope of assistance was moderate compared to the countries' needs. Parallel to Operation Enduring Freedom, U.S. assistance was boosted both in quality and amount (Table 8.2). Central Asian presidents became familiar faces at the White House. In December 2001 U.S. president George W. Bush and Kazakh president Nursultan Nazarbaev agreed to a strategic partnership, and in March

2002, U.S. secretary of state Colin Powell and Uzbek foreign minister Adulaziz Kamilov went a step further by signing a five-point Strategic Partnership and Cooperation Framework Agreement according to which the United States undertakes to "regard with grave concern any external threat to the security and territorial integrity of the Republic of Uzbekistan."[73] The document also lays out fairly specific goals that the United States and Uzbekistan aim to work to achieve jointly, including building a strong and open civil society, establishing a genuine multi-party system and independent media, strengthening non-governmental structures, and improving the judicial system.

If in the first few months of the war on terrorism the Central Asian leaders had hoped that "coffers of foreign assistance from Washington would be placed at their feet," they soon lost their illusions about how much U.S. aid to expect.[74] There has been a dramatic increase in U.S. foreign assistance, but it still represents a fraction of these states' needs. As Table 8.2 shows, most of the funding has been directed toward security, which at best enables these countries to begin a decades long process of rebuilding their military and security forces. In 2003, all countries except Kazakhstan experienced a dramatic decline in aid to levels recorded prior to the war on terrorism. This decline can be attributed to several factors.

The first is related to geopolitical developments: U.S. military attention quickly shifted to Iraq, and Operation Iraqi Freedom absorbed huge resources. Second, the United States has not yet developed a coherent strategy toward the Central Asian states in general and Uzbekistan in particular. Alongside Operation Enduring Freedom, the U.S. seems to have pursued an ad hoc, "band-aid" approach toward Central Asia.[75] As none of the Central Asian leaders has been willing to improve human rights and democracy in his countries, the initial enthusiasm that marked the strategic partnerships has cooled considerably. Uzbek president Islam Karimov in particular is suspected of paying mere lip service to major elements of the 2002 agreement. The Rose Revolution in Georgia that swept away President Eduard Shevardnadze has put Central Asian rulers on their guard against a similar fate. In these circumstances it is unlikely that these leaders will voluntarily introduce greater democracy. Furthermore, there are serious doubts about whether the money is being spent efficiently and concerns that funds are being siphoned off into the pockets of senior leaders and their networks.[76] Reacting with greater caution and suspicion, Congress has tied further support to stricter

Table 8.2

U.S. Assistance to Central Asia (in millions of dollars)

Central Asian country	Cumulative obligations FY 1992–2002	Cumulative obligations FY 2001[a]	FY 2002 budgeted		FY 2003 budgeted	
Kazakhstan	886	75.5	Security and law enforcement	41.6	Security and law enforcement	49.2
			Market reforms	14.0	Economic and social reforms	23.4
			Social services	6.0		
			Democracy programs[b]	13.7	Democracy programs	13.9
			Community development	11.5	Cross-sectoral initiatives	5.0
			Humanitarian assistance	3.2	Humanitarian assistance	0.5
			Total	90.0	Total	92.0
Kyrgyzstan	634	36.7	Security and law enforcement	37.4	Security and law enforcement	10.3
			Market reforms	17.6	Economic and social reforms	19.9
			Social services	11.7		
			Democracy programs	16.1	Democracy programs	13.5
			Community development	6.0	Cross-sectoral initiatives	3.8
			Humanitarian assistance	6.2	Humanitarian assistance	9.1
			Total	95.0	Total	56.6
Tajikistan	508	67.4	Security and law enforcement	21.5	Security and law enforcement	1.1
			Market reforms	9.4	Economic and social reforms	14.3
			Social services	12.2		
			Democracy programs	12.4	Democracy programs	7.3
			Community development	10.4	Cross-sectoral initiatives	4.5
			Humanitarian assistance	75.6	Humanitarian assistance	21.8
			Total	141.5	Total	49.0

Country		Category		Category	
Turkmenistan	218	13.7	Security and law enforcement	8.0	Security and law enforcement	1.4
			Market reforms	0.9	Economic and social reforms	2.4
			Social services	1.8		
			Democracy programs	5.2	Democracy programs	4.7
			Community development	1.7	Cross-sectoral initiatives	2.1
			Humanitarian assistance	0.5	Humanitarian assistance	0.5
			Total	18.1	Total	11.1
Uzbekistan	508	54.7	Security and law enforcement	79.0	Security and law enforcement	30.2
			Market reforms	10.9	Economic and social reforms	18.2
			Social services	45.5		
			Democracy programs	26.2	Democracy programs	14.7
			Community development	5.5	Cross-sectoral initiatives	4.5
			Humanitarian assistance	52.7	Humanitarian assistance	8.5
			Total	219.8	Total	86.1
Totals	2,754	248.0		564.4		294.8

Sources:: Martha Brill Olcott, "Taking Stock of Central Asia," in *Journal of International Affairs* 56, no. 2 (Spring 2003): 15; Jim Nicol, *Central Asia's New States. Political Developments and Implications for U.S. Interests.* Issue Brief for Congress. Congress Research Service. The Library of Congress. Updated April 1, 2003, p. 16; and U.S. Department of State. Bureau of European and Eurasian Affairs, *Fact Sheets on U.S. Assistance to Central Asia,* available at www.state.gov/p/eur/rls/fs/29487pf.htm, accessed July 19, 2004.

[a]*Freedom Support Act,* other Function 150 funds, and Agency funds. Function 150 is the International Affairs category of the Federal Budget, which includes funding for the programs and activities of four cabinet departments, seven independent agencies, three foundations, and numerous other international organizations.

[b]Democracy Programs vary from academic and professional exchanges to projects that support independent media, political parties, and nongovernmental organizations (NGOs). For more detailed information, please refer to the 2004 Fact Sheets on U.S. Assistance to Central Asia, Bureau of European and Eurasian Affairs; U.S. Department of State.

conditions. Unless Uzbekistan and Kazakhstan show substantial and continuing progress on human rights, democratization, and economic reforms, the first "war on terror" allies could face a mandatory cutoff of direct foreign aid. This step would enable the United States to circumvent the credibility trap in the "war of ideas" and avoid the "Pahlavi effect," that is, losing face when unpopular leaders to which the United States has given unconditional support lose power.[77] It is a common complaint in the Arab and Muslim world that the United States exhibits double standards by promoting democracy and human rights on the one hand, while supporting regimes that repress their own people and deny them basic political and civil rights on the other hand. U.S. interests in oil and other raw materials as well as America's demands for military bases and access are viewed as undermining Washington's declared concern for democracy and human rights, thus showing up the United States as the ultimate hypocrite. On the other hand, strategic considerations could force Washington to accept trade-offs rather than upset its major Central Asian partner.[78] President Islam Karimov responded to American calls for democratization by closing the Tashkent office of the U.S.-based NGO Open Society Institute in April 2004.[79] The Strategic Partnership Treaty Karimov signed with Russia in June 2004 may also be taken as indicative of his disappointment with the results of his policy of closer relations with the West.[80]

Central Asian Reorientation Toward Russia and China?

If Operation Enduring Freedom was a marriage of convenience between the United States and its new Central Asian allies, different perceptions of democratization, economic reform, and Operation Iraqi Freedom soon put an end to the honeymoon. Recent agreements with Russia and China reflect growing disenchantment with U.S. policy in Central Asia and signal the Central Asian leaders' intentions of moving from a pro-Western to a so-called multidirectional foreign policy:

- The aforementioned Strategic Partnership Treaty between Uzbekistan and Russia seeks to enhance political and military cooperation and strengthen economic ties.
- Economic cooperation quickly moved to center stage when Lukoil, Russia's largest oil company, and Uzbekneftegaz, Uzbekistan's national oil and gas company, signed a thirty-five-year, $1 billion

production sharing agreement to develop the Kandym gas field. Furthermore, Gazprom, the Russian state-owned gas monopoly, plans to invest $1 billion to develop gas-condensate fields in the Ustyurt region.[81]

- Also in June 2004, the China National Petroleum Corporation (CNPC) and Uzbekneftegaz signed an agreement to develop a closer partnership to survey and drill for oil and gas.
- Russian president Vladimir Putin and his Tajik counterpart Imomali Rakhmonov entered into a swap arrangement in June 2004. In exchange for Moscow writing off approximately $300 million in debt, Tajikistan granted Russia the rights to the Nurek space surveillance center. In addition, Russian companies will participate in the development of Tajik hydroelectric projects, and Russian border guards will continue to guard Tajikistan's frontier with Afghanistan until at least 2006.
- During the summit of the Shanghai Cooperation Organization (SCO) in Tashkent in mid-June 2004, China offered to provide member states (Russia and all Central Asian states except Turkmenistan) with $900 million in loans and trade credits.
- In October 2003, the Russian airbase at Kant, Kyrgyzstan was officially opened.[82] Up to 500 Russian personnel and over twenty combat aircraft will be stationed at the base, which will serve as the staging area for a rapid deployment force under the aegis of the Collective Security Treaty Organization (CSTO), a partnership between Russia, Armenia, Belarus, Kazakhstan, Kyrgyzstan, and Tajikistan that has evolved out of security treaties signed by the six countries as members of the Commonwealth of Independent States (CIS).

A multidirectional foreign policy, which seeks to exploit perceived opportunities with a view to promoting a regional balance of power through ties with the regional powers Russia and China, while pragmatically cooperating with the United States, has been the official stance of the Kazakh government since independence. It could prove to be the preferred approach of the political leaders in the region, as it would enable them to revive relations with Russia and China, which are unlikely to demand improvements in human rights and democratization.

Russia still suspects that Washington seeks to undermine its few remaining positions of power, and sees evidence of this in the expansion

of NATO (of which the Baltic states are now members); the launching
of a missile defense program and the withdrawal from the Anti-Ballistic
Missile (ABM) Treaty; the war against Iraq; and single-minded U.S.
support for the Baku-Ceyhan pipeline, which will carry oil from
Azerbaijan (and perhaps eventually Kazakhstan) to Turkey, circumvent-
ing Russia. With bases in Khanabad and Manas, America has also established its power on Russia's southern flank.[83]

Ironically, thus, relationships between most of the Central Asian states
and Moscow are today better than they were before the United States
opened bases in the region. Russian president Putin has sought to make
a virtue out of necessity, working to redefine the Kremlin's relationships with the United States and its near neighbors in Central Asia. With
regard to the United States, Putin hopes to benefit from a general co-
operativeness, the payoff for which is expected in the shape of arms
control, economic assistance, better relations with NATO, and a more
understanding American attitude toward the war in Chechnya. Unlike
his predecessor, President Putin bases his policy toward Central Asia
not on an imperial approach, but on a public show of respect. For the
foreseeable future, Russia will not have the means to dominate the
region as it did during the Soviet era. But it will retain important influence because of its near-monopoly on pipeline routes out of Central
Asia and because of its importance as a migrant labor market for many
Central Asians.

The "war on terror," particularly in Afghanistan and Central Asia,
provided a limited basis for cooperation between Washington and Beijing,
while the "persistent, underlying sources of contention" between them
have not changed significantly.[84] Over the last two years, the Sino-American relationship has remained curiously disaggregated. At one level,
Washington and Beijing have emphasized their common interests in the
region and been at pains to profess their appreciation of each other in a
way that stretches credibility. On another and more fundamental level,
both are aware that their perspectives and interests continue to diverge.[85]
Beijing views the U.S. National Security Strategy of September 2002
with suspicion, welcoming neither the many references to Washington's
leadership role in the international system, nor its mention of the need
to build "a balance of power favoring human freedom," which Beijing
interprets as a reference to China's authoritarian political system.[86]

On the other hand, the Chinese leadership had an obvious interest in
joining the U.S.-led coalition against terrorism, as it is increasingly

worried about linkages between Al-Qaeda elements in Afghanistan and Islamist radicals and separatists in Xinjiang, an energy-rich province adjoining Central Asia, whose indigenous people, the Turkic-Mongol Uighurs, are culturally and ethnically closer to Central Asians than to Han Chinese. Therefore, Chinese leaders have made the suppression of Uighur separatist movements a focal point of their security-related relations with Xinjiang's immediate neighbors (Kazakhstan and Kyrgyzstan).

Despite some nervousness about China's interests, there is great admiration among Central Asian leaders for their Chinese colleagues' ability to achieve high rates of economic growth while keeping the country under tight political control.[87] The Chinese have established a major trading presence throughout the region, though this is not always reflected in official statistics that record their share of trade. Chinese "access" to Central Asia can be expected to continue, assuming that Chinese economic and political power continues to grow. The opening of U.S. bases in the region has done little to challenge China's confidence that its regional influence will steadily increase, a view not yet contested by Russia. On the contrary, long before September 11, a common security interest in Central Asia had already led to closer Sino-Russian relations.

The U.S.-led "war on terror" gave Russia and China a pretext to reinvigorate the Shanghai Cooperation Organization (SCO), a nascent cooperation forum, founded at the instigation of Russia and China and consisting of the two regional powers and Kazakhstan, Kyrgyzstan, Tajikistan, and Uzbekistan.[88] The member countries have pledged themselves to combat terrorism, extremism, and separatism. Joint anti-terrorist maneuvers between Chinese, Kyrgyz, Kazakh, and Russian forces in autumn 2003 sought to broaden the SCO's security dimension. Advocates envisage the forum developing beyond security to provide a promising framework for trade and cultural relations, thereby becoming "the region's authoritative voice."[89] The group could emerge as a powerful regional player if the organization develops an autonomous structure and is not exploited as a mouthpiece for the two most powerful members. Two permanent institutions, a secretariat in Beijing and an anti-terror office in Tashkent, give the SCO an organizational structure.[90] In the first years of its existence, Western observers and politicians did not pay much attention to the SCO, as the organization's efforts were modest, and all Central Asian leaders paid lip service to regional cooperation, without producing any results.[91]

But the SCO's summit in Tashkent in June 2004—or rather, the various behind-the-scenes agreements (see above)—provided a new thrust for the future development of regional cooperation. The anti-terror office was officially opened and a willingness to improve cooperation was signaled by inviting the Afghan president Hamid Karzai to attend as a guest—evidence that the group's common interest is still the fight against terrorism. Given this basis for cooperation, the United States will probably watch developments in the SCO more closely or even seek observer status with the organization.

To summarize: The military presence of the United States has considerably curtailed political options for Russia and China in Central Asia on the one hand. On the other hand, this geopolitical objective is not a major motivation for a prolonged presence. Russia and China will remain regional powers trying to extend their zones of influence, while the Central Asian leaders will pragmatically try to take advantage of rivalries and interests among the major powers. However, topics of common concern, like the war against terrorism, will require more intensive cooperation.

Conclusion

Central Asia, including Afghanistan, has very often been a meeting point of world politics, an area where interests clashed and "great games" were played. But a "new great game" is an inappropriate label for contemporary politics involving a new player, the United States. First, the resources of fossil fuels in the Caspian Basin are not extensive enough to justify such terminology. Second, the reason for the enhanced U.S. presence in the region still unifies major powers. For this reason, the military aspect of the "war on terror" is central to U.S. relations with Afghanistan and Central Asia for the moment. In the near future, with the approach of Bases Realignment and Closing (BRAC) in 2005 and the reallocation of responsibility for rebuilding Afghanistan, the United States is likely to restructure rather than reduce its presence, as it will want to preserve its ability to respond quickly in the "war on terror," especially the pursuit of terrorists in Afghanistan.

To achieve these goals, the United States will be forced to cooperate with some awkward partners. Russia and China have their own specific agendas in the region, but are probably aware of their limited capabilities to provide security. The Afghan government is completely dependent on America's presence and development aid, as it still lacks the monopoly of power and administrative capacity to run the country. A sudden withdrawal of the U.S. troops would jeopardize the existence of the Afghan government. For this reason, the Afghan government will not question the U.S. agenda on Afghanistan. The relationship between the United States and the Central Asian states is different. Central Asia's authoritarian leaders seek to take advantage of their countries' exposed position in the "war on terror." They are unlikely to democratize, fearing instability and the loss of power. The United States risks a conflict of goals structurally similar to the quandaries of the Cold War period, albeit with different consequences. Development aid in the region intended to promote liberalization, democratization, and the strengthening of human rights could alienate allies in the "war on terror." But without these objectives, the "war of ideas" will definitely be lost. Aside from the operational problems and risks, there is no strong domestic lobby for a U.S. presence in Central Asia. There will be little support among the American public for protracted involvement in the messy affairs of distant Central Asian states—and without this support, it will be hard to sustain any policy that implies material costs, setbacks, frustration, and the loss of American lives.

Notes

1. Hermann Kreutzmann, "Vom 'Great Game' zum 'Clash of Civilizations': Wahrnehmung und Wirkung von Imperialpolitik und Grenzziehungen in Zentralasien," *Petermanns Geographische Mitteilungen* 141, no. 3 (1997): 163–85.

2. Andreas Kappeler, *Russland als Vielvölkerreich: Entstehung, Geschichte, Zerfall* (Munich: C.H. Beck, 1993).

3. U.S. Congress, Office of Technology Assessment, *U.S. Oil Import Vulnerability: The Technical Replacement Capability,* OTA-E-503 (Washington, DC: U.S. Government Printing Office, October 1991), p. 38.

4. Leon B. Poullada and Leila D.J. Poullada, *The Kingdom of Afghanistan and the United States, 1828–1973* (Lincoln, NE: Dageforde, 1995).

5. Conrad Schetter, *Kleine Geschichte Afghanistans* (Munich: C.H. Beck Beck'sche Reihe, 2004) p. 157. While the Soviet Union carried out infrastructure projects north of the Hindu Kush, the American projects were concentrated in the south; the Soviet Union concentrated on training and supporting the Afghan armed forces, and the United States focused on Afghan education and the private sector. Despite this peaceful coexistence between the two superpowers in Afghanistan, U.S. development aid was influenced by Cold War geostrategic considerations: The United States constructed a huge airport near Kandahar for American military use should the Cold War escalate. However, the airport was never used for this purpose, even when the situation escalated in 1979. In addition, for the U.S., its involvement in the region raised the issue of balancing its relations with Afghanistan and Pakistan,

which had repeatedly clashed over territorial claims (the Pashtunistan dispute) since the early 1950s.

6. John K. Cooley, *Unholy Wars: Afghanistan, America, and International Terrorism* (London: Pluto Press, 2000), p. 17.

7. Amalendu Misra, *Afghanistan* (Cambridge, UK: Polity Press, 2004) p. 27. The main architect of the new U.S. policy toward Afghanistan was Zbigniew Brzezinski, the national security adviser of President Jimmy Carter.

8. Jean-Charles Brisard and Guillaume Dasquié, *Die Verbotene Wahrheit: Die Verstrickungen der USA mit Osama bin Laden* (Reinbek: Rowohlt, 2001).

9. Marvin Weinbaum, "War and Peace in Afghanistan: The Pakistani Role," *The Middle East Journal* 45, no. 1 (1991): 75.

10. This strategy was widely practiced in the 1980s as part of the Reagan policy of arming Third World anti-communist insurgencies.

11. Gennadi Botscharow, *Die Erschütterung: Afghanistan—Das sowjetische Vietnam* (Vienna: Zsolnay, 1990).

12. The Geneva Accord of 1988 concentrated on the withdrawal of Soviet troops and did not include any peace arrangements. Both sides, the Soviet Union as well as the United States, insisted on providing their allies with military support. This approach became known as "positive symmetry."

13. Barnett Rubin, *The Fragmentation of Afghanistan* (New Haven, CT: Yale University Press, 1995).

14. Andreas Wimmer and Conrad Schetter, "Putting State-Formation First: Some Recommendations for Reconstruction and Peace-Making in Afghanistan," *Journal for International Development* 15 (2002): 525–39; and Christine Noelle-Karimi, Conrad Schetter, and Reinhard Schlagintweit, eds., *Afghanistan: A Country Without a State?* (Frankfurt: IKO-Verlag, 2002).

15. Emmanuel Karagiannis, "The U.S.-Iranian Relationship After September 11, 2001 and the Transportation of Caspian Energy," *Central Asian Survey* 22, no. 2–3 (2003): 151–62.

16. The capture of Kabul by the Taliban in 1996 was reportedly noted as a positive development by the executive vice president of Unocal International. Richard S. Ehrlich, "Taliban Claims Oil Fuels U.S. Bombing," *Washington Times* (Oct. 14, 2001).

17. Ahmed Rashid, *Taliban: Militant Islam, Oil and Fundamentalism in Central Asia* (London: Tauris, 2000), p. 171.

18. Oliver Roy, "Die Taliban als Wächter der Scharia und der Pipeline," *Le monde diplomatique* (Nov. 12, 1996).

19. Richard Mackenzie, "The United States and the Taliban," in William Maley, ed., *Fundamentalism Reborn? Afghanistan and the Taliban* (London: Hurst, 1998), p. 90.

20. Ibid., p. 90. Washington did not establish diplomatic relations with the Taliban government; the only countries to do so were Pakistan, Saudi Arabia, and the United Arab Emirates.

21. To build the pipeline Unocal needed financial assistance from international development organizations such as the World Bank. However, a peaceful environment is a precondition for providing funding for major projects such as this.

22. UNODC (United Nations Office on Drug and Crime), *Afghanistan: Opium Survey 2003* (New York: United Nations, Oct. 2003).

23. In 1999, by which time the United States had already dissociated itself from the Taliban, these sectarian tensions almost caused a military confrontation between the Taliban and Iran. The assassination of Iranian diplomats during the takeover of the northern Afghan town of Mazar-i Sharif by the Taliban in August 1999 led Iran to station 500,000 soldiers on the Afghan border and threaten military intervention in November 1999.

24. Norbert Holl, *Mission Afghanistan: Erfahrungen eines UNO-Diplomaten* (Munich: Herbig, 2002), pp. 182–84; and Zalmay Khalilzad and Daniel Byman, "Afghanistan: The Consolidation of a Rogue State," *Washington Quarterly* 23, no. 1 (2000): 66.

25. Rashid, *Taliban*, p. 182.

26. Mavis Leno, wife of Jay Leno, a well-known TV entertainer, donated $100,000 to the campaign, and Feminist Minority, an influential NGO, organized a charity party for the women of Afghanistan on the occasion of the Oscar awards ceremony in 1999. In a speech in April 1999, Hillary Clinton, then first lady, denounced the Taliban not only for the "physical beating" of women, but also for the "destruction of the spirit of these women" (Associated Press, Apr. 29, 1999).

27. Kenneth Katzman, *Afghanistan: Current Issues and U.S. Policy—Report for Congress* (Library of Congress, Jan. 28, 2003), available at http://fpc.state.gov/documents/organization/17335.pdf, accessed June 18, 2004, p. 20.

28. Mackenzie, "The United States and the Taliban," pp. 90–103; and Rashid, *Taliban*. Other changes underlining the new importance of Afghanistan for the State Department were the appointments of Thomas Pickering as undersecretary of state and of Karl Inderfurth, a former Afghanistan correspondent, as assistant secretary for South Asia.

29. Reuters (Nov. 18, 1997).

30. UNODC, *Afghanistan;* and UNODC (United Nations Office on Drug and Crime), *The Opium Economy in Afghanistan: An International Problem* (New York: United Nations, 2003). After initial reluctance to act against poppy cultivation, the Taliban effectively prohibited the production of opium in 2001. In that year, production fell from 3,276 metric tons to 185 metric tons.

31. Rashid, *Taliban*, p. 174.

32. Inderfurth met periodically with leaders of the Taliban and Bill Richardson initiated peace talks between the Taliban and the Northern Alliance in Islamabad on April 26, 1998.

33. Katzman, *Afghanistan*, p. 19; and Amin Saikal, "The Afghanistan Conflict: International Terrorism and the U.S. Response," *Perceptions* (Mar.–May 2002): 80.

34. Sebastian Mallaby, "The Reluctant Imperialist: Terrorism, Failed State, and the Case for American Empire," *Foreign Affairs* 81, no. 2 (Mar.–Apr. 2002): 11–12; and Misra, *Afghanistan*.

35. William Maley, *The Afghanistan Wars* (London: Palgrave/Macmillan, 2002).

36. Robert O. Keohane, "The Public Delegitimation of Terrorism and Coalition Politics," in Ken Kooth and Tim Dunne, eds., *Worlds in Collision: Terror and the Future of Global Order* (New York: Palgrave/Macmillan, 2000), pp. 141–51.

37. Alexander Thier, "The Politics of Peace-Building: Year One—From Bonn to Kabul," in Antonio Donini, Norah Niland, and Karin Wermester, eds., *Nation-Building Unraveled? Aid, Peace and Justice in Afghanistan* (Bloomfield, CT: Kumarian Press, 2003), pp. 39–60.

38. Antonio Giustozzi, *Respectable Warlords? The Transition from War of All Against All to Peaceful Competition in Afghanistan,* Jan. 29, 2003, available at www.crisisstates.com/download/others/SeminarAG29012003.pdf, accessed June 18, 2004.

39. Conrad Schetter, "Afghanistan: Gewaltwirtschaft und "Warlords," *Blätter für deutsche und internationale Politik* 10 (2003): 1233–36.

40. To mention just the most important operations: Operation Anaconda in February–March 2001, Operation Champion Strike in September 2002, Operation Valiant Strike and Operation Desert Lion in March 2003, Operation Viper in April 2003, Operation Resolute Strike in April 2003, Operation Haven Denial and Operation Warrior Sweep in September–October 2003, Operation Avalanche in November 2003, and Operation Mountain Storm in March 2004.

41. David W. Barno, *Afghanistan: The Security Outlook,* presentation at the Center for Strategic and International Studies (CSIS) (Washington, DC: May 14, 2004), available at www.csis.org/isp/pcr/040514_barno.pdf, accessed June 18, 2004.

42. Nick Childs, *U.S. Wants More Help for Afghanistan,* Aug. 15, 2002, available at http://news.bbc.co.uk/1/hi/world/south_asia/2196468.stm, accessed June 18, 2004.

43. Andreas Wimmer and Conrad Schetter, "Putting State-Formation First: Some Recommendations for Reconstruction and Peace-Making in Afghanistan," *Journal for International Development* 15 (2002): 525–39.

44. Although Germany has been helping to rebuild the police force, the United States introduced an alternative three-month training program for policemen because it deemed the German training periods of two years as too time-consuming and too slow given the country's huge demand for police officers.

45. The so-called Beiruti Boys, Ashraf Ghani (finance minister), Zalmay Khalilzad (U.S. representative for Afghanistan), Anwar-ul-Haq Ahady (president of the Bank of Afghanistan), and Akbar Popal (rector of the University of Kabul), studied at the American University of Beirut. In the mid-1990s, Hamid Karzai (president) and Zalmay Khalilzad were consultants for Unocal. Khalilzad also worked for the State Department in the 1990s. Ahmad Jalali (interior minister) was head of the Afghan broadcasting service of the Voice of America.

46. Karzai received only two votes out of twelve in an internal election of the members of the Rome group during the Bonn conference. Conrad Schetter, "Hamid Karzai: Übergangspräsident für Afghanistan," *Orient: Zeitschrift des deutschen Orient-Instituts* 43, no. 1 (2002): 9–19.

47. Christina Bennet, Shawa Wakefield, and Andrew Wilder, *Afghan Elections: The Great Gamble* (Kabul: AREU [Afghan Research Unit], Nov. 2003), available at www.areu.org.af/publications/elections%20brief/areu%20elections%20brief.pdf, accessed June 18, 2004; and Conrad Schetter and Bernd Kuzmits, "Why a Further Afghanistan Conference," *ZEF Policy Brief,* no. 1 (Bonn: Center for Development Research [ZEF], Mar. 2004).

48. ICG (International Crisis Group), *The Afghan Transitional Administration: Prospects and Perils,* Asia Briefing (July 30, 2002); and Thier, "The Politics of Peace-Building," p. 55; Khalilzad announced Zahir Shah's change of mind at a press conference before the latter had a chance to make any comment, a fact that further underlines Washington's strong influence.

49. Subodh Atal, "At a Crossroad in Afghanistan: Should the United States Be Engaged in Nation-Building?" *Foreign Policy Briefing* 81 (Washington, DC: Cato

Institute, Sept. 24, 2003); and United States Institute of Peace, *Unfinished Business in Afghanistan: Warlordism, Reconstruction, and Ethnic Harmony,* Washington, DC: 2003, available at www.usip.org/pubs/specialreports/sr105.pdf, accessed July 19, 2004, p. 10.

50. National Intelligence Council, *Afghanistan and Regional Geopolitical Dynamics After September 11,* Conference proceedings, Apr. 18–19, 2002, available at www.cia.gov/nic/PDF_GIF_confreports/afghanistan.pdf, accessed July 19, 2004.

51. Schetter, Hamid Karzai: Übergangspräsident für Afghanistan, pp. 9–19.

52. Markus Kaim and Lars Berger, "USA," in Udo Steinbach and Marie-Carin von Gumppenberg, eds., *Zentralasien Lexikon* (Munich: C.H. Beck, 2004): 291–96; and Rajan Menon, "The New Great Game in Central Asia," *Survival* 45, no. 2 (2003): 187–204.

53. Fiona Hill, "Central Asia and the Caucasus: The Impact of the War on Terrorism," in Freedom House, *Nations in Transit 2003: Democratization in East Central Europe and Eurasia* (Lanham, MD: Rowman & Littlefield, June 2003), pp. 39–50.

54. Martha Brill Olcott, "Taking Stock of Central Asia," *Journal of International Affairs* 56, no. 2 (Spring 2003): 3–17.

55. Richard Giragosian, "The U.S. Military Engagement in Central Asia and the Southern Caucasus: An Overview," *Journal of Slavic Military Studies* 17, no. 1 (Mar. 2004): 43–77.

56. J.D. Crouch, II, assistant secretary of defense for international security policy, Senate Foreign Relations Committee hearing on the United States Department of Defense Security Cooperation in Central Asia, June 27, 2002.

57. In late 2001 and early 2002, Astana repeatedly sought closer military links with Washington to compensate for the build-up of U.S. forces at Khanabad. In the end, the United States signed an agreement with Astana designating three airfields—Chimkent, Lugovoi, and Almaty—that could be used by U.S. and coalition forces for emergency landings.

58. The base at Mary is ideally situated from a military planning perspective. The facility can be utilized not only in the context of Afghan contingencies, but also to leverage Central Asia as a "back door" to the Gulf.

59. Kazakhstan and Uzbekistan had major chemical and biological warfare facilities in the Soviet era. Both states are among the world's top producers of low-enriched uranium. Jim Nichol, *Central Asia's New States: Political Developments and Implications for U.S. Interests,* Issue Brief for Congress, Congress Research Service (Library of Congress, updated Apr. 1, 2003), p. 12.

60. Ibid., p. 13.

61. Svante E. Cornell, "The United States and Central Asia: In the Steppes to Stay?" *Cambridge Review of International Affairs* 17, no. 2 (July 2004), pp. 240–41.

62. Nichol, *Central Asia's New States,* p. 11.

63. Giragosian, "The U.S. Military Engagement," p. 3.

64. Jacquelyn K. Davis and Michael J. Sweeney, *Central Asia in U.S. Strategy and Operational Planning: Where Do We Go from Here?* (Washington, DC: Institute for Foreign Policy Analysis, Feb. 2004).

65. There are no accurate figures of the amount of drug money from Afghanistan and Central Asia that ends up in the pockets of terrorists, who are by no means the only beneficiaries of poppy cultivation. It was estimated that the Taliban received 80 percent of its income from opiate-related activities at the height of its power in

Afghanistan. Frank Cilluffo, *The Threat Posed from the Convergence of Organized Crime, Drug Trafficking, and Terrorism*, testimony before the House of Representatives, Judiciary Committee, Subcommittee on Crime, Dec. 13, 2000, available at www.csis.org/hill/ts001213cilluffo.html, accessed July 20, 2004. Juma Namangani, former leader of the IMU, used his interest in the heroin trade to fund much of the IMU's activity. He reportedly paid recruits between $100 and $500 per month, a fortune given the low standard of living. Ahmed Rashid, *Jihad: The Rise of Militant Islam in Central Asia* (New Haven and London: Yale University Press/World Policy Institute, 2002), p. 209.

66. UNODC (United Nations Office on Drugs and Crime), *Illicit Drugs Situation in the Regions Neighbouring Afghanistan and the Response of ODC*, Discussion Paper, Nov. 2002, available at www.unodc.org/pdf/afg/afg_drug-situation_2002-11-01_1.pdf, accessed June 18, 2004.

67. Davis and Sweeney, *Central Asia in U.S. Strategy.*

68. The dispute focuses on whether the Caspian is a sea or a lake and whether this has implications for both the applicability of the UN Convention on the Law of the Sea and the negotiation of boundaries, which affect the claims of the littoral states to significant oil deposits under the waters. On the great game, see Lutz Kleveman, *The New Great Game: Blood and Oil in Central Asia* (London: Atlantic Books, 2003).

69. The Caspian Basin is divided among Azerbaijan, Iran, Kazakhstan, Russia, Turkmenistan, and Uzbekistan.

70. The military side of the Department of Defense has moved faster in this respect. Long before September 11 it had already altered its unified command boundaries to transfer the Central Asian states (and Afghanistan) to the same area of responsibility (AOR) as the rest of the Greater Middle East under U.S. Central Command (CENTCOM).

71. In 2002, Congress also adopted an FSA for Afghanistan.

72. Brigitte Vassort-Rousset, "The U.S. Silk Road Strategy: American Geostrategy for Central Asia," *Ares* 20, no. 1 (Feb. 2003): 92.

73. U.S. Department of State, *United States-Uzbekistan Declaration on the Strategic Partnership and Cooperation Framework*, Mar. 12, 2002, available at www.state.gov/r/pa/prs/ps/2002/8736.htm, accessed June 18, 2004.

74. Olcott, "Taking Stock of Central Asia," p. 5.

75. Davis and Sweeney, *Central Asia in U.S. Strategy*, p. 2.

76. Martha Brill Olcott, *Central Asia: Terrorism, Religious Extremism, and Regional Stability*, Testimony before the U.S. House of Representatives, Committee on International Relations, Subcommittee on Middle East and Central Asia, Oct. 29, 2003 (Carnegie Endowment for International Peace), available at www.carnegieendowment.org/publications/index.cfm?fa=view&id=1387&prog=zru, accessed June 18, 2004.

77. Ariel Cohen, *Radical Islam and U.S. Interests in Central Asia*, testimony before the U.S. House of Representatives, Committee on International Relations, Subcommittee on Middle East and Central Asia (Heritage Foundation, Oct. 29, 2003), available at www.heritage.org/Research/RussiaandEurasia/Test102903.cfm, accessed June 18, 2004.

78. Victor Mauer, "Die geostrategischen Konsequenzen nach dem 11. September 2001," *Aus Politik und Zeitgeschichte* (B 3–4, Jan. 19, 2004): 18–25.

79. Earlier in the year, the Uzbek government promulgated new rules that required all domestic and international NGOs to reregister. All U.S.-funded NGOs except for the Open Society Institute, but no opposition parties, have been reregistered. The National Democratic Institute, the International Republican Institute, and Freedom House received warnings that if they continued working with unregistered parties they would lose their status.

80. Radio Free Europe/Radio Liberty, *Central Asia Report* 4, no. 24, June 23, 2004, available at www.rferl.org/reports/centralasia/2004/06/24–230604.asp, accessed June 18, 2004.

81. Ibid.

82. Aleksandr Bogatyrov, "The Russian Outpost at Tyan-Shan: Kant Is Acquiring the Status of a Collective Rapid Reaction Forces Airbase, Kraznaya Zvezda," Oct. 23, 2003, cit. in Davis and Sweeney, *Central Asia in U.S. Strategy*, p. 65.

83. Menon, "The New Great Game in Central Asia."

84. Aaron L. Friedberg, "September 11 and the Future of Sino-American Relations," *Survival* 44, no. 1 (2002): 33.

85. Adam Ward, "China and America: Trouble Ahead?" *Survival* 45, no. 3 (2003): 35–56.

86. National Security Strategy—Foreword by President George W. Bush, cit. in Ward, "China and America," p. 42.

87. Olcott, "Taking Stock of Central Asia."

88. The SCO evolved out of the Shanghai Five, a loose security group formed in 1996 by the current SCO members except Uzbekistan as a confidence-building measure to enable member states to cooperate on solving border disputes. Uzbekistan joined the group in 2001. In the same year, the Shanghai Five gave itself a new name and organizational structure.

89. Sergei Blagov, cit. in Sean L. Yom, "Power Politics in Central Asia: The Future of the Shanghai Cooperation Organization," *Harvard Asia Quarterly* (Autumn 2002), available at www.fas.harvard.edu/~asiactr/haq/200204/0204a003.htm, accessed June 18, 2004.

90. It was initially intended to open the office in Bishkek, the capital of Kyrgyzstan. As a gesture to Uzbekistan, the most populous and most recent Central Asian member, the office was relocated at the suggestion of Russia and China.

91. Yom, "Power Politics in Central Asia."

9

United States and Africa

"Uncle Sam" or "Uncle Scrooge"?

Peter J. Schraeder

Scholars and policy analysts from the northern industrialized democracies are increasingly attempting to take stock of the successes and failures associated with the restructuring of Africa's once moribund economic and political systems—the so-called African renaissance—that gathered strength in the post–Cold War era. An important point of departure of these analyses is an optimistic belief in both the willingness and the ability of democratically elected leaderships in the northern industrialized democracies to correct past deficiencies in Africa policies and ultimately play a supporting role on the African continent. In the case of the United States, Michael Clough captured the inherent optimism of the American Africanist community in the immediate aftermath of the fall of the Berlin Wall by arguing that the United States was "free at last" of the conceptual and ideological "shackles" of its Cold War competition with the former Soviet Union and could henceforth embark on a bold new relationship with the African continent.[1] For Clough and others, including myself, the Cold War's end had rendered obsolete a formerly interventionist policy built upon the twin themes of anti-communism and containment, especially after Washington's primary perceived adversary, the Soviet Union, had followed in the footsteps of other great empires throughout history, fragmenting into a host of smaller, independent, and ultimately less-threatening countries.

Much to our chagrin, however, the Cold War's end in many respects reinforced the historical tendency among U.S. policy makers to treat Africa as a "back-burner" issue. In a play on words of the Reagan administration's much-debated policy of "constructive engagement" toward South Africa, Clough poignantly argued that the post–Cold War tendency to downgrade Africa was captured by the de facto policy of "cynical disengagement" of the first Bush administration (1989–93) in which policy was guided by three principles:

- Do not spend much money [on Africa] unless Congress makes you.
- Do not let African issues complicate policy toward other, more important parts of the world.
- Do not take stands that might create political controversies in the United States.[2]

Although no two administrations are ever alike, most scholars would agree that these three principles have significantly guided U.S. policy toward Africa during both the Clinton administration (1993–2001) and the second Bush administration (2001–present), and in fact were reinforced in the aftermath of two decisive political-military turning points during the first years of both administrations: the October 1993 deaths of eighteen U.S. soldiers serving in Mogadishu, Somalia, as part of a UN-mandated intervention commonly referred to in the United States as Operation Restore Hope; and the September 11, 2001, terrorist attacks against the World Trade Center in New York and the Pentagon in Washington, DC, which resulted in the deaths of more than 2,000 civilians.

Having recently celebrated the "crystal" (fifteen-year) anniversary of the Cold War's end (which coincided with the 2004 U.S. presidential elections) against the backdrop of an ever-widening global war against terrorism, the time appears ripe for a reassessment of U.S. policy toward Africa.[3] Although many complex issues must be considered as part of any healthy foreign policy debate, one guiding question in particular stands out: Should the United States draw on its idealist-inspired "Uncle Sam" mythology and seek to play a more benevolent, proactive role in the African renaissance, or will a continued emphasis on other regions of greater perceived interest, most notably in the post–September 11 era, invariably reinforce a more realist-inspired "Uncle Scrooge" policy in which Africa at best remains neglected by U.S. policy makers?

Historical Context: From the Revolutionary War of 1776
to the War on Revolutionary Terrorism (2001–present)

A common thread of contemporary Africanist scholarship is that U.S. policy toward Africa during the Cold War was marked by indifference at worst, and neglect at best. A corollary of this argument is that, regardless of who has occupied the White House, policies were marked more by continuity than change. In his presidential address to one of the annual meetings of the African Studies Association, for example, Crawford Young underscored the "essential continuity" of U.S. policy toward Africa since the founding in 1958 of a separate Bureau of African Affairs within the State Department. Although he carefully added that "noteworthy fluctuations" had occurred, he nonetheless concluded that "these variations have been above all of style, tone, and the subtler chemistry of policy articulation, and not its underlying substance."[4] Five years later (and one year prior to the fall of the Berlin Wall), Brian Winchester concurred, noting that U.S. foreign policy "demonstrated remarkable coherence and regularity despite the differences between Republican and Democratic administrations and the tenure of nine different Assistant Secretaries of State for African Affairs."[5]

The adoption of a more extended historical perspective demonstrates that one can distinguish between at least five periods of continuity and change in which U.S. involvement on the African continent either expanded or contracted:

- 1776–1861: Revolutionary fervor and expansion
- 1861–1947: Civil War, retrenchment, and restrained involvement
- 1947–89: Cold War struggle and renewed expansion
- 1989–2001: Partial retrenchment in the Cold War's aftermath
- 2001–present: War on terrorism—contradictory trends

The first century of the American republic (1776–1861) was marked by the gradual expansion of foreign policy activity as demonstrated by the gradual spread of consulates and embassies to all regions of the African continent.[6] Many of these diplomatic missions were downgraded or closed, however, as a result of the U.S. Civil War (1861–65) and the retrenchment that followed, as the U.S. federal government focused on internal reconstruction and development. During this period of retrenchment, the Berlin Conference of 1884–85, which the United States attended as an observer, not only consecrated the formal creation of European empires and spheres of influence throughout Africa, but significantly restrained the pace of U.S. efforts at regaining levels of influence enjoyed prior to the U.S. Civil War. This second period of U.S. involvement (1861–1947) is thus best described as one of retrenchment in which future involvement was restrained by the African continent's subdivision into formal European colonial empires.

A renewed period of U.S. expansion occurred during the Cold War era (1947–89). The combination of declining colonial influence of Belgium, Britain, Germany, Italy, Portugal, and Spain (with France being the exception) with the growing diplomatic activities of the Soviet Union and its allies prompted Washington to open embassies in almost every African country that achieved independence. The hallmark of this era was the enunciation of a variety of presidential doctrines, beginning with the Truman Doctrine in 1947 and culminating in the Reagan Doctrine of the 1980s, that underscored Washington's self-appointed right to intervene against communist advances throughout the world, including in Africa.[7] This approach transcended partisan loyalties as both Democratic and Republican administrations sought to enlist African leaders on the side of the United States in an emerging East-West rivalry with the communist bloc. The policy makers of Charles de Gaulle's France, Mao Zedong's China, and Nikita Krushchev's Soviet Union shared Washington's perception of Africa's importance in the emerging Cold War environment of the 1950s. As a result, they were equally fervent in the pursuit of African allies, contributing to Africa's emergence as an arena of great power competition.

The fall of the Berlin Wall in 1989 signaled the end of the Cold War but not the end of international rivalry in Africa. As deftly noted by Jeffrey E. Garten, former undersecretary of commerce for international trade in the Clinton administration, the ideologically based Cold War between the United States and the Soviet Union was replaced by a "cold peace" in which the great powers increasingly struggled for economic supremacy in all regions of the world, including in Africa.[8] Although I have argued elsewhere that this cold peace manifested itself in rising U.S.-French tensions in francophone Africa during the 1990s, not least of all due to an expanding U.S. economic presence in this region, the Cold War's end not surprisingly fostered a reevaluation that resulted in a certain degree of political-military retrenchment from 1989 to 2001, albeit not nearly on the same scale as what occurred in the aftermath of the U.S. Civil War.[9] Perceptions of Africa's decreased political-military importance in the post–Cold War era were aptly captured by three trends: the State Department downsized its Bureau of African Affairs and closed several consulates in Africa, the Central Intelligence Agency (CIA) closed fifteen "stations" (centers of operation) in Africa and withdrew dozens of case officers, and only the "eleventh-hour intervention" of the Congressional Black Caucus prevented the Foreign Affairs Committee of the House of Representatives from merging its subcommittees on African and Latin American affairs.[10] "We have never been in Africa to report on Africa," explained one CIA official. "We went into Africa as part of the covert activity of the Cold War, to recruit [as spies] Soviet, Chinese, Eastern European and sometimes North Korean officials under circumstances that were easier to operate under than in their home countries."[11]

The most recent turning point in U.S. policy toward Africa resulted from the terrorist attacks of September 11 and their aftermath. These attacks exerted a profound influence on U.S. foreign policy as the Bush administration announced a global war on terrorism, replete with an official doctrine (the Bush Doctrine) and pledges to aid countries threatened by terrorism, that harkened back to the initial stages of the Cold War, when President Truman in 1947 pledged to aid countries threatened by communism. If current U.S. policy toward Africa follows in the footsteps of its Cold War predecessor, we are potentially at the beginning of a renewed period of U.S. expansionism on the African continent as this and future administrations seek African allies in the war on terrorism. It is equally possible, however, that the war on terrorism will lead to U.S. retrenchment as valuable resources are diverted to the geopolitical center of this conflict: the Middle East and South Asia.

Although it is risky to draw conclusions from unfolding events, it appears that at the very minimum the events of September 11 are prompting U.S. policy makers to de facto divide Africa into at least two spheres of variable U.S. foreign policy interest: those regions (North and East Africa) destined to receive a greater degree of U.S. attention due to their proximity to the Middle East, the perceived epicenter of the global war on terrorism; and the remainder of Sub-Saharan Africa (Central, Southern, and West Africa) which, except for some prominent cases, such as Nigeria and South Africa, is destined to be relegated to the back burner of U.S. foreign policy. It is striking to note, for example, that the microstate and former French colony of Djibouti emerged in 2003 as the site for the Defense Department's Combined Joint Task Force–Horn of Africa (CJTF-HOA), the primary responsibility of which is to gather intelligence and wage war on potential terrorist groups in neighboring Eritrea, Ethiopia, Kenya, Somalia, Sudan, and Yemen.[12] The country enjoys the distinction of hosting the only formal U.S. military base on the African continent. In the aftermath of hosting several high-ranking official U.S. visitors, most notably Secretary of Defense Donald Rumsfeld, Djibouti also agreed to station on its territory Radio Sawaa, Washington's post–September 11 Arabic language program that is beamed to all Middle East countries (as well as Sudan), twenty-four hours a day, seven days a week. Djibouti's rising fortunes are clearly linked to its status as an "island of stability" in a troubled region (the Horn of Africa) that sits astride the strategically important Straits of Bab-el-Mandeb and the Arabian Peninsula.

Competing Foreign Policy Interests

A hallmark of U.S. policy toward Africa is the lack of consensus within the policy-making establishment over Africa's importance to the United States. In many respects, the determination of U.S. interests in Africa varies depending on the portion of the policy-making establishment that is defining those interests. The Congressional Black Caucus and other lobbying groups derivative of the African-American community are quick to emphasize the importance of cultural interests, due to the important reality that more than 34 million U.S. citizens (roughly 12 percent of the U.S. population according to the 2000 U.S. census) claim an African-American heritage.[13] Other members of Congress underscore the importance of U.S. humanitarian interests in alleviating chronic drought and famine. The Department of Commerce not surprisingly focuses on economic interests, most notably increasing U.S. exports to the African continent and ensuring U.S. access to African petroleum reserves. The Department of State focuses on political interests, including the potential electoral weight of fifty-three African votes in the United Nations. The Department of Defense naturally focuses on security interests, including Africa's geographic proximity to the strategically important regions of Europe and the Middle East.

These differences notwithstanding, two sets of interests—security and economic—have both dominated and historically competed for preeminence in U.S. policy toward Africa. From a broad historical perspective, the pursuit of economic self-interest historically has been in the forefront of U.S.-African relations since the founding of the American republic in 1776. Returning once again to our five major phases of contraction and expansion, economic interests prevailed during three periods: 1776–1861, 1861–1947, and 1989–2001. When viewed from this long-term historical perspective, Washington's pursuit of strategic interests during the Cold War era (1947–89), most notably the ideologically inspired interest of containing the Soviet Union and its communist allies, represented an anomaly in an otherwise economically inspired approach to U.S. policy toward Africa.

The U.S. response to the terrorist attacks of September 11 nonetheless signifies the continued importance of national security interests in U.S. policy toward Africa during the contemporary era (2001–present). In North Africa, for example, the construction and opening in December 2002 of a new $42 million U.S. embassy in Tunis demonstrated Tunisia's rising strategic importance as an Arab country that offers strong support for the war on terrorism. Tunis boasts a State Department office for assessing regional threats, a Pentagon regional training center for U.S. Special Forces destined for combat in the Arab world, and a Foreign Service Institute for teaching the Arabic language to numerous U.S. government personnel who are preparing to work in Arabic-speaking countries. Tunisia is not unique, but rather indicative of the strengthening of U.S. security ties with North and East African countries deemed important to the Bush administration's war on terrorism.

Cold War Trends

The fact that U.S. policy toward Africa appears once again to be entering an anomalous period in which strategic interests predominate warrants a few words as to the dominant trends in its Cold War predecessor (1947–89). Two themes aptly illustrate how U.S. policy makers perceived Africa's role in the various strategies of containment applied to Africa in varying forms during the Cold War era.[14] First, policy makers perceived the African continent as a means for solving non-African problems. Rather than being regarded as important in their own right, African countries were perceived by U.S. policy makers as a means for preventing the further advances of Soviet communism, and therefore U.S. relationships with African regimes evolved according to their relative importance within an East-West framework. Emperor Haile Selassie was courted from the 1940s to the 1970s, for example, due to Ethiopia's

strategic location and partnership in a global telecommunications surveillance network directed against the Soviet Union. When the security
relationship between the United States and Ethiopia shattered during
the 1970s, the United States turned to Siad Barre primarily because access to bases in Somalia could enhance the U.S. military capability to
counter any Soviet threat to Middle Eastern oil fields. Similarly, Washington policy makers viewed Mobutu Sese Seko and a host of Afrikaner
governments positively because the Democratic Republic of the Congo
(Congo-Kinshasa; formerly Zaire) and South Africa could serve as regional bulwarks against communism. In each of these cases, an overriding preoccupation with anti-communism led Washington to overlook
the authoritarian excesses of these regimes in favor of their willingness
to support U.S. containment policies in Africa.[15]

The second major outcome of Washington's containment policies was
the emergence of the African continent as a battlefield for proxy wars as
both the United States and the Soviet Union became involved in regional conflicts. In almost every case, regional conflict was exacerbated
by one superpower's reaction to the other's involvement in a particular
crisis. Soviet involvement, as well as merely the "threat" of Soviet involvement, was enough to capture the attention of the White House, and
usually provoke an escalation of the conflict. In the case of Congo-
Kinshasa, the political instability of the early independence years, even
when coupled with only relatively limited Soviet involvement, was
enough to warrant White House–authorized covert assassination attempts,
as well as military operations involving U.S. troops and transport aircraft. During the 1975–76 Angolan civil war, Soviet-Cuban involvement
led to a tacit U.S.–South African–Congolese alliance in which Washington supported the direct involvement of Congolese and, more onerous
from the point of view of most African countries, South African troops.
The Reagan administration continued in this tradition and seized upon
the Ethiopian-Somali border conflict of 1982 to demonstrate renewed
U.S. resolve to stand by anti-communist allies who were threatened by
Soviet-backed, communist regimes. In these and other cases, local conflicts having little, if anything, to do with the ideological concerns of
communism or capitalism threatened to become East-West flashpoints
in the face of growing U.S.-Soviet involvement.

A full array of interventionist tools, listed in order from the least to
most coercive, were employed by Washington throughout the African
continent in the name of anti-communism:

- The pursuit of classic diplomacy, most notably inviting key African allies, such as Mobutu Sese Seko of Congo-Kinshasa, to make official head-of-state visits to the White House in Washington, DC;
- The provision of economic and military aid to anti-communist client states, such as the regime of Ethiopian emperor Haile Selassie;
- The attachment of political conditionalities to the foreign policy relationship, as in the case of the Carter administration making the strengthening of U.S.-Somali ties contingent on the Siad Barre regime's promise to refrain from further military intervention in the Ogaden region of Ethiopia;
- The imposition of economic sanctions against perceived "radical" regimes backed by the Soviet Union, such as that of Egypt's Gamal Abdul Nasser;
- The pursuit of covert intervention, including the successful assassination of Patrice Lumumba, the nationalist leader of Congo-Kinshasa;
- The funding of paramilitary intervention, as witnessed by U.S. assistance to the União Nacional para a Independência Total de Angola (UNITA) guerrilla forces of Jonas Savimbi to overthrow a self-proclaimed Marxist regime in Angola;
- The use of military intervention, as witnessed by the Johnson administration's decision to send U.S. combat troops to Congo-Kinshasa.

The provision of economic and military aid was the most extensively utilized tool of intervention during the Cold War era, and as such merits special attention. Three conclusions can be drawn from a larger statistically oriented project that two colleagues and I undertook to assess the foreign aid motivations of a variety of northern industrialized democracies, including the United States, toward Africa during the last decade of the Cold War.[16] First, our analysis confirmed widely held presumptions that U.S. Africa policies were largely driven by strategic interests. The existence of military access agreements in particular ensured the generous provision of foreign aid. The most notable example of such an arrangement was the Carter administration's negotiation of military access agreements with Egypt, Kenya, Somalia, and Sudan at the end of the 1970s. These security agreements served as the basis for extensive foreign aid relationships during the 1980s, although only the agreements with Egypt and Kenya lasted throughout the decade.

Our analysis also confirmed widely held assumptions of the importance of ideological concerns in U.S. Africa policies.[17] During the 1980s, the U.S. government denied foreign aid to the self-proclaimed Marxist regimes of Angola, Ethiopia, and Mozambique, whereas it treated capitalist countries such as Congo-Kinshasa, Kenya, and Senegal as ideological allies deserving of aid. Socialist regimes were neither strongly supported nor strongly opposed. This finding is clarified by calculating the percentages of U.S. aid provided to each type of ideological regime during the 1980s. Whereas capitalist regimes annually received 88 percent of all U.S. aid to the African continent, Marxist and socialist regimes received only 6 percent each.

Our statistical analysis also demonstrated the existence of a negative relationship between U.S. aid levels and the gross national product (GNP) per capita of African recipients (i.e., higher aid levels were enjoyed by countries with a low GNP per capita). This finding reflects the fact that U.S. aid consistently was provided to African regimes that had "consistently worse economic growth rates" than those enjoyed by other African countries.[18] For example, one of the largest recipients of U.S. aid in 1989 was the regime of Mobutu Sese Seko, an authoritarian leader who in 1965 assumed power in a military coup d'état, and who increasingly relied upon the Congolese army and foreign aid to maintain himself in power as his popular support progressively eroded throughout the 1980s. Similar to the foreign policy relationships cultivated with other authoritarian African allies, such as Egypt, Liberia, Somalia, and Sudan, which were among the top recipients of U.S. foreign aid during the 1980s, preoccupations with anti-communism led American policy makers to overlook rising economic deterioration and government repression as long as African leaders supported U.S. containment policies.[19]

Policy-Making Process: Bureaucratic Influence Amid White House and Congressional Neglect

The formulation and implementation of U.S. policy toward Africa is effectively explored by treating the U.S. policy-making establishment as a series of three concentric circles: the inner White House circle that includes the president and his principal foreign policy advisors, most notably the national security advisor; a second circle that comprises the bureaucracies of the executive branch; and an outer circle that includes Congress and the larger African affairs constituency.[20]

White House Neglect of the African Continent

Beginning with the innermost circle, it is typically assumed by foreign observers that presidents and their principal foreign policy advisors will be the most influential and the most activist in shaping U.S. policy toward Africa. Throughout the Cold War and its aftermath, however, presidents traditionally have devoted less attention to Africa than to regions of perceived greater concern, most notably Western Europe, Eastern Europe (including Russia and the other countries that were once part of the Soviet Union), and more recently the Middle East and South Asia.

Neglect of Africa at the highest reaches of the U.S. policy-making establishment is the direct result of a wide variety of factors: a president's typical lack of knowledge and therefore the absence of a deep-felt interest in a region that historically enjoyed few enduring political links with the United States as compared with the former European colonial powers; a tendency to view Africa as the responsibility of those same European colonial powers, especially France, whose leaders were often willing to take the lead in crises; the impracticality of one person monitoring relations with nearly 200 countries worldwide, including 53 in Africa, and therefore the necessity of delegating responsibility for handling foreign policy for those regions considered marginal to the White House; and, most important, the necessity of balancing domestic priorities with foreign affairs necessities, especially during a first term in office in which the ultimate priority of all presidents is to assure reelection, with simple electoral logic typically suggesting that Africa is not a priority for the vast majority of the voting public. It should therefore come as no surprise that Clinton's historic trips to the African continent in 1998 and 2000, which raised awareness of Africa within the United States to levels previously unseen in the country's history, were undertaken during his second term in office. In this regard, although these trips raised the foreign policy bar as concerns Africa for subsequent administrations, the efforts of the Clinton White House must be assessed against the larger backdrop of the president's more activist approach during his second term toward all regions of the world, in which Africa relatively speaking still remained the region of least concern.[21]

President George W. Bush's early statements of his administration's self-proclaimed "realist" policy toward Africa offered clear evidence of the continent's decreased standing at the level of the White House from the high benchmark set by the Clinton administration during its second term. Two statements during the presidential election campaign of 2000 were particularly revealing. In response to a question concerning Africa's place within a future Bush administration, Bush noted that the continent did not "fit into the national strategic interests" of the United States "as far as I [Bush] can see them."[22] This response, consistent with a realist approach that perceives Africa as marginal in terms of U.S. national security interests, was followed by a statement concerning the lack of U.S. intervention in Rwanda in 1994 to prevent genocide in that country. "No one liked to see it on our TV screens," explained Bush, who further noted that the Clinton administration had done "the right thing" in deciding not to intervene.[23] This latter statement captured Bush's strong aversion to U.S. involvement in peacemaking operations, often derisively referred to during the presidential campaign as ill-conceived exercises in "nation-building" (discussed further below).

The realist tendencies of the Bush White House ensure that Africa remains marginalized by a White House team that does not perceive the continent as an important part of the overall international strategic landscape. As signaled by President Bush's selection of Mexico as the country to be honored with the first presidential visit of the new administration (since World War II it was Canada that was so honored), as well as his high-profile involvement in the April 2001 Summit of the Americas and presidential tour of Chile, El Salvador, and Mexico in April 2002, Latin America was supposed to be the region of the Southern hemisphere to receive priority attention from the Bush White House. This foreign policy focus changed, of course, with the terrorist attacks of September 11 and the emergence of the Middle East as the focal point of a global war on terrorism. Even Bush's highly trumpeted visit to five African countries (Botswana, Nigeria, Senegal, South Africa, and Uganda) in July 2003 failed to reverse perceptions of Africa's marginalization at the level of the White House. In fact, for many observers, the July presidential visit (originally set for earlier in the year but canceled due to the looming war in Iraq) actually reinforced perceptions of Africa's neglect in the Bush White House. African reporters, who dubbed Bush's visit as that of a "cowboy in Africa" and representative of "Tarzan politics," were especially critical of the shortness of the stopovers (often lasting only a few hours) that were limited to small, choreographed audiences, suggesting that the visit was designed more to achieve sound bites destined for audiences in the U.S. (most notably the African-American community) than to provide serious engagement with African policy makers and their peoples.[24]

Congressional Neglect of the African Continent

The outer concentric circle of the policy-making process revolves around Congress (the Senate and the House of Representatives) and a variety of African affairs interest groups, such as the Congressional Black Caucus and other African-American groups (e.g., the African American Institute), and a wide array of lobbyists representing the interests of various African countries (the so-called K street crowd).[25] The Africa Subcommittee of the International Relations Subcommittee (House of Representatives) and the African Affairs Subcommittee of the Foreign Relations Committee (Senate) historically were the two most important congressional watchdogs of U.S. policy toward Africa during the Cold War era. In the Cold War's aftermath, however, other congressional committees have become increasingly important in debates over issues such as the importance of aid versus trade, the proper U.S. role in peacemaking and peacekeeping, and the normative goal of promoting democracy. Among the influential committees in the Senate (which have counterparts in the House) are the Foreign Operations Subcommittee of the Appropriations Committee, the International Finance Committee of the Banking, Housing, and Urban Affairs Committee, and the International Trade Committee of the Finance Committee.

A variety of constitutionally mandated prerogatives, including the confirmation of presidential appointees, the convening of hearings, and the drafting of and voting on key legislation, suggests that Congress theoretically should play an important role in defining U.S. foreign policy toward Africa. Like their White House counterparts, however, members of Congress historically have neglected Africa relative to other regions of perceived greater interest. Reelection pressures and time constraints imposed by terms of office (two years for representatives and six years for senators) force them to select and prioritize the domestic and the international issues that will receive their attention. Since the primary objective of most members is to be reelected, and since most U.S. citizens know or care very little about the African continent, conventional wisdom suggests that it is politically unwise to incur the possibility of alienating their constituencies by focusing on Africa. Membership in the Africa subcommittees is among the least desired congressional positions in both houses of Congress, and is therefore relegated to relatively junior representatives and senators.

An important impact of congressional neglect of Africa is that even highly motivated chairpersons of the Africa subcommittees face an uphill task in pushing African issues to the forefront of congressional debate. In the absence of crisis, partisan and ideological differences within Congress prevent activist groups from achieving congressionally mandated changes in U.S. policy toward Africa. Even during short-term crises when an issue may attract the attention of a significant number of members of Congress, control of the policy-making process naturally flows to the White House and the bureaucracies of the executive branch. In this regard, the resurgence of guerrilla activity in the eastern provinces of Congo-Kinshasa at the beginning of 1999, let alone the involvement of several foreign armies in this conflict (what some policy makers typically referred to as "Africa's First World War"), failed to rise to the level of a policy-making crisis in the non-ideological context of the post–Cold War era, a far cry from the crisis atmosphere that prevailed in the 1960s when a guerrilla insurgency within the same region was perceived by U.S. policy makers as threatening to install a pro-Soviet regime under the leadership of Patrice Lumumba.

Historical congressional neglect of Africa and therefore the absence of congressional activism as concerns U.S. policy toward Africa was reinforced by the Democratic Party's stunning defeat in the November 1994 congressional elections that led to Republican control over both the House and the Senate for the first time in decades. From January 1995 to January 2001, a Democratic White House had to deal with an increasingly hostile, Republican-controlled Congress that was at odds with many aspects of White House foreign policy, including that directed toward the African continent. The likelihood of congressional activism in Africa is further hindered by the slim margins of Republican Party control of both houses of Congress in the aftermath of the November 2004 elections. Whereas the Republicans hold a majority of 55 seats in the Senate as opposed to 44 seats for the Democrats and one for the independents, they hold 231seats in the House as opposed to 202 for the Democrats and 1 for the independents (as well as 1 vacancy as of this writing). In both cases, slim partisan majorities militate against activist policies in regions considered to be of minor concern (i.e., Africa), as both parties seek to avoid missteps in preparation for the congressional elections of November 2006.

Bureaucratic Influence in the Policy-Making Process

The net result of White House and congressional neglect of Africa is that U.S. policy toward Africa, perhaps more so than that toward any other region of the world, essentially is delegated to the high-level bureaucrats and political appointees within the bureaucracies of the executive branch. In order to fully understand continuity and change in that policy, one must therefore focus on the policies and interactions of the African affairs bureaus of the traditional national security bureaucracies, such as the State Department, the Pentagon, and the CIA, as well as their counterparts within the increasingly important economic realm, most notably the Department of Commerce. What I have elsewhere referred to as "bureaucratic influence" in the policy-making process will more often than not characterize the formulation and implementation of U.S. policy toward Africa in "routine" situations (i.e., during the absence of crisis).[26]

Secretary of State Colin Powell and the State Department, most notably its Bureau of African Affairs under the leadership of Walter Kansteiner III, emerged at the beginning of the Bush administration as the lead bureaucratic voice in the formulation and implementation of U.S. policy toward Africa. An African American who enjoyed a distinguished thirty-five-year military career that included serving as national security advisor to President Reagan and as chairman of the Joint Chiefs of Staff under both Bush (senior) and the first year of the Clinton administration, Powell underscored his determination to make Africa a priority under the new Bush administration by making the Africa Bureau the first stop of his numerous get-acquainted meetings at the State Department. Along with Condoleezza Rice, the first African-American woman to head the National Security Council (NSC), Powell's African-American heritage was viewed by many as a natural bridge to ensure effective relations with African leaders and their respective diplomatic corps.

Early press reports suggested cautious optimism on the part of several African leaders that Powell and others in the Bush administration would elevate Africa's standing in Washington. "My impression was that he has a very keen interest in African affairs," explained Seth Kimanzi, secretary general in the Ministry of Foreign Affairs of Rwanda, a country considered one of the "favorites" of the Clinton administration. "He may prove different from what has been propagated in [the] media—that the Bush administration is ignorant of African affairs."[27]

This image was reinforced by Powell's week-long tour of four African countries (Kenya, Mali, South Africa, and Uganda) during May 2001, less than four months after the inauguration of the new administration. Others, of course, lamented what they perceived as a potential turn for the worse under a Republican administration, as witnessed by the question posed in the headline of *Africa Business* magazine: "After the Clinton Smile, Will It Be the Bush Snarl?"

Regardless of whether Powell is remembered by the history books as having succeeded where his predecessors failed in cajoling a recalcitrant White House and Congress to improve Africa's standing in the U.S. foreign policy hierarchy (an unlikely conclusion as unfolding events forced Powell to focus on other regions of more immediate concern), an important outcome of bureaucratic influence in the policy-making process is that, in the absence of active coordination of policy at the highest reaches of the U.S. government (i.e., the White House), U.S. policy toward each African country tends to become fragmented and interpreted differently, according to the established organizational missions of bureaucracies that were historically created to deal with different aspects of the foreign policy relationship.[28] Each bureaucracy essentially fosters a unique institutional culture that both supports its mission and socializes individuals into working toward its attainment. Although other sources of bureaucratic behavior such as the substantive views and personal ambitions of individual bureaucrats are important, the critical point here is that members of a bureaucracy often become the advocates of their agencies and tend to interpret U.S. foreign policy according to their agency's role and mission in the foreign policy establishment, often leading to a less than harmonious relationship. Bureaucracies do not run wild within a political void, but rather constitute part of a domestic political process—in this case, bureaucratic politics. To this end, they bargain and compromise, ultimately seeking to maximize their own positions within the policy-making establishment.[29]

A textbook example of foreign policy fragmentation is the Clinton administration's handling of Operation Restore Hope.[30] In this case, the absence of high-level White House attention to an inherited, ongoing U.S. intervention in Somalia resulted in the reinforcement of an already fragmented policy in which various executive branch bureaucracies were pursuing different, often contradictory, goals. While the State Department was emphasizing the need for political reconstruction and negotiated outcomes among all of the various clan militia groups, the Pentagon was carrying out military operations designed to militarily defeat and capture militia leader Mohammed Farah Aidid, leading to a policy-making situation in which an emphasis on political reconstruction was at best contradicted by an exclusionary military approach favored by military officials in the field.[31] Most important, the first high-level analysis of growing contradictions in U.S. policy toward Somalia only occurred as a result of a crisis—the deaths of eighteen U.S. soldiers in October 1993—approximately eight months after the Clinton administration assumed office. To his credit, Clinton recognized the shortcomings of the policy as it had evolved and quickly announced the impracticality of a military solution imposed from abroad, as well as the ultimate withdrawal of U.S. troops. However, the structural problem inherent in the Clinton administration's foreign policy apparatus, that is, the lack of high-level attention and coordination of U.S. Africa policies except when a crisis or domestic politics forced those policies to the top of the foreign policy agenda, continued to foster a variety of unevenly applied policies.

Foreign policy fissures have also emerged in the Bush administration between the conservative and moderate wings of the Republican Party, as witnessed by rising bureaucratic competition between the Pentagon under Secretary of Defense Donald Rumsfeld and the State Department under Secretary of State Powell. As concerned the brewing debate in 2003 over what should constitute the proper U.S. response to the intensification of civil conflict in Liberia, Rumsfeld fiercely opposed the involvement of U.S. ground troops, preferring instead that a regional peacekeeping force led by Nigeria and composed of African troops take responsibility for military action.[32] Powell, who also preferred that Nigerian troops take the lead, nonetheless supported the introduction of a few U.S. troops to secure the port and capital city, as well as nearby relief corridors. Although observers correctly noted that the White House decision to send in a force of 200 ground troops on August 14, 2003, represented somewhat of a victory for Powell, he nonetheless was increasingly marginalized within the Bush administration, and was ultimately replaced by Condoleezza Rice as secretary of state after Bush's victory in the 2004 elections.

One must be careful, however, not to overestimate the impact of a new administration on promoting change in U.S. policy toward Africa. An important outcome associated with bureaucratic influence in the policy-making process—the dominant feature of U.S. Africa policy—is the creation of a bureaucratic mindset among a career civil service elite that fosters a fundamental resistance to change or a predilection toward maintenance of the status quo. Among the most important factors contributing to bureaucratic conservatism are the safety of relying on established and accepted standard operating procedures, as well as the realization that undue risk taking may permanently damage one's career by effectively blocking upward mobility through the ranks. As explained in a classic study by Morton A. Halperin, the net result is that the "majority of bureaucrats prefer to maintain the status quo, and only a small group is, at any one time, advocating change."[33] Consequently, members of a bureaucracy, especially its politically appointed head, will often put up a fierce fight rather than submit to changes they perceive as infringing on their "territory," or threatening the integrity of their organization's bureaucratic mission. In short, the inherent conservativism of bureaucracies prompts their members to resist change.

The self-interested nature of bureaucracies nonetheless propels their members to attempt to expand their realm of influence within the policy-making establishment. Since, as was noted earlier, members of a bureaucracy tend to identify national security in terms of their agency's mission in the foreign policy establishment, it follows that these same members will seek to widen the role of their organization. The primary means of achieving this has typically been through the expansion of bureaucratically inspired activities associated with each of Africa's fifty-three countries. These have included the Africa Bureau's (State Department) pursuit of White House visits for African heads of state; the Pentagon's interest in strengthening joint military maneuvers with African militaries, most notably the expansion of a wide array of military assistance programs with Nigeria; the CIA's willingness to share intelligence findings with friendly African regimes, such as the Kagame regime of Rwanda; and the Commerce Department's interest in securing new trade and investment accords, with South Africa and the various oil-producing states (e.g., Angola) serving as the centerpiece of U.S. economic policy. Regardless of the particular strategy pursued in strengthening ties with a particular African country, the term "incrementalism" best captures the resulting process of change: once a foreign policy relationship is established with an African country, the self-interested nature of bureaucracies often contributes to the maintenance and/or gradual enhancement of relations that are difficult to reverse.

Defense Department planning as concerns Africa's strategic role in the post–September 11 era offers an impressive example of incrementalist logic at work. According to an interview that General James Jones, head of the U.S. European Command (which oversees most U.S. military operations in Africa), provided to the *New York Times,* the Defense Department is gradually strengthening U.S. military ties with select African countries as it enlists them in the Bush administration's war on terrorism.[34] Jones is particularly interested in ensuring U.S. access to a "family of bases" in friendly African countries, including "forward operating bases each with an airfield nearby that could house up to a brigade, 3,000 to 5,000 troops," as well as "bare-bones bases that Special Forces, Marines or possibly an infantry rifle platoon or company could land at and build up as the mission required."[35]

The process of incrementalism nonetheless helps explain the rarity of dramatic shifts in U.S. policy toward the vast majority of Africa's fifty-three countries, even when a new administration with seemingly different beliefs than its predecessor takes power (as in the shift in power from the Clinton to the Bush administrations). As noted earlier, the time constraints associated with relatively short terms of office for presidents and most members of Congress, coupled with the traditionally low level of attention they pay to African issues, favor bureaucratic influence, and therefore generally support policies of maintaining the status quo. Perhaps the most significant barrier to change, however, is that the numerous activities of the bureaucracies simply do not fall within the realm of presidential action. As President Johnson's secretary of state, Dean Rusk, commented during the transition from the Johnson to the Nixon administrations: "A transition is not so earth-shaking. Of the thousand or so cables that go out of here every day, I see only five or six and the President only one or two. Those who send out the other 994 cables will still be here [long after the administration is gone]." Adopting a train metaphor to clarify his thoughts, Rusk noted that a transition "is a little bit like changing engineers on a train going steadily down the track. The new engineer has some switches he can make choices about—but 4,500 intergovernmental agreements don't change."[36]

Although somewhat exaggerating the importance of bureaucracies during presidential transitions, Rusk's train metaphor is correct in one key respect. It suggests that established bureaucratic missions greatly increase the possibility that U.S. policy toward the vast majority of African countries will continue to chug along on established tracks until some event (such as a crisis) potentially attracts the attention of the White House or other U.S. domestic actors and provides the basis for a reassessment. In the absence of crisis, White House attention will invariably be focused elsewhere, and established policies will continue to be maintained and strengthened by the bureaucratic train. As a result, although policy toward some African countries may shift, due to the secretary of state's reordering of U.S. priorities or the idiosyncratic interests of certain members of Congress or an ascendant African affairs interest group (such as the Christian coalition), U.S. policy toward Africa under the Bush administration, even in the post–September 11 era, will demonstrate strong threads of continuity with its Democratic predecessor, the Clinton administration.

Foreign Policy Challenges and Responses

Every newly elected administration attempts to set a new tone in U.S. policy toward Africa by underscoring what it will do differently than its predecessors, especially when the change in office is the result of partisan rivalry, as when the Clinton administration entered office after twelve years of Republican control of the White House (1981–93). The inauguration in January 2001 of George W. Bush as the forty-third president of the United States was no different. As was the case with two previous presidential transitions in which Republican presidents took office after a period of Democratic Party control of the White House (Nixon's replacement of Johnson in January 1969 and Reagan's replacement of Carter in January 1981), the Bush foreign policy team castigated the Clinton administration as having pursued an overly idealistic and ultimately unsuccessful "feel good" policy toward Africa that was long on rhetoric but short on substance. The corrective, according to the newly minted foreign policy triumvirate of Secretary of State Powell, Secretary of Defense Rumsfeld, and National Security Advisor Rice, was a more "realist"-oriented foreign policy reminiscent of the Reagan and especially the Nixon administrations that emphasizes a more "hardheaded" analysis of concrete U.S. interests. The essential thrust of this realist approach with regard to Africa, which was reinforced by the events of September 11 and its aftermath, can be summarized as follows: "Forget the rhetoric and boost the geopolitics."[37]

To be sure, there do indeed exist important differences in how Democratic and Republican administrations assess and understand the nature of political-military and socioeconomic changes on the African continent. Those who tend to focus on the internal dimensions or origins of change can be conceptually referred to as regionalists.[38] For these policy makers, typically prominent in Democratic administrations, domestic instability and conflict are due primarily to the internal shortcomings of any given regime. Any solution, therefore, must focus on the reform of that regime, including support for the protection of human rights, the promotion of socioeconomic development, and the adoption of democratic practices, often in conjunction with regional and international organizations, most notably the African Union and the United Nations. In sharp contrast, those who tend to focus on the international dimensions or origins of change can be conceptually referred to as globalists.[39] For these policy makers, typically prominent in Republican administrations, international influences are often at the heart of rising domestic instability and conflict. The proper solution, according to the globalists, is the containment of these foreign threats, as was the case with the U.S. policy of containment of communism during the Cold War era. In addition to emphasizing the importance of strategic cooperation with threatened countries, these individuals are typically wary of U.S. involvement in international organizations, most notably the United Nations.

The differences between regionalists and globalists are significantly mitigated, however, by the simple reality of bureaucratic influence in the policy-making process as concerns Africa. Specifically, the prominent role played by the State Department and especially its Bureau of African Affairs in the formulation and implementation of U.S. policy toward Africa under both Democratic and Republican administrations has fostered a great deal of consistency in how Africa's key problems are assessed, especially during the post–Cold War era. For example, regardless of whether one reviews the Senate confirmation hearings for Assistant Secretary of State for African Affairs Susan Rice (under the Clinton administration) or Assistant Secretary of State for African Affairs Walter Kansteiner III and his successor, Constance Berry Newman, under the Bush administration, one is struck by the consensus over the problems that plague the African continent. In these and other confirmation hearings, five sets of foreign policy challenges are typically described as worthy of U.S. attention:

- reversing grinding poverty and the lack of sustainable growth and development;

- mitigating the deleterious impacts of corruption and authoritarianism;
- stemming the multiplication of civil conflicts;
- containing and eliminating transborder threats;
- halting the spread of HIV/AIDS.

Foreign Policy Challenge #1: Reversing Grinding Poverty and the Lack of Sustainable Growth and Development

The U.S. foreign policy solution for reversing grinding poverty and the lack of sustainable growth and development involves basically the promotion of economic liberalization in overly statist African countries, in which trade and foreign investment gradually replace foreign aid as the preferred economic tools of U.S. statecraft. Especially during the Clinton administration, the predilection of conservative Republican members of Congress to oppose foreign aid, combined with Africa's low priority compared to other regions of greater perceived interest at the level of the White House, reinforced a post–Cold War trend of reducing U.S. foreign aid commitments. According to one authoritative estimate, U.S. bilateral aid to Sub-Saharan Africa (inclusive of development assistance, economic support funds, food aid, and foreign disaster relief) fell from a peak level of $1.93 billion in 1992 to $933 million in 2000, a 52 percent decrease in overall aid.[40] Although foreign aid resources to the African continent have in fact increased in the post–September 11 era as part of the Bush administration's overall expansion of foreign aid programs, Africa remains marginalized in a foreign aid hierarchy that continues to favor other regions of perceived greater concern, most notably the Middle East.[41]

To its credit, the Clinton administration in 1996 unveiled the first formal trade policy for aggressively pursuing new markets throughout Africa. This report included the formal launching of an interagency Africa Trade and Development Coordinating Group, which was jointly chaired by the National Economic Council (NEC) and the National Security Council (NSC). The centerpiece of this economic strategy was congressional legislation, the Africa Growth and Opportunity Act (AGOA), designed to enhance U.S.-African trade. Although sharply criticized by African leaders, such as former president Nelson Mandela of South Africa, as well as influential members of the U.S. African affairs constituency, most notably the Congressional Black Caucus, a compromise bill was passed by both the House of Representatives and the Senate in 2000, and subsequently embraced by the Bush administration. The stakes associated with U.S.-African economic ties, although small when compared to U.S. economic ties with its leading trade partners of Japan, Canada, and the European Union, are nonetheless substantial: approximately $24 billion in trade and $10 billion in U.S. direct investment as of 2002.

The Bush administration has sought to build on the Clinton administration's successes by strengthening and extending AGOA, ensuring high-level participation in business-oriented summits, such as the Corporate Council for Africa's biannual U.S.–Africa Business Summit held in June 2002, and offering rhetoric in favor of the aims embodied in the New Partnership for Africa's Development (NEPAD). It is highly unlikely, however, that the foreign aid and investment recommendations of a NEPAD peer review mechanism would be followed by an administration focused on promoting U.S. national security, and that in any case remains predisposed to favor trade over aid. Like his post–Cold War predecessors, Powell in particular argued that foreign policy should serve as the facilitator of U.S. private enterprise in all areas of the world, including Africa. "Open trade is an enormous force," he explains. "It powers more than just economic reform and growth; it creates better relations between nations."[42]

The Bush administration's primary focus in U.S.-African trade ties not surprisingly has involved ensuring U.S. access to and investment in Africa's burgeoning oil sector. This is the direct result of the Bush administration's national energy policy (which places an overriding emphasis on enhancing the supply of oil available to the U.S. economy) and the search for new markets outside of the Middle East in the post–September 11 era, not to mention the extremely close ties of senior Bush administration officials with the oil industry. Not only does Bush himself come from a family involved in the oil business, Cheney was the chief executive officer of Halliburton (a major oil services corporation) and Rice was a senior manager with Chevron (with the company even naming an oil tanker after her). In this regard, specialists in U.S. policy toward Africa are well advised to focus on evolving U.S. economic ties with such oil-rich African countries as Angola, Chad, Congo (Brazzaville), Equatorial Guinea, Gabon, and Nigeria.[43]

A final element of U.S. economic policy under both the Clinton and Bush administrations has been a rejection of Washington's past support for Europe's privileged economic role in its former colonies in favor of a more aggressive approach to promoting U.S. trade and investment (although both administrations have pressed the European allies to be more assertive in their former colonies in the political-military realm). "The African market is open to everyone," explained former assistant secretary of state for African affairs Herman Cohen in a 1995 speech in Libreville, Gabon. "We must accept free and fair competition, equality between all actors."[44] Such an approach not surprisingly has contributed to the intensification of economic competition between the United States and the other northern industrialized democracies, most notably France, as they compete for economic influence in the highly lucrative petroleum, telecommunications, and transport industries throughout Africa.

Foreign Policy Challenge #2: Mitigating the Deleterious Impacts of Corruption and Authoritarianism

The U.S. foreign policy solution for dealing with the deleterious impacts of corruption and authoritarianism has been to offer both diplomatic and financial support for democratization. Entering office when democratization movements were multiplying throughout the African continent, the Clinton administration even went so far as to set out an official democracy promotion doctrine, the "policy of enlargement," that was intended to replace the outmoded strategy of containment.[45] Although as an official doctrine enlargement proved to be short-lived, it nonetheless embodied the belief of both Clinton and Bush that promoting democracy is a worthy U.S. foreign policy goal. As such, it has infused official administration statements, as when Powell denounced President Robert Mugabe's continuation in office as an impediment to Zimbabwean democracy, or when Bush called upon President Charles Taylor to step down from power as an important first step in establishing democracy in Liberia.

One of the guiding principles of U.S. democracy promotion programs is that democracy is best served by fostering a regularized political process that has as its basis the holding of free and fair elections, as well as the nurturing of effective state institutions, most notably an independent legislature and judiciary and a civilian-controlled military. One result of this approach is that U.S. policy makers are often prone to portray even significantly flawed election results, especially in countries closely allied to the United States, as nonetheless constituting "important starting points" in the transition to democracy, which can be improved in later rounds of more democratic elections. It is precisely for this reason that critics have often criticized U.S. democracy promotion as placing too much faith in elections, as well as favoring a "top-down" approach to democratization that is too elite centered.[46]

Democracy promotion, however, has never served as the principal foreign policy interest of the northern industrialized democracies, including the United States. At best it has played a secondary role behind more self-interested pursuits.[47] Equally important, rhetoric has not always conformed with actual policies. The cornerstone of Clinton administration policy toward Congo-Kinshasa, for example, was a permutation of the "Mobutu or chaos" thesis that dominated the thinking of the State Department, the Pentagon, and the CIA from the 1960s through the 1980s.[48] This bureaucratically inspired consensus embodied the firm belief that "chaos," meaning territorial disintegration, regional instability, and ultimately communist expansion into the heart of Africa, was the only alternative to Mobutu's continued hold over power. The Mobutu or chaos thesis suggested the necessity for a strong (but not necessarily democratic) leader if the region is to avoid socioeconomic and political-military chaos. "Regardless of the fact that we are no longer faced with a communist threat," explained a member of the State Department's Africa Bureau, "the destabilization of Zaire [Congo-Kinshasa]—which borders nine other African countries—could have a tremendously negative impact on regional stability."[49] With the experiences of Somalia and Rwanda still etched in their minds, the Africa specialists of the executive branch bureaucracies successfully argued for the need to tread softly as, according to another member of the State Department's Africa Bureau, the situation in Congo-Kinshasa "could easily turn into a Somalia and a Rwanda rolled into one, although this time in one of Africa's largest and most populous nations."[50]

It was particularly striking during interviews to hear members of the State Department's Africa Bureau argue that, like his predecessor at the beginning of the 1990s, Kabila was both "part of the problem and part of the solution" to resolving the crisis in the Great Lakes region. Once again returning to current manifestations of the Mobutu or chaos thesis, there was a tendency for U.S. diplomatic personnel to argue against pushing Kabila too hard or too fast for fear that this would intensify an already chaotic political-military situation. As a result, initial U.S. support for the Kabila regime placed a heavy premium on his promise to create a "responsive and accountable" (but not necessarily democratic) government capable of restoring order and ensuring the territorial integrity of the nation. Toward this end, contemporary U.S. policy toward Congo-Kinshasa under the Bush administration continues to emphasize: stability, territorial integrity, and the cessation of transborder threats, even if the successful achievement of all three comes at the short-term expense of democracy.

Especially in the aftermath of the terrorist attacks of September 11, the Bush White House has had to weigh the benefits of democracy promotion when such a policy would potentially alienate important African allies in the war on terrorism. In the case of Djibouti, for example, a decision to make democracy promotion the principal U.S. foreign policy objective theoretically would have precluded the stationing on Djiboutian soil of hundreds of U.S. Special Forces. Indeed, all three of Washington's North African allies (Egypt, Morocco, and Tunisia) in the war on terrorism lack democratic political systems. "In short," explained a member of the U.S. embassy in Tunis in 2003, "foreign policy is about choosing, and in this case there is no question that the security interest of combating global terrorism with our allies in North Africa is more important than the degree to which the peoples of these countries enjoy democratic forms of governance."[51] The problem with such rationales, according to proponents of democracy promotion, is that the emerging anti-terrorist consensus in U.S. foreign policy is fostering a return to a strategic approach to the African continent reminiscent of the Cold War era in which national security interests overshadowed the normative goals of promoting democracy and fostering economic development.

Foreign Policy Challenge #3: Stemming the Multiplication of Civil Conflicts

The U.S. policy response to Africa's multiplying civil conflicts has been to limit White House exposure by curtailing U.S. involvement in United Nations–sponsored interventions and stressing a brand of conflict resolution that de facto embraces the theme "African solutions for African problems." The turning point in the post–Cold War era occurred in October 1993, when dozens of U.S. soldiers were killed or wounded in a fierce battle in Mogadishu, Somalia, as part of Operation Restore Hope, a humanitarian military mission initially launched by President Bush (senior) after he was defeated in the 1992 presidential elections. The

Somali "debacle," as it came to be known, served as the cornerstone of a policy directive, Presidential Decision Directive 25 (PDD 25), that announced an extremely cautious approach to ethnically and religiously based conflicts in Africa. When confronted in 1994 with rising popular demands for U.S. intervention in Rwanda, for example, the Clinton administration, fearful of being drawn into "another Somalia," not only initially blocked the dispatch of 5,500 troops requested by UN secretary-general Boutros Boutros-Ghali, it instructed administration spokespeople to avoid labeling the unfolding ethnic conflict as "genocide" lest such a label further inflame American public sympathy and demand American intervention as was the case in Somalia, or trigger American obligations under international treaties dealing with genocide and its prevention.[52]

As noted earlier in this chapter, President Bush had made a public statement during the 2000 election campaign that the Clinton administration had "done the right thing" in deciding not to intervene. This statement clearly captured Bush's strong aversion to U.S. involvement in peacemaking operations, often derisively referred to during the presidential campaign as ill-conceived exercises in "nation-building." As a result, the Bush White House remains hesitant to support United Nations–sponsored attempts at peacemaking on the African continent, and will continue to be extremely reluctant to authorize the involvement of U.S. troops even in less-threatening peacekeeping operations in which all parties to the conflict desire the placement of a third-party military force on the ground. It is precisely for this reason that in 2003 the Bush administration resisted initial pleas from within the West African region and the international community to commit large numbers of U.S. troops to stem fighting in Liberia, offering instead a limited deployment of small numbers of U.S. troops designed to provide logistical support to a larger West African peacekeeping force led by Nigeria.

White House hesitation to become involved in United Nations–sponsored military interventions in Africa reflects growing concerns, especially among Republicans in the U.S. Congress, about the general role of the U.S in the United Nations. As aptly noted by Daniel P. Volman, a specialist of the congressional role in U.S. policy toward Africa, Republican members of Congress have drawn on "public concern about the role of the United States in the United Nations to bolster their demands for cuts in U.S. financial support for the international body and for the curtailment of UN peace keeping activities in Africa and other parts of the world."[53] It is precisely this global mindset that allowed Senator Jesse Helms (Republican–North Carolina), the former chair of the Senate Foreign Relations Committee, to hold back U.S. funding for the UN until that body finally agreed to reduce the U.S. contributions to the overall UN budget (from 25 percent to 22 percent) and the UN peace-keeping budget (from 30 percent to 27 percent), with significant implications for UN activities in Africa.[54] Indeed, the congressional furor during May 2001 over the U.S. loss of its seat on the Human Rights Commission of the United Nations Economic and Social Council prompted the passage of congressional legislation withholding $244 million in unpaid dues until the seat was reinstated.

The White House's hesitancy in supporting United Nations–sponsored peacekeeping missions has led to de facto support for African military solutions under the guise of "African solutions for African problems." It is precisely for this reason, argued critics of U.S. policy toward Africa, that the Clinton administration originally proposed the creation of an African Crisis Response Force (ACRF), subsequently reformulated under the guise of the African Crisis Response Initiative (ACRI). Africans, not Americans, were to take the lead in resolving African conflicts—a regional dynamic that stood in sharp contrast to extensive White House attempts at resolving the Arab-Israeli conflict in the Middle East and the series of crises in the Balkans in Western Europe.

The experience in Somalia also significantly affected the Clinton administration's approach to conflict resolution, most notably by re-solving a debate between two currents of thought in the administration. The first emphasized the classic belief that African issues unnecessarily distract the administration and potentially plunge the White House into unwanted domestic political controversies. According to this viewpoint, U.S. involvement (even in terms of conflict resolution) should be re-stricted in order to avoid entanglement in "future Somalias." A second, more activist approach also derived from the Somali experience but un-derscored that the massive costs associated with Operation Restore Hope could have been avoided by earlier, preventive action. "The choice is not between intervening or not intervening," explained a policy maker at the beginning of the Clinton administration. "It is between getting involved early and doing it at a cheaper cost, or being forced to inter-vene in a massive, more costly way later."[55] As witnessed by the Clinton White House's cautious approach to the initial stages of the Rwandan conflict, the events of October 1993 in Somalia clearly strengthened the position of those warning against getting too closely involved in "intractable" conflicts in Africa.

The Bush administration clearly shares its predecessor's maxim of avoiding undue U.S. involvement in African conflicts. As explained by Powell during his Senate confirmation hearings, the newly elected administration agreed with its predecessor that Africans needed to "do more for themselves" in the realm of conflict resolution. "In Sierra Leone, Liberia, Angola, the Congo [Kinshasa] and elsewhere, this means stopping the killing, taking the weapons out of the hands of children, ending corruption, seeking compromises, and beginning to work in peace and dialogue rather than war and killing," explained Powell. "It means giving the profits from oil and diamonds and other precious resources to schools and hospitals and decent roads instead of to bombs, bullets, and feuding warlords."[56] According to what can be labeled the Powell Doctrine for Africa, African diplomats and military forces, and not those of foreign powers (including the United States) must take the lead in responding to African crises and conflicts. U.S. forces, if to be used at all, must be perceived as the source of last resort, and in any case must be severely limited in terms of size, mission, and timetable. This vision is integral to the Bush administration's military training program known as the African Contingency Operations Training and Assistance (ACOTA) program, which in turn replaced ACRI. The primary difference between ACRI and ACOTA is that the latter focuses on training for "offensive" military operations, including the ability of African troops to conduct operations in hostile environments.

U.S. foreign policy has particularly evolved as concerns the potential threat posed by state failure of varying degrees in Africa and other regions of the Southern hemisphere. Especially during the 1990s, the breakdown of central state authority fostered the emergence of several "warlord states" (in which vast stretches of the hinterland are actually controlled by regional military leaders opposed to the state) and "collapsed" or "failed" states (in which regime failure leads to the complete breakdown of central state authority over a given territory).[57] The test case of the post–Cold War era for how the United States would respond to such states, of course, was U.S. intervention in Somalia, which made both the Clinton and Bush administrations wary of becoming involved in similar cases. Indeed, it is striking that Somalia was (and remains) permitted to drift without an effective centralized state structure since the collapse of the Siad Barre regime in 1991.

In the post–September 11 era, the Bush administration has come to the realization that failed states run the risk of becoming "breeding grounds" for terrorist activities. This realization, however, has led to neither the elaboration of an official policy as concerns failed states nor a willingness to commit U.S. troops in such situations. The de facto policy has become one of relying on the interventionist efforts of three sets of actors: African regional powers or regional organizations with direct stakes in the conflict, as in the case of Nigerian-led intervention in Liberia; former colonial powers, as in the case of French intervention in Côte d'Ivoire; and United Nations–led peacekeeping forces, as in the case of Congo-Kinshasa.

Foreign Policy Challenge #4: Containing and Eliminating Transborder Threats

The U.S. policy of containing and eliminating transborder threats, most notably the deadly 1998 terrorist attacks against U.S. embassies in Nairobi, Kenya, and Dar es Salaam, Tanzania, and later terrorist attacks in 2002 against tourist targets in Mombasa, Kenya, has followed a three-fold approach. First and foremost, the United States has sought to cultivate ties with strategically placed African powers. As explained by Powell, the Bush administration has focused its energies on Africa's leading regional powers, most notably Nigeria in West Africa and South Africa in Southern Africa, harkening back to the Nixon administration's strategy of relying on such powers to ensure stability within their given regions. This worldview represents somewhat of a departure from the Clinton administration's approach of relying on what was often referred to as the "new bloc" of African leaders, including Isaias Afwerki of Eritrea, Meles Zenawi of Ethiopia, Yoweri Museveni of Uganda, and Paul Kagame of Rwanda, who control battle-hardened guerrilla armies and who are committed to militarily reordering African international relations. Apart from the fact that they control the reins of power, these regimes were supported by the Clinton administration due to their ability to maintain stability and their commitment to creating "responsive and accountable" but not necessarily democratic governments.[58]

Critics of the Clinton administration's policy, which like that the Bush administration emphasizes the importance of maintaining stability over the normative goal of democracy promotion, argue that its shortcomings were clearly demonstrated by the emergence of interstate conflicts between the members of this new bloc, including the border war between Ethiopia and Eritrea and the military clashes between Uganda and Rwanda in Congo-Kinshasa. According to this argument, the primary problem with the Clinton administration approach was to rely on personalized links with leaders who for whatever reason held the upper hand at any given moment, regardless of the true power of their countries—as in the case of Rwanda's undue influence over its much larger neighbor, Congo-Kinshasa. A more effective long-term approach, according to the Bush administration's realist worldview, is to focus on true regional powers that combine both the economic and military capabilities (not to mention the political intention) to ensure stability within their given regions. It is precisely for this reason, for example, that the Bush administration has pressured South Africa to play a more proactive role in resolving an intensifying political crisis in Zimbabwe, as well as support the decision of Nigeria to lead a peacekeeping force to Liberia.

A second element of U.S. containment and elimination of transborder threats has involved an aggressive policy toward regional pariah states, most notably Libya and Sudan. Especially in the early months of the Bush administration, a more bellicose conservatism overrode the more moderate instincts of Powell and the State Department. For example, the Bush administration refused to drop U.S. sanctions against Libya although the Qaddafi regime had finally handed over two suspects associated with the 1988 Lockerbie air disaster (in which a bomb destroyed Pan Am Flight 103, killing all on board), and an international court in January 2001 had found one of the suspects guilty, while releasing a second. As part of a conservative-inspired "get tough" policy with regional pariah states, the newly elected Bush administration raised new conditions for the suspension of sanctions, which included the Qaddafi regime's formal admission of guilt and payment of compensation to the families of the deceased.[59]

U.S. foreign policy toward the Sudanese regime of Omar Hassan al-Bashir, although it had taken certain steps to marginalize the Islamist forces of Omar Hassan al-Turabi, further demonstrated the Bush administration's "get tough" policy with regional pariah states in its early months. Whereas the Clinton administration focused on the regional threat associated with Sudan's attempts to export its brand of Islamic revivalism, the Bush administration had initially focused on the human rights abuses associated with that country's eighteen-year-old civil war, the longest running in Africa. Powell noted in congressional testimony on March 7, 2001, for example, that there exists "perhaps no greater tragedy on the face of the earth today."[60]

The principal driving force in U.S. policy toward Sudan, however, was not Powell's personal interest but rather rising pressures from a wide array of Christian groups—one of the Bush administration's most important grassroots constituencies—to "do something" to stop what they perceive as a genocidal policy that a northern-based Islamic regime is carrying out against a southern-based, predominantly Christian population. Christian groups are especially outraged by the ongoing practice of southern Christians being sold as slaves in northern Sudan, and have joined with sympathetic members of Congress, most notably Sam Brownback (Republican–Kansas), to call for a more aggressive U.S. policy stance.[61] In the aftermath of the terrorist attacks of September 11, however, the Bush administration softened its rhetoric due to Sudan's diplomatic support for Washington's global war against terrorism.

The third element of the U.S. approach to containing and eliminating transborder threats involves a series of interconnected anti-terrorist efforts. At the heart of these efforts is a significantly expanded embassy construction budget for upgrading the security of embassies at risk, as well as expediting the building of new embassies, such as the $42 million facility in Tunis, Tunisia, that now house once geographically dispersed buildings within one walled compound. The so-called hardening of U.S. diplomatic targets, which includes the construction of new diplomatic facilities in Nigeria and South Africa, is complemented by a series of anti-terrorist diplomatic initiatives, such as a $100 million counter-terrorism package for East Africa, designed to promote regional cooperation against a variety of terrorist threats in conjunction with U.S. intelligence and law-enforcement agencies, most notably the CIA and the Federal Bureau of Investigation (FBI).

Foreign Policy Challenge #5: Halting the Spread of HIV/AIDS

The centerpiece of the U.S. foreign policy approach to halting the spread of HIV/AIDS has been funding for HIV/AIDS programs in the United States (Center for Disease Control), targeted African countries (such as Uganda, the continental leader in HIV/AIDS prevention), and the international system (such as the United Nations Global Fund to Fight AIDS,

Tuberculosis and Malaria). Although the Clinton administration had supported low levels of funding for a variety of HIV/AIDS programs throughout the 1990s, a "tipping point" was reached in the latter half of 1998, in the aftermath of Clinton's twelve-day presidential visit to the African continent, which led to a series of policy initiatives.[62] Of particular importance was an executive order signed by Clinton in May 2000 that would allow African countries confronted by medical emergencies to pursue two courses of action without risk of U.S. sanctions:

- "parallel imports" (purchasing patented pharmaceuticals from an inexpensive source in a Third World country);
- "compulsory licensing" (commissioning a domestic firm to produce a medication after forcing negotiated terms with the patent holder, so long as they were not in formal violation of the World Trade Organization's international property rights agreement).[63]

The momentum in the U.S. approach to the HIV/Aids pandemic was strengthened at the beginning of the Bush administration by a White House commitment to provide $200 million to the United Nations' Global Fund. Although some applauded this new direction, with others criticizing the $200 million as an extremely paltry amount that in reality did not even begin to address the true extent of the problem throughout Africa, most observers remained wary due to the simple fact that prominent leaders within both the Republican-dominated White House and Congress have typically not been sympathetic to a wide array of progressive social policies. For example, almost immediately upon taking the presidential oath, President Bush, with the firm backing of his conservative allies, reinstated the ban originally imposed by the Reagan administration (but overturned during the Clinton years) on providing U.S. federal aid to overseas entities that provide, or counsel in favor of, abortion services, an action that has had severe implications for the family planning programs of African governments.

Africanists were nonetheless heartened by Powell's very public focus on African efforts to combat HIV/AIDS and a variety of other communicable diseases, most notably malaria and tuberculosis, during his week-long tour of four African countries in May 2001. The more realist underpinnings of the trip were nonetheless demonstrated by the fact that conflicts in neighboring countries and what Africans could do to resolve them with U.S. support served as an important component of private discussions with host country leaders. Among the regional hotspots that dominated the bilateral talks were: Guinea, Liberia, and Sierra Leone with President Alpha Oumar Konaré of Mali; Angola, Congo-Kinshasa, and Zimbabwe with President Thabo Mbeki of South Africa; Congo-Kinshasa and Sudan with President Daniel arap Moi of Kenya; and Congo-Kinshasa and Sudan with President Yoweri Museveni of Uganda. Realism also pervaded high-level discussions that focused on strengthening U.S.-African trade relationships via AGOA, an area of common national self-interest regardless of whether Powell was dealing with a democratic South Africa under Mbeki's leadership or an undemocratic Kenya under Moi.

To its credit, the Bush administration has made the necessity of fighting HIV/AIDS an important component of official administration rhetoric, and, by the beginning of 2003, was promising to provide $10 billion in "emergency" funds to fight HIV/AIDS in Africa as part of a $15 billion global effort that would be spread over five years. Skeptics nonetheless point out that, despite its "emergency" label, the Bush administration's budget provided no new funds for 2003.[64] "The $10 billion in new money would start small, with much less than $1 billion disbursed in 2004 and with no guarantee that it would not be edged out of future budgets by rising costs of war in Iraq or other priorities pushed by powerful lobbyists," explains Salih Booker, William Minter, and Ann-Louise Colgan, three scholars associated with Africa Action. "Also *The New York Times* noted that the increase in AIDS funds comes partly by cutting nearly $500 million from international child health programs."[65] In short, these and other critics argue that funding is not at the level that was either promised by the Bush administration or that is necessary to deal with the HIV/AIDS pandemic, and remaining foreign aid resources are increasingly being targeted toward counter-terrorism and other national security objectives at the expense of development.

Toward the Future

The African continent and U.S. policy toward Africa are at important turning points as both African and American leaders grapple with decisions designed to strengthen the African renaissance at the beginning of the new millennium. African leaders are confronted with the reality that even the best of intentions are often not enough as they struggle with a variety of political-military and socioeconomic challenges. American leaders are similarly confronted with the reality that attempts at facilitating the African renaissance require an enormous amount of political will and understanding of an extremely diverse African mosaic that historically has not constituted a priority concern within the global hierarchy of U.S. foreign policy.

Even the best of American intentions, which attempt to draw on America's benevolent Uncle Sam mythology in the active pursuit of facilitating the African renaissance, can be deemed contradictory, inadequate, or, in the extreme, as essentially constituting an Uncle Scrooge policy devoid of either true interest or sincerity. It is clear that the vast majority of African leaders and intellectuals at the very minimum perceive U.S. policies toward Africa as being both contradictory and inadequate. Although several recent high-profile events, most notably presidential visits to the African continent by Clinton in 1998 and 2000, and Bush in 2003, were designed to reverse this perception, and indeed are indicative of rising U.S. interests, such high-level attention is typically fleeting and therefore has been unable to convince the majority of Africans that the United States is seriously interested in African problems. Even in the case of Clinton's presidential visits to the African continent, which on average were more positively and warmly perceived than that undertaken by Bush in 2003, many African leaders and policy makers appreciated Clinton's warm rhetoric and sincere interest in African affairs, but were highly critical of the fact that rhetoric often was not followed by the implementation of concrete policies.

Observers of U.S. Africa policies are particularly critical of the impact of U.S. Cold War policies on the African continent. The Cold War tendency to perceive the African continent as a tool for solving non-African problems (i.e., through the East-West lens of containment of communism and the Soviet Union), which in turn ensured the emergence of the African continent as a battlefield for proxy wars as both the United States and the Soviet Union became involved in regional conflicts, often exerted a negative impact on the African countries that became witting or unwitting pawns on this East-West chessboard. To be sure, U.S. policy toward Africa achieved notable successes during the Cold War era, as demonstrated by the way adult Africans fondly remember their Peace Corps teachers and the educational opportunities that were opened up to tens of thousands of Africans through a vast array of cultural exchange programs. It is the broad strokes of policy that matter, however, and in this regard the broad strokes, at least during the Cold War, suggested that Africans were not important in their own right.

It is precisely for this reason that many observers of U.S. foreign policy look with trepidation upon the Bush administration's ever-widening global war against terrorism. Specifically, the emerging anti-terrorist consensus in U.S. foreign policy appears to be fostering a return to a strategic approach to the African continent reminiscent of the Cold War era in which national security interests overshadowed the normative goals of promoting democracy and fostering economic development. Although many observers hoped that the Cold War's end would usher in a new era in U.S. policy toward Africa, the emergence of what some are now referring to as a "second Cold War" (albeit in this case against international terrorism) makes it highly likely that Africa will once again be viewed by American policy makers through a strategic prism that more likely than not will have little (if anything) to do with the reality confronted by most African states. Indeed, as a result of the events of September 11, the motto attributed to the initial months of the Bush administration's policy toward Africa—"Forget the rhetoric and boost the geopolitics"— is potentially being replaced by an even more negative variant—"Forget democracy and development and boost anti-terrorism"—with severe implications for an entire generation of African citizens.

Notes

1. Michael Clough, *Free at Last? U.S. Policy Toward Africa and the End of the Cold War* (New York: Council on Foreign Relations Press, 1992), p. 2.

2. Michael Clough, "The United States and Africa: The Policy of Cynical Disengagement," *Current History* 91, no. 565 (May 1992): 193–98.

3. For other recent examples, see Stephen J. Morrison and Jennifer G. Cooke, eds., *Africa Policy in the Clinton Years: Critical Choices for the Bush Administration* (Washington, DC: Center for Strategic and International Studies Press, 2001); David F. Gordon, David C. Miller, Jr., and Howard Wolpe, *The United States and Africa: A Post–Cold War Perspective* (New York: W.W. Norton, 1998); and Karl P. Magyar, ed., *United States Interests and Policies in Africa: Transition to a New Era* (New York: St. Martin's Press, 2000).

4. Crawford Young, "United States Foreign Policy Toward Africa: Silver Anniversary Reflections," *African Studies Review* 27, no. 3 (Sept. 1984): 14.

5. N. Brian Winchester, "United States Foreign Policy Toward Africa," *Current History* 87, no. 529 (May 1988): 193.

6. See Peter Duignan and L.H. Gann, *The United States and Africa: A History* (Cambridge, UK: Cambridge University Press, 1984).

7. F. Ugboaja Ohaegbulam, "Containment in Africa: From Truman to Reagan," *TransAfrica Forum* 6, no. 1 (Fall 1988): 7–34.

8. Jeffrey E. Garten, *A Cold Peace: America, Japan, Germany, and the Struggle for Supremacy* (New York: Twentieth Century Fund, 1993).

9. Peter J. Schraeder, "Cold War to Cold Peace: U.S.–French Competition in Francophone Africa," *Political Science Quarterly* 115, no. 3 (2000): 395–420.

10. Steven A. Holmes, "Africa: From Cold War to Cold Shoulders," *New York Times* (Mar. 7, 1993): E4.

11. Quoted in Walter Pincus, "CIA Plans to Close 15 Stations in African Cutback," *Washington Post* (June 23, 1994): A20.

12. For an overview, see Cherif Ouazani, "L'Enquête Djibouti: En première ligne," *Jeune Afrique l'Intelligent,* no. 2195 (Feb. 2–8, 2003): 36–41.

13. For example, see Randall Robinson, *The Debt: What America Owes to Blacks* (New York: Dutton, 2000). For a contrarian view, see Keith B. Richburg, *Out of Africa: A Black Man Confronts Africa* (New York: BasicBooks, 1997).

14. For a fascinating portrayal by a career diplomat, see Donald Petterson, *Revolution in Zanzibar: An American's Cold War Tale* (Boulder, CO: Westview, 2002).

15. For example, see Sean Kelly, *America's Tyrant: The CIA and Mobutu of Zaire* (Washington, DC: American University Press, 1993).

16. Peter J. Schraeder, Steven W. Hook, and Bruce Taylor, "Clarifying the Foreign Aid Puzzle: A Comparison of American, Japanese, French, and Swedish Aid Flows," *World Politics* 50, no. 2 (Jan. 1998): 294–323.

17. Ibid.

18. Clough, *Free at Last?*, p. 77.

19. Ibid., pp. 76–100.

20. For a more extended analysis, see Peter J. Schraeder, *United States Foreign Policy Toward Africa: Incrementalism, Crisis and Change* (Cambridge, UK: Cambridge University Press, 1994).

21. See the articles in a special issue, "The Clinton Administration and Africa (1993–1999)," *Issue: A Journal of Opinion* 26, no. 2.

22. Quoted in Ian Fisher, "Africans Ask If Washington's Sun Will Shine on Them," *New York Times* (Jan. 21, 2001): A3.

23. Quoted in Howard W. French, "Shrinking from Democracy: In Congo, A Lesson in Where Easy Paths Lead," *New York Times* (Jan. 21, 2001): A3.

24. For a sampling of these views, see Seul Mouammar Kaddafi, "La politique de Tarzan," *Jeune Afrique l'Intelligent,* no. 2218 (July 13–19, 2003): 17–20; and Francis Kpatindé, "Un cow-boy en Afrique," *Jeune Afrique l'Intelligent,* no. 2217 (July 6–12, 2003): 56–58.

25. For a useful overview, see Kim Olsen, ed., *Contact: Africa 2001, A Directory of U.S. Organizations Working on Africa,* 4th ed. (Washington, DC: Africa-America Institute, 2001).

26. Peter J. Schraeder, "Bureaucratic Incrementalism, Crisis, and Change in U.S. Foreign Policy Toward Africa," in Jerel A. Rosati, Joe D. Hagan, and Martin W. Sampson III, eds., *Foreign Policy Restructuring: How Governments Respond to Global Change* (Columbia: University of South Carolina Press, 1994), pp. 111–37.

27. Quoted in Fisher, "Africans Ask If Washington's Sun Will Shine on Them," p. A3.

28. The primary mission of the State Department's Bureau of African Affairs, for example, is the maintenance of smooth and stable relationships with all African

governments. The emphasis is on quiet diplomacy and the negotiated resolution of any conflicts that may arise. In sharp contrast, the primary bureaucratic mission of the CIA's Africa Division traditionally was to carry the ideological battle against the Soviet Union and communism to the African continent in efforts that ranged from the cultivation of local agents to the mounting of covert operations. Openly contemptuous of self-proclaimed Marxist and other "leftist" regimes, liberation movements, "radical" Islamist regimes, and, more recently, terrorist movements, the CIA prefers close liaison with the security services of European allies and friendly African regimes. In the case of the Pentagon, the primary bureaucratic mission of the Office for African Affairs (International Security Affairs) is to ensure continued access to strategically located bases and other facilities for responding to local crises and, most important, military contingencies in Europe and the Middle East. Finally, the primary bureaucratic mission of the Africa Office within the Department of Commerce is to foster U.S. trade and investment throughout the African continent.

29. For fascinating insights provided by a political appointee, see Smith Hempstone, *Rogue Ambassador: An African Memoir* (Sewane, TN: University of the South Press, 1997).

30. For an excellent introduction, see Walter Clarke and Jeffrey Herbst, eds., *Learning From Somalia: The Lessons of Armed Humanitarian Intervention* (Boulder, CO: Westview, 1997).

31. For a good overview, see Terrence Lyons and Ahmed I. Samatar, *Somalia: State Collapse, Multilateral Intervention, and Strategies for Political Reconstruction* (Washington, DC: Brookings Institution, 1995).

32. Steven R. Weisman and Thom Shanker, "U.S. Facing Rising Pressure for Liberia Role," *New York Times* (Aug. 9, 2003): A1, A4.

33. See Morton H. Halperin, *Bureaucratic Politics and Foreign Policy* (Washington, DC: Brookings Institution, 1974).

34. Eric Schmitt, "U.S. Military Plans African Expansion," *International Herald Tribune* (July 5–6, 2003): 1, 4.

35. Quoted in ibid., p. 4.

36. Quoted in Halperin, *Bureaucratic Politics and Foreign Policy,* p. 292.

37. See Peter J. Schraeder, "'Forget the Rhetoric and Boost the Geopolitics': Emerging Trends in the Bush Administration's Policy Towards Africa, 2001," *African Affairs,* no. 100 (2001): 387–404.

38. Charles F. Doran, "Regionalists vs. Globalists," in Peter J. Schraeder, ed., *Intervention into the 1990s: U.S. Foreign Policy Toward the Third World* (Boulder, CO: Lynne Rienner, 1992), pp. 55–74.

39. Ibid.

40. Donald Rothchild, "The U.S. Foreign Policy Trajectory on Africa," *SAIS Review* 21, no. 1 (Winter/Spring 2001): 179–211.

41. Samir Gharbi, "Afrique: Augmentation de l'aide américaine en trompe l'oeil," *Jeune Afrique l'Intelligent,* no. 2207 (Apr. 27–May 3, 2003): 94.

42. A statement of Secretary of State-Designate Colin L. Powell prepared for the Confirmation Hearing of the U.S. Senate Committee on Foreign Relations, Jan. 17, 2001, p. 12.

43. See Stephen Ellis, "Briefing: West Africa and Its Oil," *African Affairs* 102, no. 406 (Jan. 2003): 135–38; Jean-Pierre Favennec and Philippe Copinschi, "Les Nouveaux enjeux pétroliers en Afrique," *Politique Africaine,* no. 89 (Mar. 2003): 127–48.

44. Copy of speech provided by the U.S. embassy in Libreville, Gabon.

45. Anthony Lake, "From Containment to Enlargement," address at the School of Advanced International Studies, Johns Hopkins University, Washington, DC, Sept. 21, 1993.

46. Thomas Carothers, *Aiding Democracy Abroad: The Learning Curve* (Washington, DC: Carnegie Endowment for International Peace, 1999), pp. 136–40.

47. Peter J. Schraeder, ed., *Exporting Democracy: Rhetoric vs. Reality* (Boulder, CO: Lynne Rienner, 2003).

48. Michael G. Schatzberg, *Mobutu or Chaos? The United States and Zaire, 1960–1990* (Lanham, MD: University Press of America, 1991).

49. Quoted in Schraeder, *United States Foreign Policy Toward Africa,* p. 107.

50. Personal interview.

51. Personal interview.

52. Douglas Jehl, "Officials Told to Avoid Calling Rwanda Killings Genocide," *New York Times* (June 10, 1994): A8.

53. Daniel P. Volman, "The Clinton Administration and Africa: Role of Congress and the Africa Subcommittees," *Issue: A Journal of Opinion* 26, no. 2 (1998): 14.

54. Barbara Crossette, "U.N. Agrees to Cut Dues Paid by U.S., Easing an Irritant," *New York Times* (Dec. 23, 2000): A1, A6.

55. Jim Cason and Bill Martin, "Clinton and Africa: Searching for a Post–Cold War Order," *ACAS Bulletin,* no. 38–39 (Winter 1993): 3.

56. *U.S. International Engagement: A Time of Great Opportunity, Statements by Secretary of State Colin Powell on Key Foreign Policy Issues;* opening statement, confirmation hearing before the Senate Foreign Relations Committee, Jan. 17, 2001, available at http://usinfo.state.gov/journals/itps/0301/ijpe/pj61powe.htm, accessed July 27, 2004.

57. For a more extensive discussion, see Peter J. Schraeder, *African Politics and Society: A Mosaic in Transformation,* 2nd ed. (Belmont, CA: Wadsworth/Thomson Learning, 2004). For example, see I. William Zartman, ed., *Collapsed States: The Disintegration and Restoration of Legitimate Authority* (Boulder, CO: Lynne Rienner, 1995).

58. Dan Connell and Frank Smith, "Africa's New Bloc," *Foreign Affairs* 77, no. 2 (Mar./Apr. 1998): 80–94; and Marina Ottaway, *Africa's New Leaders: Democracy or State Reconstruction?* (Washington, DC: Carnegie Endowment for International Peace, 1999).

59. Jane Perlez, "Unpersuaded by Verdict, Bush Backs Sanctions," *New York Times* (Feb. 1, 2001): A8.

60. Quoted in Anthony Lewis, "'No Greater Tragedy,'" *New York Times* (Mar. 24, 2001): A27.

61. Jane Perlez, "Pair of Views About Sudan: Help Rebels or End War," *New York Times* (Feb. 25, 2001): A5.

62. J. Stephen Morrison, "U.S. Policy Toward HIV/AIDS in Africa: Momentum, Opportunities, and Urgent Choices," in Morrison and Cooke, eds., *Africa Policy in the Clinton Years,* p. 20.

63. Ibid., pp. 19–20.

64. Salih Booker, William Minter, and Ann-Louise Colgan, "America and Africa," *Current History* 102, no. 664 (May 2003): 195–99.

65. Ibid., p. 196.

10

Conclusion and Perspectives

U.S. Policy Toward the Global South
After September 11, 2001

Jürgen Rüland

U.S. Post–Cold War Policies in the Global South:
Lack of Coherence

In the previous chapters U.S. policies toward key regions of the global South have been examined. At least six major conclusions can be drawn from these analyses. First, at the domestic level there is no lack of vocal lobbies and civil society organizations in the United States representing the interests of the countries and the people in the global South. They lobby for a more equitable and just global economic order, for more democracy, poverty alleviation, and environmental protection. They castigate the excesses of neoliberal globalization and unprincipled collusion with authoritarian regimes and they expose corruption, social injustices, ethnic and religious discrimination, and other human rights violations in countries of the South. A broad array of think tanks, often with explicit ideological predispositions and partisan links, and well-established area studies programs in the universities, provide unrivaled scholarly expertise on most regions of the developing world, with the possible exceptions of Central Asia and a few closed regimes such as Iran, North Korea, and Iraq. Unfortunately, however, foreign policy makers often seem averse to utilizing the available scholarly expertise.[1]

As congressional influence on foreign policy making has markedly increased in the post-Vietnam era, most NGOs and civil society groups seek congressional backing for their demands. However, given the fragmentation, the lack of coordination, and, usually, the mostly single-issue agendas of these groups, their activities may have contributed to a pluralization of U.S. foreign policy making, but hardly to more effective representation of Third World interests. Most of these Third World lobbies are unable to mobilize enough backing in Congress to change government policies. Representatives and senators normally respond only to issues that help them in their reelection bids, that is, issues that generate publicity or have an immediate bearing on the interests of their constituents and their campaign financiers. Given the limited interest of the American public in foreign policy and in regions where no or only marginal American interests are at stake, Third World affairs normally attract only limited attention in Congress.[2] The exceptions are major security threats originating in the regions of the South, such as international terrorism after September 11, 2001. In such cases, however, the momentum in policy making shifts from Congress to the executive branch.

Second, more than in the Cold War period, the 1990s were characterized by a lack of coherence and continuity in American foreign policy toward countries of the South. Whereas during the Cold War, the position of Third World countries in the superpower rivalry primarily defined American policies toward them, in the period between the collapse of the Eastern Bloc and September 11, 2001, there was no singular global issue that determined U.S. foreign policy to the same extent. Moreover, in the absence of major security threats and the growing importance of "low politics" in foreign policy making with its concomitant pluralization of actors, policy outcomes became less predictable than in the Cold War era. After September 11, the U.S.-led war on terrorism is rapidly becoming the new "North Star" guiding Washington's relations with the global South. Although the renewed priority of security issues in U.S. foreign policy has strengthened the president and the executive, this does not necessarily mean that inconsistencies have ceased. Foreign policy decisions are still the result of bureaucratic politics involving the State Department, the Pentagon, the National Security Council, and the economic departments. Moreover, they also reflect the influence of the ideologues in the administration and the foreign policy-making apparatus. Whereas, as Howard J. Wiarda (Chapter 4) argues, the ideologues may have greater influence shortly after an administration comes into office, over time the foreign and security bureaucracies, with their more pragmatic outlook, regain their influence.[3]

Third, inconsistencies in U.S. policies in the 1990s have, third, been particularly noteworthy in the promotion of democracy and human rights. While the policy of "enlargement" has at least temporarily given higher priority to democratization and human rights in U.S. policies toward the global South, they have still been subordinated to other objectives: in the Cold War era to the twin objectives of anti-communism and containment of the Soviet Union and in the 1990s to economic objectives. Cases in point are the policies vis-à-vis China, Russia, and the "new generation of African leaders." Promotion of democracy and human rights were frequently criticized as policies applying double standards.

Fourth, while "benign neglect" goes too far as a characterization of U.S. relations toward the global South in the post–Cold War period, it is indisputable that as a U.S. foreign policy priority the South was considerably downgraded and relations with it were much more selective. Despite the symbolic politics of the second Clinton administration, Central Asia, South Asia, and Africa received the least interest of all major regions of the South. In the 1990s, these regions lost their geopolitical and strategic value, although Central Asia with its oil and gas reserves and South Asia after India's economic liberalization have become economically attractive to the United States. Africa, once a pawn on the East-West chessboard, was relegated to a "back-burner" of U.S. policy in the 1990s. With the current Bush administration's war on terror looming high among the priorities of the U.S. foreign policy agenda, observers worry that the continent may slide back into a second Cold War where strategic objectives rank higher than normative goals such as promoting democracy and poverty alleviation.[4]

Southeast Asia, too, ceased to receive the attention it had during the Cold War. No singular event could be more symbolic of the downscaled strategic interest of the United States in Southeast Asia than the closing of the military bases in the Philippines—even if the closing was preceded by a vote of the Philippine Senate ending the right of the United States to maintain bases in the country. The loss of the bases was at least partly compensated for by visiting rights for the U.S. Navy in Singapore and, in 1999, a Visiting Forces Agreement with the Philippines.[5] They provide the United States with logistical support to protect the sea lanes across Southeast Asia through which Japan, a major U.S. ally in East Asia, imports 80 percent of its energy. How Southeast Asia ranks in U.S. policy makers' priorities is to some extent a function of America's China policies. The more the U.S. regards China as a "strategic competitor," the more attention it must devote to Southeast Asia, a region traditionally considered by China as a sphere of influence.

Latin America as the backyard of the United States has always attracted American attention. The North American Free Trade Agreement (NAFTA), which includes Mexico, and moves toward a Free Trade Area of the Americas (FTAA) are manifestations of the continued interest of the United States in Latin America. The Middle East also remained a priority region in the 1990s. In the Gulf, the United States pursued a strategy of "dual containment" directed against Iraqi ambitions to acquire weapons of mass destruction (WMD) and alleged Iranian designs to export its theocratic system of government to the region. The centerpiece of its Middle Eastern policy, however, was the search for a settlement of the Arab-Israeli conflict, with the United States becoming a prime mover in the Oslo peace process. Yet, the perceived American bias in the Arab-Israeli conflict was a major reason for the dramatic loss of American "soft power" in the region and among Muslims in general. Confidence in U.S. policies further eroded under the current Bush administration, which is widely suspected in the Muslim world of giving a free hand to Israeli prime minister Sharon to use unrestrained military force in retaliation against Arab suicide bombings. Unilateral air strikes by the Clinton administration against Iraq and targets in Sudan in the 1990s further fueled anti-Americanism in Islamic countries. It reached new heights in the aftermath of the campaign against the Taliban, during the Israeli military incursions into the West Bank in the first half of 2002, the Iraq War, and after the revelation of gross human rights violations by American security personnel in occupied Iraq.

After September 11, 2001, attitudes of American foreign policy makers toward the global South changed profoundly, so much that international terrorism has become the main criterion defining relations with Third World countries. It is thus hardly surprising that regions considered to be breeding grounds for terrorism, such as the Middle East, Central Asia, and parts of South Asia, attracted most American attention. However, more surprising was the fact that Southeast Asia, a region hitherto known for its more tolerant brand of Islam, was designated by Pentagon planners as a "second front" in the fight against international terrorism. These overly alarmist concerns were obviously guided by the Islamic revival in the region, the growing political space of Islamist groups after democratization in Indonesia, and ethno-religious conflicts in peripheral regions of Indonesia, the Philippines, and since early 2004 in the south of Thailand.[6]

Fifth, while "hard" security issues were downgraded in American Third World policies during the 1990s, economic issues gained in priority. They were part and parcel of an American strategy to overcome the perceived weaknesses exposed during the so-called Western decline debate and to restore the economic fundamentals of U.S. power. Even though "low-intensity conflicts" and so-called nonconventional security threats such as illegal immigration, piracy, narcotics trafficking, environmental degradation, and AIDS and other epidemics increasingly caught the attention of U.S. policy makers, no sense of urgency was attached to them. Hence, development and foreign aid—including that channeled through multilateral organizations—were deemed dispensable and consequently dramatically scaled back. Even worse, in a Republican-dominated Congress preoccupied with America's national interest, poverty alleviation was discredited as "welfare aid" and as a waste of resources. In the quest for strengthening American economic competitiveness in a globalizing world, U.S. policies concentrated on the economically most advanced regions of the Third World: selected countries in Southeast Asia and Latin America and, outside these regions, economies like India and South Africa. Trade promotion and American investment opportunities were the prime motivations behind this policy. In the regions marginalized by globalization, American economic interests concentrated mainly on the extractive sector, most notably oil and gas. A systematic development policy concentrating on basic needs, sustainable development, poverty alleviation, and investment in human capital was abandoned, and the role of USAID as the agency responsible for development cooperation was questioned and downgraded.

Sixth, and last, multilateralist policies pursued in the first years of the Clinton administration increasingly gave way to a more unilateralist approach. American displeasure was particularly directed against the United Nations. James M. McCormick (Chapter 3) notes that this shift marks an adjustment to a Republican-dominated Congress, reflected also in Clinton's appointment of William Cohen, a Republican senator, as defense secretary. Anthony Lake, Clinton's erstwhile national security advisor, aptly summarized the ensuing trend toward a more conservative foreign policy when he stated that "only one overriding factor can determine whether the United States should act multilaterally or unilaterally, and that is America's interests."[7]

The Aftermath of September 11, 2001: The Rediscovery of the Global South?

The younger Bush came into office in January 2001 with an avowed disinterest in Third World affairs. Typical in this respect was an election campaign statement that Africa does not "fit into the national strategic interests" of America.[8] His administration also had low regard for nation-building in failed states, peacekeeping, and international institution building, especially if they curtailed U.S. policy options. The Bush administration's foreign policy orientation has been described by analysts as "great-power realism."[9]

The terrorist attacks of September 11, 2001, led to a rethinking of these premises. The U.S. government responded swiftly to the security threats emanating from international terrorist networks such as Al-Qaeda. Although these threats were not entirely new, they were magnified by the apparent vulnerability of the American homeland. The conclusions drawn from this traumatic experience are documented in the new National Security Strategy (NSS) of the U.S. government published on September 20, 2002.

Some analysts rightfully maintain that the NSS also contains elements of idealism and is thus not just a strategy that paves the way for unilateral policies and legitimizes preemptive or even preventive military strikes, as frequently criticized in the European media.[10] Yet, it is a document pervaded by the notion that the United States is operating in an anarchic international environment. This anarchy is illustrated by terrorist threats and rogue states seeking to acquire WMDs and suspected of supplying terrorists with access to them. International relations are thus driven by power, and power is primarily understood in military terms. It follows from this that U.S security must be based on military superiority, which must be maintained by all means. It is in fact a strategy based on U.S. dominance.[11] Thus, even though the NSS contains idealist and institutionalist paradigms, they are subordinate to the overriding objective of security. Democratization, for instance, is not promoted for its own sake, but rather as a device to bring to power governments that share some common values with the United States and hence may be expected to be more accommodating to American security interests. The distrust of the Bush administration of international institutions as illustrated by the withdrawal from the negotiations on climatic change (after the U.S. Senate had already voted against ratification of the Kyoto Protocol in 1997), the opposition to the International Criminal Court, the rejection of the verification regime of the Biological Weapons Convention, and the annulment of the Anti-Ballistic Missile (ABM) Treaty, also finds expression in the NSS.[12] The Bush administration obviously views international institutions in the realist sense as merely another arena for power struggles. Therefore, Washington is prepared to invest in international institution building only insofar as it fits its security interests. Its approach to institutions is thus best characterized by the paradigm of hegemonic stability; but unlike in the immediate post–World War II period, the United States is now much more of a cunning than a benign hegemon.[13]

As the NSS outlines the parameters of U.S. foreign policy for the coming years, the subsequent sections are conjectures about its consequences for U.S. policies toward the global South.

Consequences for Global Governance

The Iraq crisis was the test case for the doctrine of preemption as outlined by the NSS. Unable to secure a UN mandate for the use of force, the United States formed a coalition of the willing and acted unilaterally, eventually defeating and overthrowing Saddam Hussein. Although the war against Iraq was a military success, its repercussions for international institution building and the evolving system of global governance will be far-reaching. The war left the United Nations in a state of disarray for it was unable to prevent the unilateral use of force by the U.S.-led coalition. Relegated by the United States to a subsidiary organization of post-conflict peace building, the UN has lost in stature and prestige as a collective security mechanism. Only the mounting difficulties in the reconstruction of Iraq and the building of a democratic society, illustrated by dozens of casualties every day, convinced the Bush administration that the UN must play a role in postwar Iraq.

The war against Iraq also further eroded the "legitimacy norm for the legitimate use of force" as spelled out by Article 51 of the UN Charter.[14] The Kosovo war had already raised serious questions in this respect. Yet, the ethnic cleansing of the Albanian population by the Serbian Milosevic regime provided some legitimacy for the view that severe crimes were being committed against humanity and that the war was a humanitarian intervention. In the case of Iraq, however, it was more difficult to portray the war as a humanitarian intervention despite the undeniable fact that Saddam's record of human rights violations was one of the worst in the world. If human rights violations and lack of democracy were indeed the main reasons for the intervention, then many other regimes beyond the so-called axis of evil of Iraq, Iran, and North Korea would face replacement by military intervention.[15] Moreover, the Iraq War was not a preemptive, but a preventive strike. While preemption is acceptable by the standards of international law where an armed attack on a state is imminent, prevention is not. Prevention is directed against an adversary who in the more distant future may evolve into a security threat and therefore needs to be contained. Iraq did not pose an immediate threat to the United States that justified a preemptive strike.[16] Neither the UN weapon inspectors nor the U.S. occupation forces found convincing evidence that Iraq possessed WMDs at the time of the intervention. Similarly unsubstantiated were claims that the Saddam regime had established links to Al-Qaeda.

The Iraq War has not only weakened the UN, but also caused divisions in the European Union (EU) and the North Atlantic Treaty Organization (NATO). A closer look at institutions involving regions of the South also reveals collateral damage. The Asia-Pacific Economic Cooperation (APEC), for instance, originally designed as a trade-facilitating forum, has increasingly been transformed into a security forum as the United States seeks to extend its anti-terrorism coalition to the Pacific Rim.[17] In Southeast Asia, strengthening regional cooperation under the auspices of the Association of Southeast Asian Nations (ASEAN) has never been a major U.S. policy objective. Although the United States had been in dialogue with ASEAN since the 1970s, it preferred a bilateral approach. However, under the terrorist threat the United States rediscovered ASEAN as a regional organization and has been promoting ASEAN cooperation for the sake of greater efficiency in fighting terrorism.[18] Yet, as the bumpy nature of this cooperation has shown and in the face of the regional grouping's internal crisis in the aftermath of the Asian currency crisis, it is farfetched to expect the United States to be an external federator for ASEAN.[19]

While it is indeed simplistic to portray the NSS exclusively as a blueprint for unilateral action, it is equally misleading to attach to it a multilateral dimension—"American style," "selective," "imperial," or otherwise.[20] This "multilateralism with adjectives" differs from an institutionalist version of multilateralism in two important aspects: (1) it does not rest on durable institutions, and (2) as a consequence of (1), it does not create the actor predictability multilateral frameworks are expected to provide. What is mistaken by many analysts as multilateralism in the NSS is, in effect, plain and simple coalition building. Coalitions have the advantage of being flexible and adaptable to changing circumstances. They are of limited duration, tend to change with the issue, impose fewer commitments on their members than more cohesive institutions, and do not generate the governance costs usually associated with institution building.[21] Established institutions such as the EU or NATO may be gradually hollowed out by such coalitions. They lose their cohesion and the will to compromise. To portray coalition building as an "advanced form" of multilateralism obviously misses the point.[22]

Through its coalition building, the United States is in reality pursuing bandwagoning for dominance.[23] However broad these coalitions may be, the history of international relations shows that there is a great likelihood that dominance breeds counter-coalitions. One such counter-coalition has already emerged in the UN Security Council, with the axis Paris-Berlin-Moscow-Beijing opposing unilateral American action in Iraq. Other coalitions, though so far not activated, could emerge between Russia and China, China and India, or even between a tripartite alliance of Russia, China, and India. While it is true that the common interests of these powers and the United States still outweigh the disagreements, the incentives for counterbalances increase as the United States's lead in the area of military technology widens (culminating in plans to establish a Missile Defense Shield, MDS) and the U.S. presence in the "front line states" of the Middle East and Central Asia is prolonged.[24] At least in Moscow and Beijing this could arouse fears of encirclement, which will hardly be tolerated.

It does not need much imagination to predict that the U.S. doctrine of preemption will readily find imitators elsewhere. In the strife-torn Third World, especially where no major interests of the United States or other major powers are at stake, regional powers could be tempted to apply the U.S. reasoning for preventive actions against their adversaries. It would allow them to attack their opponents on the basis of a pretext, without obliging them to provide the necessary evidence beforehand. India, for instance, in view of the terrorist threats originating from Pakistan, has already made clear that it claims the right of preemptive strikes.[25] UN secretary-general Kofi Annan summarized these concerns in his address to the UN General Assembly in the following words:

"My concern is that, if it [the U.S. doctrine of preemption] were to be adopted, it would set precedents that result in a proliferation of the unilateral and lawless use of force, with or without credible justification."[26]

With the NSS and the war against Iraq, military hard power assumes a higher priority than institution building. Current American foreign policy is thus reversing the institutionalist belief that in the light of the growing economization of international relations, complex interdependence and the diffusion of weapons technology, military power is increasingly unable to influence actor behavior in policy arenas other than the military domain.[27] The overwhelming military dominance of the United States, as exemplified in the Second Gulf War, in the Kosovo war, the Afghanistan war, and buttressed once more in the Iraq War, has made U.S. decision makers overconfident that wars can be won with a lean army and a minimum of U.S. casualties and that, if needed, the use of force or the threat thereof may create political solutions favorable to the United States.[28] While the reliance on superior military power may indeed tempt U.S. decision makers to intervene in countries of the global South whenever they seem to harbor serious security risks, the post–Iraq War events show how difficult it is even for a superpower to translate a military victory into the desired political outcome.

Spiraling defense spending is another consequence of the renewed importance of military power. According to data provided by the Stockholm International Peace Research Institute (SIPRI), global defense spending grew by 6 percent in 2002. The United States alone, however, accounted for three-fourths of the increase. In 2002, global defense spending was 14 percent higher than in 1998, though still 16 percent below the level of 1988.[29] The fact that Iraq had obviously abandoned its biological and chemical weapons program, yet was still attacked by the U.S.-led coalition, while at the same time the United States was reluctant to respond with force to North Korea's admission of a nuclear weapons program, may have taught rogue states the wrong lesson if they conclude that the possession of WMDs deters the United States from attacking them. The dispute over the Iranian nuclear program seems to point in this direction.

Development Aid

Reversing the Bush administration's early pronouncements, the NSS has declared development a "moral imperative and one of the top priorities of

U.S. international policy." The renewed attention devoted to development is explained by the fact that the NSS has identified poverty as one, albeit not the only, condition for breeding terrorism and creating political instability. Accordingly, the NSS has set for "the United States and other developed economies" the ambitious goal of doubling the size of the world's poorest economies within a decade. The NSS is thus in accordance with President Bush's call for a "new compact for global development," which he made on March 14, 2002, at the Monterrey Conference on Financing for Development when he announced the establishment of the UN Millennium Challenge Account (MCA). The MCA would increase U.S. development aid by $5 billion a year, phased over a three-year period ($1.7 billion in fiscal year 2004, $3.3 billion in fiscal year 2005, and $5 billion in fiscal year 2006).[30] This is equivalent to a 50 percent increase in U.S. spending on development, a target confirmed by the NSS. The funding of the account would not replace, but complement existing development aid. A new entity, the Millennium Challenge Corporation (MCC), would be entrusted with the administration of the aid. The MCC will be run by a chief executive officer appointed by the president and controlled by a cabinet-level board headed by the secretary of state.[31]

The MCA has not only been greeted by the administration but also by independent development experts and NGOs as promising "to bring about the most fundamental change to U.S. foreign assistance policy since President John F. Kennedy introduced the Peace Corps and the U.S. Agency for International Development (USAID) in the early 1960s."[32] As the Heritage Foundation emphatically exclaimed, "it reverses the traditional aid formula; instead of giving aid to get the hoped for reforms, it is based on reform before aid."[33] Aid will henceforth be given very selectively only to developing countries that govern justly, invest in their people by upgrading health and education, and encourage economic freedom. Selection is based on sixteen indicators in three selection categories (see Table 10.1). Only countries qualifying as better performers in all three categories are eligible for MCA funding. Final selection will be made by the president on the recommendation of the MCC board. Selected countries will be invited to propose projects to the MCA, which, after screening them, will sign contracts with these countries specifying mutual commitments and agreed performance benchmarks. On May 6, 2004, the MCC board selected the first batch of sixteen countries eligible to apply for MCA assistance in fiscal year 2004. They

Table 10.1

Eligibility Criteria for the Millenium Challenge Account

Indicator	Source
A. Ruling justly	
1. Civil liberties	Freedom House
2. Political rights	Freedom House
3. Voice and accountability	World Bank Institute
4. Government effectiveness	World Bank Institute
5. Rule of law	World Bank Institute
6. Control of corruption	World Bank Institute
B. Investing in people	
7. Public primary education spending/GDP	World Bank
8. Primary education completion rate	World Bank
9. Public expenditure on health/GDP	World Bank
10. Immunization rate: DPT and measles	WHO/World Bank
C. Economic freedom	
11. Country credit rating	Institutional Investor
12. Inflation	IMF
13. Three-year budget deficit/GDP	IMF/ World Bank
14. Trade policy	Heritage Foundation
15. Regulatory quality	World Bank Institute
16. Days to start a business	World Bank

Source: U.S. Department of State, *Millenium Challenge Act of 2003: Section-by-Section Analysis of Proposed Legislation*, February 5, 2003, available at www.state.gov/e/eb/rls/othr/19458.htm, accessed July 24, 2004.

include Armenia, Benin, Bolivia, Cape Verde, Georgia, Ghana, Honduras, Lesotho, Madagascar, Mali, Mongolia, Mozambique, Nicaragua, Senegal, Sri Lanka, and Vanuatu.[34]

In absolute terms, the MCA will entrench the United States for a long time as the world's leading aid donor in absolute terms, a position it regained in 2002 for the first time since 1992. U.S. official development assistance (ODA) in 2002 amounted to $10.9 billion, a slight increase in its share of the GNP from 0.10 percent to 0.11 percent (see Table 10.2).[35] Yet, despite the massive infusion of funding through the MDA, the United States will still rank last among industrial nations in relative terms, a fact that experts believe remains unchanged even if the substantial private U.S. aid is included.[36]

But aside from the MCA's enthusiastic reception as an "exciting new program with enormous potential," the development community has listed an array on potential shortcomings that could prevent the program from achieving its lofty objectives.[37]

Table 10.2

Ten Major Recipients of U.S. Official Development Assistance Between 1980 and 2000

Countries	ODA (constant 1999 dollars, in millions)
Egypt	35,857.8
Israel	29,053.7
El Salvador	5,619.0
India	4,272.0
Philippines	4,124.3
Bangladesh	4,016.2
Pakistan	3,863.1
Turkey	3,161.2
Honduras	2,982.3
Indonesia	2,739.9

Source: Brett D. Schaefer, *The Millenium Challenge Accout: An Opportunity to Advance Development*, Heritage Lecture no. 753, July 27, 2002, available at www.heritage.org/Research/TradeandForeignAid/loader.cfm?url=/commonspot/security/getfile.cfm&PageID=4864, accessed July 24, 2004, pp. 6–7.

- The MCA is based on a primarily growth-based development strategy. In line with mainstream modernization theory it assumes that economic growth produces sufficient trickle-down effects to mitigate or even eradicate poverty. Yet, four decades of development teach that growth per se is not enough. It is at best a necessary condition for poverty alleviation. If growth is distributed extremely inequitably, possibly along ethnic lines, it may not contribute to the ultimate objective of the NSS, that is, stability, but rather foment and exacerbate existing societal conflicts.
- In the later stages of the program countries with a per capita income of up to $2,975, which do not qualify as poor, become eligible. Observers suspect that this stipulation could give the administration the flexibility to support countries that play a key role in the war against terrorism. The decision to base the allocation of development aid primarily on security criteria may, however, backfire. It may be tantamount to propping up the opponents of tomorrow when regime change, changes in the regional power equation, or American policy mistakes alienate aid recipients from the United States. Iran and Iraq—major recipients of U.S. aid in the

1970s and 1980s—are cases in point. Nobody can guarantee that the same may not happen in the future with the Central Asian republics, Egypt, or Jordan.[38]

- MCA deals with the "easiest" cases among the poor countries. It does not address the problem of failed states, the states most likely to become breeding grounds of terrorism and safe havens for terrorists.[39]
- The MCA may worsen bureaucratic politics. The sidelining of USAID and the creation of the MCC as the agency responsible for managing the program could exacerbate inter-agency competition and thus neutralize the savings in transaction costs expected from the creation of the MCC.
- For a program of the size of the MCA, the MCC's initial staff of 60 rising to 200 is too small.[40] This may lead to delays and flaws in the program's management. Problems may also occur as few developing countries are able to absorb the enormous aid flows that come with program eligibility.[41]
- Development aid may not flow consistently, as recipient countries will be excluded from funding, if their performance weakens or the performance of others improves disproportionately. However, interruptions of funding may impede sustained development.
- Some analysts claim that the indicators used are faulty. This includes the risk of misclassifying countries, a problem affecting mainly borderline cases.

Apart from the overall increase in aid levels and the disbursement of $15 billion for fighting AIDS over the next five years, the NSS announced an 18 percent rise in the U.S. contributions to the International Development Association (IDA)—the World Bank's fund for the poorest countries—and the African Development Fund. Included in the 18 percent increase is an "increase of the amount of development assistance that is provided in the form of grants instead of loans." Grants should be provided particularly for investments by poor countries "in social sectors such as education, HIV/AIDS, health, nutrition, water, and sanitation."

It remains to be seen how serious the administration is in its drive for development and poverty alleviation and to what extent the MCA enables the United States "to reassert its leadership role in foreign assistance."[42] Apart from the growth bias of the MCA and the NSS, other actions of the Bush administration are clearly at variance with the objective of poverty alleviation. One is—as will be shown below—trade policies; another is the Bush administration's decision to end U.S.-financed family planning programs distributing contraceptives. Such a policy was first introduced by the Reagan administration, but repealed by Clinton. The U.S. government subsequently terminated its contributions to the United Nations Fund for Population Activities (UNFPA). Instead, the $34 million committed to the fund are to be disbursed to USAID for the latter's health programs.[43] Although poverty is a complex phenomenon, and the causal relationship between it and population growth is contested, it is nevertheless a fact that the population in poor countries is growing faster than that in wealthier countries.[44] It has also been convincingly shown that the absence of family planning programs may lead to an increase in the number of abortions and the spread of HIV/AIDS.

Nor is there any mention in the NSS of the environmental aspects of development, the sustainable use of natural resources, and environmental protection. In fact, the Bush administration's rejection of the Kyoto Protocol and the appointment of a pro-business head of the Environmental Protection Agency in August 2003 shows where it stands on these issues. The withdrawal from the Kyoto Protocol also sets a negative precedent for developing countries, which argue that economically advanced countries are primarily responsible for climate change and view costly environmental protection as a neocolonial ploy to slow down their development.

Trade

The suspicion that poverty alleviation as laid out in the NSS is merely a palliative in an otherwise neoliberal agenda is corroborated by a closer look at the economic development strategy that the United States promotes. It repeats the free trade and free market mantra of the Washington Consensus. Although the NSS called on the IMF to improve its management of financial crises, there is no explicit criticism of the structural adjustment policies the fund pursues as its standard medicine and no suggestion of how to avoid their socially disruptive effects. As structural adjustment leads to deep cuts in state funding of social policies, it also contradicts the Bush administration's goal of poverty alleviation.

Free trade agreements benefit above all strong economies. Thus, as long as there are no asymmetric provisions giving economically less advanced countries more time to adjust their economic competitiveness to lowered tariffs and other forms of market opening, the effect on them will inevitably be detrimental. Yet, to be fair, at least as far as Africa and the Caribbean are concerned, the United States indeed seems to be prepared to provide greater trade preferences to these countries than in the past. On the other hand, U.S. behavior in WTO trade liberalization rounds does not give much credence to its propositions of a more development-friendly trade policy. U.S. attempts to maintain subsidies for cotton have caused "anger and bitterness" among poor African producer countries such as Benin, Burkina Faso, Chad, and Mali.[45] One year earlier, President Bush had granted massive subsidies to U.S. agriculture, which—as U.S. decision makers argue—are in the first place retaliatory measures against the protectionist agricultural policies of the EU and Japan. Moreover, apart from endearing the administration to its conservative clientele, the subsidies are obviously designed to create a bargaining chip in trade negotiations with the EU. Free trade in agricultural products works to the advantage of the highly efficient agricultural sector of the United States, Canada, Australia, and New Zealand. It would most likely also benefit some of the Southern members of the Cairns Group of agricultural exporters such as Brazil or Thailand, but hardly the majority of developing countries. Equally problematic for the majority of developing countries will be the development of genetically engineered agricultural products, which has been declared a priority by the NSS. Developing countries' dependence on giant Northern agro-multis will be cemented by these new agricultural technologies.[46]

A U.S. plan floated in the Doha Round of the WTO to reduce tariffs for all manufactured goods is also of dubious benefit for Third World countries. While it may benefit the producers of consumer products such as shoes, toys, textiles, and the like, it gives the United States and other developed economies free access to the markets of developing countries in higher added-value products. The proposal would remove protection from the more advanced industrial sectors, which in many NICs are still in their infancy, and expose the markets of least developed countries to the superior competitiveness of more advanced developing countries, with highly destructive effects for local trades and industries. Just how far national interest dominates in the U.S. proposal is shown by the Bush administration's argument that its proposal "would benefit an average four-member U.S. household with an extra $1,600 a year, while removing high foreign tariff-barriers on more than $670 billion in U.S. exports."[47]

Hardly less controversial is the shift of the United States to bilateral free trade agreements (FTAs) following the collapse of trade talks at the Cancun ministerial meeting of the WTO in September 2003. In the more recent past, the United States has concluded bilateral FTAs with Chile, Jordan, Bahrain, and Singapore (as well as with Australia, an OECD member); others with Thailand, the Philippines, and Malaysia are either already under negotiation or under consideration. While adherents of trade liberalization view them as a second best solution able to preserve the norm of trade liberalization at times when multilateral progress is difficult to achieve and as building blocks for a multilateral trade order, critics question such reasoning.[48] Bilateral FTAs are for them the economic equivalent to the coalitions of the willing in the security domain.[49] They suspect they fail to create universally accepted rules. By creating a plethora of contradictory rules (such as rules of origin), they markedly increase transaction costs, which are a greater burden for poorer countries than for the United States.[50] Moreover, bilateral FTAs allow the United States to impose on its trading partners in the South rules and norms in areas such as the protection of intellectual property, foreign investment, government procurement, and the environment where it would meet determined opposition in the WTO. Bilateral FTAs, euphemistically advertised as "WTO-Plus" agreements, may thus turn out to be a tool of U.S. foreign policy to pursue national interests in the area of trade.

Finally, trade is also used to reward countries that cooperate with the United States in the war against terrorism. During the ASEAN postministerial conference in 2002, the United States offered ASEAN a free trade agreement. Typically, however, the plan did not address ASEAN as a bloc, but rather individual countries.[51] Far from being an "external federator" for a regional organization that fell into disarray after the Asian financial crisis, the Enterprise of the ASEAN Initiative (EAI) follows the hub-and-spokes relationship the United States traditionally entertained with its Asian allies and partners.

All in all, however, in order to recover the prohibitive costs of the war against terrorism and the exploding occupation costs in Iraq, a tougher negotiation style may be expected from the United States in the WTO, the G 7/8, and other economic forums. Yet, unlike in military affairs, the power distribution in the economic realm is not unipolar but multipolar. The United States will thus face stiff resistance if it intends to extend its designs for a new world order to the economic sphere.

Democracy Promotion

Democracy promotion is the idealist or Kantian component of the NSS. It refers to the Wilsonian mission of making the world safe for democracy, thereby assuming that only a democratic world is a safer world. However, democratization is, apart from the U.S. government's plans of reorganizing international institutions, another case in which the idealist paradigm has been subordinated to a realist worldview.

By specifying that only countries implementing democratic reforms and showing progress toward good governance qualify for aid, the NSS creates a link between development assistance and democratization. The fact, however, that aid disbursements are also used to cement the coalition against terrorism creates a dilemma for the United States. Countries such as the Central Asian republics, Pakistan, Egypt, Saudi Arabia, and the Gulf emirates are autocracies showing little willingness to respond to American exhortations for reform. Even countries like Malaysia and Singapore, which have received much praise in the White House for their security cooperation, are by no means model democracies. The leverage of the United States here depends clearly on the strategic importance of these countries. Where their cooperation is indispensable, Washington's leverage is weak. It is in fact the same dilemma as during the Cold War, which illustrated only too clearly that when the objectives of security and democracy were in conflict, the United States tended to give priority to security. However, subordinating democracy promotion to economic objectives, as happened under Clinton, or to counterterrorism, as under Bush, discredits democracy promotion and gives rise to accusations of double standards.

Counter-terrorism is also likely to retard the consolidation of new democracies. Cases in point are Indonesia and Thailand, where the governments have decreed anti-terrorism measures that resemble the draconian Internal Security Acts (ISA) of Malaysia and Singapore. In the latter two countries, September 11 and its repercussions on Southeast Asia have abruptly halted discussions about the lifting of these laws. In Indonesia, the United States is also in the process of resuming aid for the armed forces. Given the government's reluctance to clamp down on Islamic extremism, and in view of the military's long-standing opposition to political Islam, the armed forces have been identified by the United States as the most reliable ally in Indonesia. Washington's choice, however, does not bode well for democratization, which parts of the armed forces have consistently opposed. They are suspected of having had a hand in much of the turmoil and violence that accompanied Indonesia's transition to democracy. U.S. support for the military is also an endorsement of those who opt for the use of force against the separatist movements in the country. The offensive started by the military in May 2003 against the rebels of the Gerakan Aceh Merdeka (GAM) in Aceh can be seen against this background.

Even more unfortunate, however, is that governments cracking down on opposition in the name of counter-terrorism, especially in the Arab world, the Middle East, and Central Asia, may use the curtailment of civil liberties in the United States itself to justify their actions. In the name of homeland security, the United States has detained some 1,200 immigrants and conducted closed deportation hearings.[52] U.S. citizens declared "enemy combatants" have been denied the right to counsel or even to contest the designation.[53] Also questionable from a human rights standpoint is the U.S. treatment of the 660 prisoners held in Guantanamo as "illegal combatants." The United States has singled out some of them for prosecution before a military tribunal, which deprives them of rights of due process.[54] By all means the worst precedent for Western-style democratization in the global South is the human rights violations committed by U.S. security personnel in Bagdad's infamous Abu Ghraib jail.

Democratization through regime change following military intervention, as in Iraq and Afghanistan, is also facing massive problems. In the war against the Taliban, the United States armed the warlords of the Northern Alliance, who have no serious commitment to the democratic reconstruction of the war-torn country. The power of the fragile Karzai government hardly extends beyond Kabul. In Iraq, the U.S. occupation forces, far from restoring public order and rebuilding the country under a democratic government, have been increasingly losing control of the situation. It soon became obvious that the adherents of the Iraq War had no blueprint for the postwar rebuilding of the country and that decision makers underestimated the political complexities. Far from spurring domino democratization in the Middle East, post-Saddam Iraq became a new battlefield for radical Islamists against America. After all, the poor record of externally imposed democratization should have warned the Bush administration. Panama, Haiti, Somalia, Grenada, and Cambodia are all countries where democracy has been hardly strengthened by American intervention or UN peace missions. Moreover, as, Thomas Carothers argues, democracy promotion U.S.-style is geared toward the election of pro-American personalities and parties with a pro-American outlook. It often ends where free elections produce results conflicting with U.S. interests.[55]

Conclusion

All in all, the NSS is a document characterized of contradictory policies. This must be attributed to the fact that the NSS complements hardnosed realism with idealist paradigms. As national interest is defined primarily in terms of national security, it must be anticipated that the idealist and institutionalist components of the NSS will take a backseat in U.S. foreign policies toward the global South. If so, then poverty alleviation and assistance for the least developed countries in Africa will be little more than symbolic politics. This will enable critics to discredit the moral imperatives of U.S. policy as an ideological mantle for hegemonial ambitions, in particular if they are wrapped in Manichean rhetoric. The loss of American "soft power" in the South will then be immense.

Notes

I am indebted to Theodor Hanf for fruitful discussions on U.S. foreign policy toward regions of the global South.

1. See the contribution of Howard J. Wiarda in this volume, and Peter J. Schraeder, *United States Foreign Policy Toward Africa: Incrementalism, Crisis and Change* (Cambridge, UK: Cambridge University Press, 1995), p. 37f.; Charles William Maynes, "America Discovers Central Asia," *Foreign Affairs* 82, no. 2 (Mar./Apr. 2003): 120; and Ibrahim Al-Marashi, "The Unexpected Aftermath of Operation 'Iraqi Freedom,'" *ISIM Newsletter* no. 12 (2003): 20.

2. See the contribution of James McCormick in this volume, and Schraeder, *United States Foreign Policy Toward Africa*, p. 37f.

3. See the contribution of Howard J. Wiarda in this volume.

4. See the contribution of Peter Schraeder in this volume. Christian Wagner, *Indiens neue Beziehung zu Amerika: Zweckbündnis oder strategische Allianz?* (Berlin: Stiftung Wissenschaft und Politik, June 2003), p. 8.

5. See the contribution of Amitav Acharya in this volume.

6. Martin Wagener, *Second Front: Die USA, Südostasien und der Kampf gegen den Terrorismus* (Trier: Universität Trier, ZOPS Occasional Paper no. 16, Oct. 2002); Joshua Kurlantzick, "Tilting at Dominos: America and Al Qaeda in Southeast Asia," *Current History* 101, no. 659 (Dec. 2002): 421–26; John Gershman, "Is Southeast Asia the Second Front?" *Foreign Affairs* 81, no. 4 (July/Aug. 2002): 60–74.

7. Quoted in James M. McCormick, *American Foreign Policy & Process*, 2nd ed. (Itasca, IL: F.E. Peacock, 1998), p. 224.

8. Salih Booker, "Bush's Global Agenda: Bad News for Africa," *Current History* 100, no. 646 (May 2001): 195.

9. Thomas Carothers, "Promoting Democracy and Fighting Terror," *Foreign Affairs* 82, no. 1 (Jan./Feb. 2003): 84.

10. Joachim Krause, Jan Irlenkaeuser, and Benjamin Schreer, "Wohin gehen die USA? Die neue Sicherheitsstrategie der Bush-Administration," *Aus Politik und Zeitgeschichte* 48 (2002): 40.

11. See also the contribution of William Quandt in this volume.

12. Bill Emmott, *Vision 20/21: Die Weltordnung des 21. Jahrhunderts* (Frankfurt am Main: S. Fischer, 2003), p. 122. The United States has begun to conclude bilateral agreements not to extradite Americans for trial before the International Criminal Court. *International Herald Tribune* (Aug. 27, 2002): 4.

13. On the concept of hegemonial stability, see Robert Gilpin, *Global Political Economy: Understanding the International Economic Order* (Princeton, NJ: Princeton University Press, 2001); and Charles Kindleberger, "Dominance and Leadership in the International Economy," *International Studies Quarterly* 25 (1981): 242–54.

14. G. John Ikenberry, "America's Imperial Ambition," *Foreign Affairs* 81, no. 5 (Sept./Oct. 2002): 51.

15. President Bush referred to the "axis of evil" for the first time in his State of the Union Address on January 29, 2002.

16. Karl-Heinz Kamp, "The National Security Strategy: Kurzanalyse der neuen amerikanischen Sicherheitsstrategie" (St. Augustin: Konrad-Adenauer-Stiftung, Sept. 25, 2002), available at www.kas.de/publikationen/2002/862_dokument.html, accessed Aug. 25, 2003.

17. *International Herald Tribune* (Oct. 24, 2002): 13. It should, however, be noted that the Clinton administration had already set a precedent in this respect. The United States used the 1999 APEC summit in Auckland to form a coalition of the willing for a humanitarian intervention in East Timor after pro-Indonesian militia rampaged in the territory following the overwhelming East Timorese vote for independence from Indonesia in a referendum held on August 30, 1999. Indonesia had annexed the former Portuguese colony in 1976.

18. See *Far Eastern Economic Review* (Aug. 15, 2002): 22.

19. Jürgen Rüland, "ASEAN and the Asian Crisis: Theoretical Implications and Practical Consequences for Southeast Asian Regionalism," *Pacific Review* 13, no. 3 (2000): 421–51.

20. Andrew Denison, "Unilateral oder multilateral? Motive der amerikanischen Irakpolitik," *Aus Politik und Zeitgeschichte* 24–25 (2003): 24. For a distinction between "cooperative," "selective" and "imperial multilateralism," see Jochen Hippler, "Unilateralismus der USA als Problem der internationalen Politik," *Aus Politik und Zeitgeschichte* 31–32 (2003): 20.

21. On the concept of governance costs, see David Lake, "Global Governance: A Relational Contracting Approach," in Aseem Prakash and Jeffrey A. Hart, eds., *Globalization and Governance* (London: Routledge, 1999), pp. 31–53.

22. Denison, "Unilateral oder multilateral?" p. 17.

23. On the concept of bandwagoning, see Stephen Walt, *The Origin of Alliances* (Ithaca, NY: Cornell University Press, 1987).

24. See Henry Kissinger, *Does America Need a Foreign Policy? Toward a Diplomacy for the 21st Century* (New York: Simon & Schuster, 2001), p. 117; Joseph S.

Nye, Jr., *The Paradox of American Power: Why the World's Only Superpower Can't Go It Alone* (Oxford: Oxford University Press, 2002), p. 25; and Harald Müller, *Amerika schlägt zurück: Die Weltordnung nach dem 11. September* (Frankfurt am Main: Fischer Taschenbuch Verlag, 2003), pp. 46ff.

25. Wagner, *Indiens neue Beziehung zu Amerika,* p. 13. Australian Prime Minister John Howard also hinted at the possibility of making preemptive military strikes against terrorist cells and organizations operating in foreign countries. Howard's announcement came on the heels of the bombing of nightspots on Bali by operatives of the terrorist Jemaah Islamiyah group in October 2002. See www.atrueword.com/index.php/article/articleview/40/1/2, accessed on May 31, 2005.

26. *New Straits Times* (Sept. 24, 2003): 1.

27. Robert O. Keohane and Joseph S. Nye, *Power and Interdependence: World Politics in Transition,* 2nd ed. (Glenview, IL: Scott, Foresman, 1989).

28. For such reasoning, see Robert Kagan, *Of Paradise and Power: America and Europe in the New World Order* (New York: Knopf, 2003).

29. *Frankfurter Allgemeine Zeitung* (June 24, 2003): 6.

30. Heritage Foundation, *The Millennium Challenge Account: Creating Effective Development Assistance,* available at www.heritage.org/Research/Features/agenda_millennium.cfm, accessed July 11, 2004, p. 2.

31. U.S. Department of State, *Millennium Challenge Account,* June 11, 2003, available at www.state.gov/e/rls/2003/21498.htm, accessed July 5, 2004.

32. Steve Radelet, "Will the Millennium Challenge Account Be Different?" *Washington Quarterly* (Spring 2003), available at www.google.de/search?q=cache:ELbMuQdK9SsJ:www.twq.com/03spring/docs, accessed July 11, 2004, p. 1.

33. Heritage Foundation, *The Millennium Challenge Account,* p. 2; U.S. Department of State, *Millennium Challenge Account,* p. 3.

34. Millennium Challenge Corporation, press release, May 6, available at www.mca.gov, accessed July 14, 2004.

35. OECD press release, Paris, May 13, 2002.

36. Radelet, *Will the Millennium Challenge Account Be Different?* p. 19; for private contributions, see Carol C. Adelman, "The Privatization of Foreign Aid: Reassessing National Largesse," *Foreign Affairs* 82, no. 6 (Nov./Dec. 2003): 9–14.

37. Radelet, *Will the Millennium Challenge Account be Different?* p. 15.

38. Ibid., p. 9.

39. Ibid., p. 9.

40. Millennium Challenge Corporation, FY 2005 Budget Justification, available at www.mca.gov, accessed July 14, 2004.

41. Ibid., p. 11.

42. Ibid., p. 19.

43. *Süddeutsche Zeitung* (July 27): 9; ibid. (Dec. 4, 2002): 6.

44. *Süddeutsche Zeitung* (Dec. 4, 2003): 6.

45. *Economist* (Sept. 20, 2003): 27.

46. See National Security Strategy of the United States of America, Sept. 17, 2002, available at www.whitehouse.gov/nsc/nss.pdf, accessed, July 21, 2004, p. 19.

47. *Wall Street Journal Europe* (Nov. 27, 2002): A2.

48. Barry Desker, "In Defence of FTAs: From Purity to Pragmatism in East Asia," *The Pacific Review* 17, no. 1 (2004): 3–26.

49. Jagdish Bhagwati, "Don't Cry for Cancun," *Foreign Affairs*, 83, no. 1 (2004): 53.

50. For the technical complexities, see Christopher M. Dent, "Networking the Region? The Emergence and Impact of Asia-Pacific Bilateral Free Trade Agreement Projects," *The Pacific Review*, 16, no. 1 (2003): 1–28

51. See the Enterprise for the ASEAN Initiative, announced by President Bush during the APEC summit in Mexico in October 2002. "Announcement on 'Enterprise for ASEAN Initiative' Marks New Chapter in US-ASEAN Relations," available at www.us-asean.org/Press_Releases/EAI.htm, accessed Dec. 11, 2002.

52. *International Herald Tribune* (Sept. 11, 2002): 8.

53. Carothers, "Promoting Democracy and Fighting Terror," p. 91.

54. *Die Zeit* (July 31, 2003): 5.

55. Carothers, "Promoting Democracy and Fighting Terror," pp. 92, 94.

Contributors

Amitav Acharya is Professor, Deputy Director, and Head of Research at the Institute of Defence and Strategic Studies at Nanyang Technological University, Singapore.

Sumit Ganguly is Director of the Indiana University Indian Studies Program and Professor of Political Science at Indiana University, Bloomington, United States.

Theodor Hanf is Professor of Sociology at the University of Frankfurt, Honorary Professor of Political Science at the University of Freiburg, Germany, and Director of the UNESCO Institute Centre des Sciences de l'Homme in Byblos, Lebanon.

Bernd Kuzmits is a research fellow in the Department for Political and Cultural Change at the Centre for Development Research at the University of Bonn, Germany.

Eva Manske is Professor of American Literature and Director of the Carl-Schurz-Haus in Freiburg, Germany.

Hanns W. Maull is Professor of Political Science and holds the Chair in Foreign Policy and International Relations at the University of Trier, Germany.

James M. McCormick is Professor of Political Science and the Chair of the Political Science Department at Iowa State University, Ames, United States.

William B. Quandt holds the Edward R. Stettinius Chair and is Professor of Politics at the University of Virginia, Charlottesville, United States.

Jürgen Rüland is Professor of Political Science at the University of Freiburg and Director of the Arnold-Bergstraesser-Institut Freiburg, Germany.

Conrad Schetter is a senior researcher in the Department for Political and Cultural Change at the Centre for Development Research at the University of Bonn, Germany.

Peter J. Schraeder is a professor in the Department of Political Science at Loyola University Chicago, United States. Currently he is at the Loyola University Rome Center, Italy.

Brian Shoup is a PhD candidate in Political Science at Indiana University, Bloomington, United States.

Howard J. Wiarda is Professor of International Affairs, the Dean Rusk Professor of International Relations, Head of the Department of International Affairs in the School of Public and International Affairs at the University of Georgia, Athens, and a Senior Associate at the Center for Strategic and International Studies (CSIS) in Washington, DC, United States.

Index